Valentin Tomberg
and the
Ecclesia Universalis

A BIOGRAPHY

HARRIE SALMAN

Valentin Tomberg
and the
Ecclesia Universalis

A BIOGRAPHY

⊕

*The Unity of
Exoteric & Esoteric
Christianity*

Angelico Press

First published in English
by Angelico Press 2022
© Harrie Salman 2022

All rights reserved

No part of this book may be reproduced or transmitted,
in any form or by any means, without permission.

For information, address:
Angelico Press
169 Monitor St.
Brooklyn, NY 11222
www.angelicopress.com

The author and publisher gratefully acknowledge the
Tomberg Archives, 24972 Steinbergkirche-Neukirchen, Germany,
and in particular Michael Frensch, for their generosity in
providing access to invaluable source documents.

978-1-62138-871-5 (pbk)
978-1-62138-872-2 (cloth)
978-1-62138-873-9 (ebook)

Cover design: Michael Schrauzer

CONTENTS

Preface 1

Introduction: From Pilgrim to Hermit 7

PART I
THE STATIONS OF VALENTIN TOMBERG'S
LIFE JOURNEY

1 Russia (1900–1918) 11

Spiritual Life in St. Petersburg [13]—The Encounter with Anthroposophy [16]

2 Estonia (1918–1938) 17

Anthroposophical Activities [19]—The Orthodox Church [24]—The Second Coming of Christ [31]—The Bible Studies [35]—The Crisis in the Anthroposophical Society [39]—The United Free Anthroposophical Groups [41]—The Lecture Tours to Western Europe [46]—The First Tour (Summer 1937) [47]—The Second Tour (Summer 1938) [50]

3 The Netherlands (1938–1944) 53

Anthroposophical Activities until May 1940 [55]—The Our Mother Prayer [65]—The Conversation with Willem Zeylmans van Emmichoven [74]—The Our Father Course [78]—A Reorientation in the Christian Tradition [86]—The Last Year in Amsterdam [96]—Valentin Tomberg in the Memory of His Friends [98]

4 Germany (1944–1948) 103

A "Second Incarnation" [105]—The Regeneration of Law and Re-Education [107]

5 England (1948–1973) 111
   The Search for Personal Certainty [115]—The Renewal of the Hermetic Tradition [118]—The Last Years [129]

PART II
THE SIGNIFICANCE OF VALENTIN TOMBERG

6 The Controversies 137
   The Criticism of Marie Steiner [139]—Willem Zeylmans van Emmichoven [144]—The Bodhisattva Question [146]—The Catholic Church [150] The Christian Community [163]— Anthroposophy [166]—Time Spirits of the Cultural Epochs [197]

7 Valentin Tomberg and the New Spiritual Thinking 207
   Platonists and Aristotelians [207]—The School of the Archangel Michael [222]—Michael, Sophia, and Christ [227]—Tomberg's Path as Platonist and Hermeticist [233]—Afterword: The Future of Human Intelligence [248]

The Writings of Valentin Tomberg 255

Preface

Russian-born Valentin Tomberg (1900–1973) was first published in the 1930s as an outstanding anthroposophical researcher. After his life took an unexpected turn in 1943, his subsequent Hermetic studies on the symbolism of the Major Arcana of the Tarot led to his recognition as the most significant Christian Hermetic philosopher of the twentieth century. More generally, Tomberg's work can be seen as part of a spiritual movement that began at the outset of the twentieth century and was aimed at developing a new spiritual culture in which human thought might regain access to the world of spirit. According to Rudolf Steiner (1861–1925), the founder of the Anthroposophical Movement, this was part of a long-prepared plan: for this purpose, individualities from the great currents that arose from the work of the Greek philosophers Plato and Aristotle were to join forces and collaborate. Steiner referred to these individuals, in a particular sense unique to his perspective, as "Platonists" and "Aristotelians."

According to Steiner, the intention of the aforementioned plan within the cultural impulse of Anthroposophy was to reach a culmination at the end of the twentieth century—and we can say that, during the first period of his life, Tomberg participated in this task. More particularly, he can be counted among the "Platonists." Unfortunately, however, conflicts arose in the Anthroposophical Society after Steiner's death in 1925 which impeded the intended cooperation between the "Platonists" and "Aristotelians." Compounding this was the chaos that lay so heavy over Europe after the First World War, for it delayed the anticipated advance in spiritual consciousness, which could only then resume making its way more deeply into the unfolding cultural context toward the end of the 1960s. Despite the conflicts that weakened its original thrust, however, Anthroposophy does still have its own role to play in this arena, alongside other spiritual currents.

Valentin Tomberg and the *Ecclesia Universalis*

In part for the reasons just given, Tomberg's work in the Anthroposophical Society did not lead to fruitful cooperation with other anthroposophists. From 1931 onwards he came under criticism by Marie Steiner, Rudolf Steiner's widow. Nonetheless, thanks especially to Elisabeth Vreede, a member of the Board of the Society until 1935, Tomberg was able to develop significant international activities from 1936 onwards, with the result that he moved from Estonia to the Netherlands. At the outbreak of the Second World War in May 1940, however (owing to issues with Willem Zeylmans, the leader of the Dutch Anthroposophical Society), he withdrew from official Anthroposophy. From 1944, Tomberg committed himself as a legal scholar to the regeneration of law in Germany. Then, from 1958 to 1967, he devoted himself to the renewal and Christianizing of the Hermetic tradition. In this way he made his own unique contribution to joining intellectuality with spirituality. To his mind, oriented as it was toward a more religious view, this connection was also a matter of meditation and prayer.

Seen from a larger perspective, Tomberg's life was dedicated to the unity of exoteric and esoteric Christianity within the spiritual space of the *Ecclesia universalis*, the universal Church that is the mystical body of Christ. It unites the Christian Churches, which belong to the Church of the apostle Peter, and the esoteric forms of Christianity, constituting the Church of the apostle John, within which Tomberg worked as an anthroposophist and an Hermeticist. In his exoteric life, Tomberg was baptized in the Lutheran Church. Around 1930 he became a member of the Greek Orthodox Church, and in 1945 he joined the Catholic Church—without leaving the Orthodox Church, in which he was still allowed to receive communion. In this way he became an ecumenical, supra-confessional Christian, as he said, connected with the spirit of the early Church, which was both exoteric and esoteric. For Tomberg, the esoteric aspect of the Church represents the "dimension of depth" that ecclesial Christianity periodically needs for its regeneration.

⊕

Through Tomberg's writings we are able to experience how very differently Eastern Europeans view spiritual life than do Western Euro-

Preface

peans (or, more generally, than do those from the Anglo-Saxon world). In 1935, Tomberg wrote about this, saying that, because of their inner constitution, Westerners focus primarily on sense-perception and conceptual thinking, which, according to Steiner's usage, characterizes the attitude of the "Aristotelian" type, who feels connected to the Archangel Michael (as understood in Anthroposophy). By contrast, before the rise of communism, Eastern Europeans had lived primarily in a world of revelations from the spiritual world in the form of imaginations, inspirations, and intuitions, which is precisely how Steiner characterized the "Platonic" type, whom we may further describe as tending to feel a connection with the being called Sophia (or Divine Wisdom). The "Aristotelian" schooling path of the Archangel Michael and the "Platonic" schooling path of Sophia are therefore quite different. Ideally, these two aspects of Anthroposophy would have been brought together in Central Europe, but unfortunately matters did not turn out this way.

By the time the Second World War had ended, Tomberg's anthroposophical work was no longer much read. But then, in the 1980s, a Tomberg renaissance began. In the United States, between 1982 and 1985, Candeur Manuscripts published his anthroposophical writings. In 1983, Achamoth Press in Germany began publishing them as well, as did the major Catholic publisher Herder. Anthroposophic Press published one of his books in 1992 and SteinerBooks two more in 2006. Three other books appeared in 2009 and 2010 under the LogoSophia imprint, and in 2019 and 2021 two more with Angelico Press (with several more in press).

The first descriptions of Tomberg's life were very incomplete and often incorrect in their details. In 1995, however, the Ramsteiner Kreis in Trier (Germany) commenced a research project on his life, work, and influence. This led to the publication of four books between 2000 and 2016.[1] The two-volume biography numbers over

---

1. Liesel Heckmann, *Valentin Tomberg*, Vol. I.1 ["Life"] (Schaffhausen: Novalis Verlag, 2001); Elisabeth Heckmann and Michael Frensch, *Valentin Tomberg*, Vol. I.2 ["Life"] (Schaffhausen: Novalis Verlag, 2005); Ramsteiner Kreis (ed.), *Valentin*

Valentin Tomberg and the *Ecclesia Universalis*

1200 pages. For this project I researched the periods of Tomberg's life in Estonia and the Netherlands, as well as the Russian Hermetic tradition and Tomberg's related work in the Netherlands. On the basis of this and subsequent research it is now possible to more accurately present Tomberg's relationship to the Christian churches and to the Hermetic tradition in general, as well as to that tradition's reappearance in a variously Christianized form especially in late nineteenth-century France.

An excellent, short English-language introduction to the life and work of Valentin Tomberg was written in 2006 by Christopher Bamford, then editor-in-chief of SteinerBooks.[2] In German, the philosopher Michael Frensch published an important biographical article in 2019, illuminating Tomberg's life from the perspective of his spiritual activity. In an epilogue, he raised the question of whether Tomberg's name should be associated with the "hidden wound of the Anthroposophical Society," namely the failure of that Society to fulfill its karmic task before the spiritual world.[3] Three years earlier, the English researcher Robert Powell had argued that Tomberg became the scapegoat of the Anthroposophical Society because he had provoked the Society's "group double" when he began speaking about the return of Christ in the etheric world.[4] "Group doubles" (which Tomberg refers to as *egregores*) are beings or entities that attach themselves to the negative habits, emotions, and thoughts of people, groups, and nations. On a psychological level, they are most often called "shadows."

In a very real and, in principle, constructive sense, Tomberg held up a mirror to the Anthroposophical Movement. In our time, a cen-

---

Tomberg, Vol. II ["Work"] (Schaffhausen: Novalis Verlag, 2000); Michael Frensch, Elisabeth Heckmann, and Esther Maria Näck (ed.), *Valentin Tomberg*, Vol. III ["Effect"] (Steinbergkirche: Novalis Verlag, 2016).

2. "Introduction to Valentin Tomberg," *Christ and Sophia* (Gt Barrington, MA: Steiner Books, 2006), vii–xxxvi.

3. "Valentin Tombergs Beziehung zur Freien Hochschule," in Elisabeth Wutte and Günter Röschert, *Perspektiven freier Hochschularbeit* (Steinbergkirche: Novalis Verlag, 2019), 84–111.

4. "Valentin Tombergs Bedeutung für die platonische Strömung," in Frensch, a.o., *Valentin Tomberg*, Vol. III, 164–88.

Preface

tury after the renewal of the Anthroposophical Society that took place at the Christmas Conference of 1923, this Movement faces the task of giving a new impulse to the culture of initiation that Steiner had hoped to establish from within the Anthroposophical Society. Such a renewal requires of us a forthright and open weighing up of the past, undertaken with an especially keen awareness of the tasks that have yet to be fulfilled. In this, Tomberg is well qualified to offer guidance, for he was the first (now over eighty years ago) to ask fundamental questions about problems in the Society, the path of schooling, and the place of the religious life and of Sophia in Anthroposophy. In truth, this biography has been undertaken with a special hope that it may contribute to such a new beginning.

To this end, this book first offers a concise description of Tomberg's life before examining the background to the controversies that arose around him. It then elaborates important themes from his work, as well as the more general significance of the "Platonic" and "Aristotelian" currents for the spiritualization of thought. The story of Tomberg's life is a dramatic one, and so it is to be hoped that, by gaining new insight into its unfolding, readers may come to a new and independent valuation and appreciation of it.

My acquaintance with Valentin Tomberg goes back to 1986, when I asked in the library of the Finnish Anthroposophical Society for a book on the spiritual history of Finland. In response, I was handed a 1931 article by Tomberg concerning the significance of the Finns for Russian culture, which led me on to his other writings. For me as a researcher of the spiritual history of Europe, this was the beginning of a rich and fruitful decades-long encounter with the anthroposophist and Christian Hermetic philosopher Tomberg. In the years that followed, I devoted several small publications to him.

After the death in 1996 of Eva Cliteur, who had been a friend of the Tomberg family, Robert Powell (a leading exponent and translator of Tomberg's work in the Anglophone world) invited me to sort out her papers, stored in some fifty bags in her home. Upon transporting them to my flat and emptying them out, I found, among

Valentin Tomberg and the *Ecclesia Universalis*

other things, correspondence about Tomberg, texts by him, and notes from his courses in Amsterdam (which in due course would be published by Achamoth Press). During this time I also met seven people who had known Tomberg fifty-five to sixty years earlier, two of whom had participated in his Our Father Course (which will be discussed later). The image I took away from these reminiscences was of a highly gifted, kind, and modest man who, as an inspired speaker, made a deep impression on those who heard his lectures.

In my research I received help from several others who had already studied Tomberg's life and work for some time. I can mention here the names of Jan Evert de Groot, Michael Frensch, Robert Powell, and Willi Seiss. Mario Betti shared with me his thoughts on the "new Platonism." With Wolfgang Gädeke I had an extensive exchange of views on Bernhard Martin's conversations with Tomberg. Markku Maula and Uberta Sebregondi gave comments on the English manuscript. In Tomberg expert and editor Michael Frensch, this book, written originally in German, has found its best commentator. My sincere thanks go to them all.

Lastly, I am very grateful to James Wetmore, the editor of this English edition, who made a substantial enrichment of the content of the book, and thereby became a dedicated collaborator of this biography.

HARRIE SALMAN
September 2022

Introduction:
From Pilgrim to Hermit

VALENTIN TOMBERG'S LIFE INSCRIBED A WIDE ARC ACROSS Europe. He was born in 1900 into an Estonian family in St. Petersburg, Russia. In 1918, during the Russian Revolution, he fled with his parents to Estonia. Two decades later (a few years before the Soviet Union, and later, Nazi Germany, occupied Estonia) he came to the Netherlands with his family at the invitation of a circle of Dutch anthroposophists. He lived in the Netherlands from 1938 to 1944, in which year, shortly before the end of the war, his friend Ernst von Hippel invited him and his family to come to Germany, where he lived for four years (1944–1948). In the unstable post-war period, when it still seemed Western Europe might be occupied by the Soviet army, Tomberg decided to emigrate to England, where he was to live for twenty-five years. He died during a holiday on the Spanish island of Majorca in 1973.

Tomberg's city of birth, St. Petersburg, is situated in the area where, according to both Rudolf Steiner and the Bulgarian spiritual teacher Peter Deunov, the coming "sixth cultural epoch" will spread from Northern Russia over the world. Thus, we may take Tomberg's appearance on the Eastern horizon of Europe and subsequent residence in five countries as an image of his journey through Europe "from the future," bearing impulses from the Slavic culture of the epoch to come. He was the first representative of the Russian tradition of Divine Wisdom, or Sophiology, within the Anthroposophical Movement. But from there he "descended" further into the past. From 1959 onwards he immersed himself in the Hermetic tradition of Egyptian antiquity, with which he had already become acquainted forty-two years earlier, in 1917, in St. Petersburg. His purpose in this immersion was, however, to *transform* it into a *Christian* tradition. Behind this tradition stands the initiate Hermes

Trismegistus ("Thrice-Great"), who is associated with the Greek god Hermes and the Egyptian god Thoth.

Although of Estonian descent, through his upbringing and schooling Tomberg was deeply grounded in the Christian culture of Russia. This culture was his soul's home. As regards his own spiritual development, it was on this Slavic foundation that he first associated himself with Anthroposophy, and later with the Hermetic tradition.

Outwardly, Tomberg lived the life of a refugee traveling through Europe. Spiritually, however, he was a pilgrim from the Russian tradition preparing the way to the next cultural epoch. He was a member, we could say, of "Eternal Israel," as he called the community of those intimately connected with Christ who, in the present, must "wander through the desert" of materialism. During his Dutch period, Tomberg made the drawing entitled *De Eeuwige Pelgrim* (The Eternal Pilgrim), reproduced on page 10, which we may surely interpret as a self-portrait.

While working on his magisterial *Meditations on the Tarot: A Journey into Christian Hermeticism*[1] in the 1960s, Tomberg was living in seclusion near London: truly, by the end of his life, the pilgrim had become a wise hermit. Following the example of the Egyptian Desert Fathers of early Christianity, he described himself as a hermit in the "modern metropolis." For this phase of his life, then, we might equally well take as his self-portrait the image of the Hermit of the Ninth Arcanum of the Tarot.

In the first part of this book, we will follow Tomberg's journey, in five chapters, through its "stations." In the second part we will discuss his significance both for Anthroposophy and for the Hermetic tradition. Here we will look at the controversies that arose around his person in the Anthroposophical Society, and at his path as an anthroposophist and Hermetic philosopher within the great project of collaboration between the "Aristotelians" and "Platonists."

---

1. Current expanded and supplemented edition (Brooklyn, NY: Angelico Press, 2019), hereafter usually referred to simply as *Meditations*.

PART I

The Stations of
Valentin Tomberg's Life Journey

The Eternal Pilgrim, a drawing by V. Tomberg

1

Russia

(1900–1918)

VALENTIN JOSEPH TOMBERG WAS BORN JUST AFTER THE end of the *Kali Yuga*, the "Age of Darkness," which, according to Rudolf Steiner, passed into the "Age of Light" in 1899—during which age, according to Steiner, people would begin to develop a new spiritual consciousness on the basis of their openness to new possibilities of both spiritual and natural clairvoyant faculties. Many young people born in the first years of the new era found their way to Anthroposophy. Steiner expected these abilities to be sufficiently developed by the beginning of the 1930s, such that many would be able to perceive what he described as the pivotal event of Christ's appearance in the "etheric" (or, living) sphere of the earth ("in the clouds" according to Matthew 24:30) at the commencement of his second coming.

More exactly, Tomberg was born in St. Petersburg on February 26, 1900 (according to the Gregorian calendar) into a family of Estonian emigrants. His father, Arnold Tomberg (1865–1940), worked as a registrar at the Petri School (where Valentin was a pupil at primary and grammar school) and later as a secretary at the Russian Ministry of Internal Affairs. Arnold was born in Vaida, near the Estonian capital of Tallinn, and died in the Estonian city of Narva. Both of Valentin's parents grew up in Estonian families that also had some connection with German culture.

At home in St. Petersburg, the family spoke Russian, German, and Estonian. Valentin had a four-year-older brother, Richard, who studied chemistry, worked later in Tallinn, and finally emigrated to Germany. After the war, the brothers met again after Richard dis-

Valentin Tomberg and the *Ecclesia Universalis*

covered quite by accident that Valentin had given a lecture somewhere in Germany.

At the end of his life, Tomberg wrote of how, when he was four years old, his mother Juliana Umblia (1868–1918/19) implanted in him a "fundamental seed-thought and seed-experience":

> One day, sixty-eight years ago, when the author was four years old, he was sitting on a colored carpet playing with building blocks. Through an open window, he could see a cloudless blue sky. The child's mother was sitting in a chair, watching him at play. Suddenly the child looked up and, gazing through the window at the blue heavens, spontaneously asked his mother: "Where is God? Is he in heaven? Does he float there? Or is he sitting there? Where?"
>
> The child's mother sat up straight and gave the following answer, which has held true for the child ever after: "God is present everywhere. We know that, even though we cannot see the air, it penetrates everything—and that it is only thanks to the air that we can live and breathe. In this same way, we live and breathe in God. And since it is in God that we live and breathe, it is from God and thanks to God that we live."
>
> This answer, so clear and convincing, was like a breath of fresh air that ever after blew away any conundrums on this question, leaving behind always the certainty of God's invisible presence everywhere. And as has been said, this seed-thought was to flourish into the heights and depths and breadths, proving to be the primal seed from which a many-branched tree of insight and faith unfolded over the following decades of the author's life.[1]

Valentin's remoter ancestors on both sides were serfs.[2] His grandfathers were carpenters and cabinet makers. The surname Tomberg was established in 1835, when serfdom was abolished in northern Estonia by Joachim von Baranoff, lord of the Väätsa estate near Paide (Estonia). This estate included the farmers of Nehatu, where Valentin's great-grandfather, Jaak of the Jaagu farm, lived at the time. The name Tomberg is common in Estonia, Finland, and Scan-

---

1. Tomberg, *The New Evolution of the Good: The Three Kingdoms and the Breath of God* (Brooklyn, NY: Angelico Press, 2022), 49–50.

2. In the first volume of the Tomberg biography (2001) it was assumed that the Tomberg family belonged to the lower nobility.

dinavia. It may be derived from Thomasberg or Domberg, and, in Estonia, perhaps from Toomberg or Toomingasberg ("hill with bird cherries").[3]

Spiritual Life in St. Petersburg

Prior to the Revolution of 1917, there was a rich "esoteric" spiritual life in Russia. Besides the older Rosicrucian and Masonic movements, this spiritual life included Martinism, Theosophy, and Anthroposophy. The French occultist and magician Gérard Encausse (known as Papus) was co-founder in 1891 of the pseudo-masonic order of the Martinists. This order had taken its name from the eighteenth-century French mystic philosopher Louis-Claude de Saint-Martin, but his Christian theosophy had nothing to do with what Papus later made of it. In 1901, Papus came to Moscow and St. Petersburg, where he gave lectures attended by the Russian Tsar and members of his court.

The activities of Papus, who was again in St. Petersburg in 1905 and 1906 (where he was consulted by the Tsar as physician and occult advisor) were also political. Rudolf Steiner spoke on April 4, 1916 of Papus' devastating influence and disastrous political role at the court of the Tsar.[4] The activity in question strengthened the anti-German alliance of France and Russia, as historian Markus Osterrieder notes.[5] In this sense, Papus was partially responsible for the First World War.

In 1910, as head of the St. Petersburg branch of the Order of Martinists, Papus appointed the mathematics teacher Grigori O. Mebes[6] as its secretary. Mebes soon founded his own Martinist lodge in 1911, which became independent of the Paris center in 1912. In this

---

3. Harrie Salman, *Forschungsergebnisse zur Geschichte der Familie Tomberg*, 2000 (unpublished).

4. See Rudolf Steiner, lecture of April 4, 1916, in *The Human Spirit Past and Present: Occult Fraternities and the Mystery of Golgotha* (Forest Row, UK: Rudolf Steiner Press, 2015), 65 (CW 167). Throughout, CW refers to the "Collected Works" numeration system of Steiner's extensive works.

5. Markus Osterrieder, *Welt im Umbruch* (Stuttgart: Freies Geistesleben, 2014), 490.

6. The surname Mebes is often transliterated as Meubes or Moebes.

lodge he introduced a hierarchy of three degrees: Martinist, Templar, and Rosicrucian.[7] To each degree corresponded an occult order, all three of which operated under his leadership.[8]

Beginning in 1902, a German-speaking Theosophical group had become active in St. Petersburg, and two years later a Russian Theosophical group was formed. Both groups had contact with Marie von Sivers, the future wife of Rudolf Steiner. When (in 1913) Steiner founded his own Anthroposophical Society, and subsequently was expelled from the Theosophical Society, member groups were also founded in Moscow and St. Petersburg that same year.[9] Already at the age of fifteen, Tomberg was introduced to this world of esotericism in St. Petersburg. In 1917 he became a member of the Theosophical Society, in whose library he came upon the book *Knowledge of the Higher Worlds and Its Attainment* and other writings by Steiner. Thus began his study of Anthroposophy.

That same year, Tomberg also read *The Holy Book of Thoth: The Great Arcana of the Tarot*,[10] published the year before by Vladimir A. Shmakov, who led a circle of "Rosicrucians" in Moscow. Shmakov, a railway engineer, had no ties with French Martinism. In his book he gave a kabbalistic interpretation of the Tarot cards, which he supplemented with references to various spiritual, philosophical, and scientific movements. In his comments on the arcana of the High Priestess and the Empress, Shmakov developed his ideas on the feminine.[11] It may have been through study of this book that the young Tomberg became acquainted with the teachings on the Divine Wisdom (Sophia) of the Russian religious philosophers Vladimir Solovyov and Pavel Florensky. Florensky, a priest and

---

7. Harrie Salman, "Valentin Tomberg und die neuere hermetische Philosophie," in *Valentin Tomberg*, Vol. II, 120–31.

8. See G.O. Mebes, *Tarot Majors* and *Tarot Minors*, two volumes (England: Shin Publications, 2020).

9. Viktor B. Fedjuschin, *Russlands Sehnsucht nach Spiritualität* (Schaffhausen: Novalis Verlag, 1988).

10. England: Shin Publications, 2022. See also *The Magi and the Fool* (England: Shin Publications, 2021), 134–77.

11. Stanislav Panin, "Cosmic Feminine in the 'Synthetic Esoteric Philosophy' of Vladimir Shmakov," in *La Rosa di Paracelso* (1/2017, www.academia.edu).

Russia (1900–1918)

polymath of astonishing erudition, attended Shmakov's circle in the early 1920s.

The young Tomberg was well acquainted with the spiritual literature of his time. In a letter to Bernhard Martin dated January 1, 1966, he wrote that, in 1917, he had studied three books by the Russian esoteric writer P. D. Ouspensky (1878–1947), who had become a disciple of Gurdjieff in 1915. These books were *Tertium Organum*, *The Symbolism of the Tarot* (both from 1912), and *Strange Life of Ivan Osokin* (1915).[12]

When the Russian Revolution broke out in November 1917, Tomberg had just begun to study law, philosophy, and history at St. Petersburg University. A few months later, in April 1918, he fled with his parents to Estonia, which had become independent from Russia. Shortly before their departure he had a profound spiritual experience that led him to take a "holy vow" about which he wrote in 1933:

Vladimir A. Shmakov (1887–1929)

> Fifteen years ago (in St. Petersburg, in Russia) it happened—on the street, amid many passers-by—that I experienced an awakening of deep soul forces. I felt the awakening. I became conscious of a powerful force of will within me that I united in the depths of my heart with a holy vow *to dedicate my whole life to the cultivation of spiritual knowledge and its manifestation to the world*. I have never forgotten this vow—others may say and think of it as they will. I can only say, before my conscience and my angel, that I have remained faithful to it in all the decisions and questions of life. It shines in me like a radiant sun that irradiates and illumines all.[13]

---

12. Archive of Christiane Martin.
13. Letter to Marie Steiner, January 19, 1933. Rudolf Steiner Nachlassverwaltung, Dornach.

Valentin Tomberg and the *Ecclesia Universalis*

The Encounter with Anthroposophy

Already in St. Petersburg, Tomberg had began to put into practice the exercises described in Rudolf Steiner's book *Knowledge of the Higher Worlds*. Whether he met anthroposophists there is not known. He said later that he had been actively engaged in Anthroposophy since his twentieth year, having found Theosophy to be one-sided and dogmatic. Regarding this, on July 28, 1920 he wrote the following letter to Rudolf Steiner,[14] which, however, probably never reached him:

> Most Honored Doctor!
> Three years ago I joined the Russian Theosophical Society, making "spiritual culture" my goal. But I could not work with theosophical one-sidedness, nor, especially, Theosophy's unrestrained suppression of every free movement of thinking. On the other hand, your writings (*Knowledge of the Higher Worlds*, *An Outline of Esoteric Science*, *Theosophy*, and *A Way to Self-Knowledge*) showed me that there existed another movement in which precisely what I missed in Theosophy was to be found: regard both for the requirements of reason and also for the uniqueness of the individual.
>
> For this reason I turned to Anthroposophy. However, the more particular reason I turn to you now with the request to be taken into the circle of your students (for it is with this alone that this letter is concerned) is that, since 1917, I have practiced the meditation exercises given by you in the books, and results have been forthcoming. This last circumstance convinces me that Anthroposophy is not charlatanism, that you know what you are talking about, and also that the area I seek to enter is a dangerous one. I do not wish to suffer the fate of that young mountain cow (of which the Buddha speaks) who, in search of fresh meadows and pastures, wandered into an unknown mountain range and fell into an abyss. These two circumstances—trust in you, and the seriousness of what I intend to undertake—are what prompt me to turn to you, Herr Doctor.
>
> Respectfully,
Valentin Tomberg

14. Letter to Rudolf Steiner, Rudolf Steiner Nachlassverwaltung, Dornach. English translation (revised) taken from *Inner Development* (Gt Barrington, MA: SteinerBooks, 1992), Introduction.

2

Estonia

(1918–1938)

AFTER THEY FLED ST. PETERSBURG, THE TOMBERG FAMILY lived first in the Estonian border town of Narva. For Tomberg this was the time (October 1918) when he immersed himself in Anthroposophy while simultaneously having to make his way in a country new to him.[1]

In November 1918, when the Red Army attacked Estonia, the Tombergs fled westward to Rakvere. In December 1918 or early January 1919, Valentin's mother was shot dead in the street by Red Army soldiers while searching for her husband and sons. This tragic event filled Valentin for many years with a sense of guilt. At the beginning of 1919, together now with his father and brother, he volunteered to serve at the front in the Estonian army, fighting against the Reds. However, he soon fell ill and was caught and imprisoned for a short time before being liberated. From 1920 to 1922 he served as a nurse in a military hospital near Tallinn. After that he earned a living with occasional work as a farm laborer, pharmacy assistant, receptionist, French and English correspondent at the Ministry of Foreign Affairs, and artist (he once drew a cartoon for a newspaper). At night he studied law, philosophy, and religion. He did not have enough money to enroll at the nearby University of Tartu.

---

1. For those readers disposed to attend to how astrological cycles play out in individual biographies, we note that this was also the time of Tomberg's first "moon node." Moon nodes repeat every 18 years, 7 months, and 9 days, when the orbits of the moon and the sun cross at the same point in the zodiac which they had occupied at birth. According to some, this nodal period can be experienced as a fresh awakening of the original birth, or destiny, impulses.

Valentin Tomberg and the *Ecclesia Universalis*

Already during his military service in Tallinn he led a weekly study group on esoteric themes.

In 1919/20, he studied the book *Encyclopaedia of Occultism* by G.O. Mebes, which was based on a lecture series on the arcana of the Tarot given in St. Petersburg, and published in 1912. Like Shmakov, Mebes based his interpretation of the arcana on the Kabbalah, and referred primarily to the French authors Eliphas Lévi and Papus.[2]

Passages from Tomberg's later *Meditations* indicate that he had not been a member of Hermetic circles, either in St. Petersburg, or, in 1920, when he met members of Mebes's lodge in Estonia, some of whom he befriended.[3] Among the members of this lodge who had fled to Estonia was the prominent Hermetic philosopher and physician Nina Roudnikova,[4] who was connected with Theosophy and with the painter and mystic Nikolai Roerich. In *Meditations* Tomberg wrote that these friends, "who belonged to the elite of the Rosicrucian group" of Mebes, told him in sincere friendship everything they knew about the work in their lodge.[5]

In an article from 1930, Tomberg described the Templar movement in European esotericism as represented in the lodge of Mebes. This movement worked with a system of symbols (the 22 Major Arcana and the 56 Minor Arcana of the Tarot) which the student did not try to penetrate with thoughts, but instead to put into the service of ceremonial magic. The intention of this movement, then, was to produce spiritual effects in the sensory world, and to obtain answers to questions.[6]

---

2. Konstatin Yu. Burmistrov, "Kabbalah and Martinism—Gregory Moebes and the Occult Renaissance in Russia of the Early 20th Century" (www.academia.edu, 2017).

3. In Heckmann, *Valentin Tomberg*, Vol. I.1, 45, and in Heckmann and Frensch, *Valentin Tomberg*, Vol. I.2, 335, 337. On the basis of this friendship, the wrong conclusion was drawn that he already in St. Petersburg had cooperated with these Hermeticists from the lodge of Mebes.

4. See Nina Roudnikova, *The Solar Way*, translated by Charlotte Cowell (England: Shin Publications, 2021).

5. *Meditations*, Letter XXI.

6. "Western Occultism, Vedanta, and Anthroposophy," in *Russian Spirituality and Other Essays: Mysteries of Our Time Seen Through the Eyes of a Russian Esoterist* (San Rafael, CA: LogoSophia, 2010), 37–42; hereafter, *Russian Spirituality*.

Estonia (1918–1938)

For his own part, in *Meditations* (arranged in twenty-two Letters to the "Unknown Friend") Tomberg criticized the use of magic for personal and collective purposes—that is, as a means to impose one's will on the invisible and visible world. In Letter XXI he discussed the work in the lodge of Mebes, in which study of the Major Arcana of the Tarot served as preparation for the study of the Minor Arcana. For Tomberg, the Major Arcana constituted an encyclopedic system of instruction in the Hermetic sciences of kabbalah, magic, astrology, and alchemy. These sciences had emerged in the West during the Italian Renaissance, but had their origins in late Egyptian culture. As has been said, the mythical figure of Hermes Trismegistus was considered the founder of this Hermetic tradition.

As he writes in Letter XXI, Tomberg received from Mebes's group only a general incentive to penetrate deeper into the symbolism of the Tarot. In his own work on the subject, he did not draw on Mebes's instructions. And he likewise rejected the ceremonial magic of Papus' Martinism, which was practiced in Mebes's lodge. His first introduction to the symbolism of the Tarot had in fact been the "magisterial" book by Shmakov, which had made such a deep impression on him in 1917 owing to its scientific and spiritual content. For Tomberg, the Major Arcana were *not* a means of ceremonial magic, but a school of meditation, a spiritual path of learning.

Anthroposophical Activities

It was on July 28, 1920, that Tomberg wrote the above-mentioned letter to Rudolf Steiner, asking to be accepted into his circle of disciples. It had become clear to him by this time that Anthroposophy was his spiritual path. In a second letter, dated July 7, 1924, he wrote to Steiner that since 1920 he had been actively involved in anthroposophical work and hoped to become a member of the School of Spiritual Science in Dornach (near Basel, Switzerland), the international center of the Anthroposophical Society.[7] A first cycle of seven years of intensive anthroposophical study (1917–1924) was thus brought to a close. On January 1, 1925, he became an official member of the Anthroposophical Society.

---

7. Letter to Rudolf Steiner, Rudolf Steiner Nachlassverwaltung, Dornach.

Valentin Tomberg and the *Ecclesia Universalis*

Stepping back now several years, after completing his military service in 1922, Tomberg had married Elena Glasenap (1881–1944), an invalid woman. She was an acquaintance of his mother and nineteen years his senior. This was a marriage of convenience, which was ended in 1932. During Tomberg's second marriage, however, Elena remained in the new family as "grandmother." In 1923, after passing an exam in constitutional law, Tomberg took a position with the Estonian Post Office in Tallinn, where, over the ensuing years, his skills and extensive knowledge of languages elevated him to head of the International Telephone Service.

As early as February 1926, Tomberg became vice-president of the Estonian Anthroposophical Society, which, in 1925, was made up of thirty-six members (Estonian, German, and Russian). He led working groups and began lecturing and writing articles. In June 1926 he sent the editorial board of the journal *Das Goetheanum* in Dornach an article entitled "Cosmic Law in the History of the Anthroposophical Society," which, however, was not published at the time.[8] At the end of July 1926 he traveled to Danzig (now in Poland), where an anthroposophical conference was held. A year later, at a second meeting in Danzig, in July 1927, he met Marie Steiner, Guenther Wachsmuth, and Elisabeth Vreede, who were members of the Executive Council of the Anthroposophical Society in Dornach. Here he was admitted to the First Class of the School of Spiritual Science.[9] According to the conference program, Tomberg (or possibly chairman Otto Sepp) was to give a lecture on the Baltic countries of Estonia, Latvia, and Lithuania, which had become independent after the First World War.

---

8. Later published in *Aufzeichnungen, Vortragsnachschriften* (Bodensee, Germany: Achamoth Verlag), 117–23. Not in English translation at this time.

9. Immediately after the founding of the General Anthroposophical Society during the Christmas Conference of 1923/24, Rudolf Steiner began to build up a School of Spiritual Science, beginning with the developmental path of the First Class, consisting of nineteen "class lessons" transmitted by him and "read" out either verbatim or "freely" by "class readers" to the members of the School. Steiner had intended to establish also a Second and a Third Class, but died before these could be established.

Estonia (1918–1938)

At this juncture, Marie Steiner had become a confidante of Tomberg. On December 3, 1928, he wrote to her about how he and four non-anthroposophical, but esoterically-minded, friends (among them Nina Roudnikova and her husband Baron Andrei von Uexküll) had caught the attention of a political-occult group with connections to the Jesuits. This latter group wanted to enlist their aid in actions opposing the Soviet Union. Tomberg asked Marie Steiner for her advice, in the event that he might discover that the intention of this group was to try to influence him by means of magic.[10] What she answered is not known.

Tomberg traveled as a representative of the Estonian Anthroposophical Society to Dornach three times (1929, 1930, and 1931) to attend meetings. In August of 1929 he became better acquainted with Albert Steffen (who had succeeded Steiner, upon his death, as president of the Anthroposophical Society) and Marie Steiner. During this first stay he must have heard about a meeting of Russian anthroposophists planned for the summer of 1930 and decided to participate in its preparation. Maria Regina Belozvetov (1893–1973), born in Saratov on the Volga as Countess Leitnecker-Demsky, and leader of the Berlin group of Russian anthroposophists founded in 1928, was the driving force behind this initiative. Of Polish-French extraction, she had grown up in Russia and been a member of the Anthroposophical Society since 1915. She studied piano in Moscow and music theory in Paris. Her father, Count Emil Demski, worked in Russia as a railway engineer; her mother, Victoria de Montfort, was a French countess. They had a home in St. Petersburg and were known at the court of the Tsar. In the wake of the Russian Revolution of 1917, Maria's father was killed by soldiers of the Red Army. Her two brothers died in prison. The story is told that when she brought them a bible, her lower jaw was broken by a blow from a rifle butt.

At Christmas 1929, Tomberg traveled to Berlin to visit Maria and her husband Nikolai Belozvetov (1892–1950). An intensive spiritual cooperation grew out of this visit. Like Tomberg, the Russian Nikolai Belozvetov had been born in St. Petersburg. Furthermore,

---

10. Letter to Marie Steiner, Rudolf Steiner Nachlassverwaltung, Dornach.

Valentin Tomberg and the *Ecclesia Universalis*

he had been accepted into the Anthroposophical Society by Rudolf Steiner in Helsinki in 1913. During the First World War, Nikolai was an artillery officer. In 1920, he fled Russia with his wife Maria, who had married him shortly before in order that she might leave Russia. The couple came to Berlin in 1921, where Nikolai became active in Anthroposophy as a speaker and writer.[11]

During his residency in Estonia, Tomberg worked, from 1926 onwards, mainly with Russian-speaking anthroposophists.[12] He led four groups: an introductory group, a circle for the study of Vladimir Solovyov, a circle in which Steiner's *Anthroposophical Leading Thoughts* were discussed, and a circle focused on Steiner's *Mystery Dramas*. As he wrote in a letter, there was among the Russians "a soul-warming, deeply enthusiastic Anthroposophy."

Now thirty years old, Tomberg wanted to build a bridge from Russian spiritual life to Anthroposophy, but also to awaken an understanding of Russian culture in Central Europe. To this end, in 1930 and 1931 he wrote thirty-two important articles for the German journal *Anthroposophie*, published in Stuttgart. Before this journal for "free spiritual life" had to be discontinued in the autumn of 1931 for financial reasons, Tomberg had contributed articles on Western and Eastern spirituality, anthroposophical esotericism, Christianity, and figures from Russian spiritual life (Dostoevsky, Solovyov, and Tolstoy).[13] These articles illustrate the independence and depth of his anthroposophical work and research. His orientation towards esoteric Christianity (that is, the Christianity of inner development), which becomes visible in these articles, stands in the tradition of Russian religious philosophy, whose leading representative,

---

11. Ludmilla Zimmermann-Belozvetov, "Eine große Freundschaft—Valentin Tomberg und Nikolai Belozvetov," in Heckmann and Frensch, *Valentin Tomberg*, Vol. I.2, 643–58. Belozvetov was the author of philosophical and anthroposophical writings. In some of them it is evident that he was inspired by Tomberg. These articles were published in 2020 by Achamoth Verlag in the book *Aufbruch zur VI. Kulturepoche* (misattributed, in this author's view, to Tomberg, apparently on the basis of similarity of content stemming from Tomberg's inspiration, as just mentioned).

12. See Tomberg's letter to Albert Steffen, July 18, 1930. Goetheanum Archive, Dornach.

13. *Russian Spirituality.*

Estonia (1918–1938)

Vladimir Solovyov, exercised considerable influence on his thinking. According to Rudolf Steiner, in Solovyov we already find a seed of the philosophy of the next culture.[14]

In Tomberg's first three articles for this journal he described how in John's gospel the activity of the hierarchies of angels becomes visible. At the same time, these articles were an introduction to esotericism, which he developed further, independently, on the basis of Rudolf Steiner's insights on the subject.[15] In the second article, the topic of moral logic announced itself. In the third, on the metamorphosis of thought, the theme of the being Sophia resounded. He wrote:

> In Eastern Christian thought there lives a remarkable figure. This figure is Mary, the Mother of God, who is at the same time Sophia, the Holy Wisdom. She is also the "Church," the principle of the *community* of all humanity, and is therefore of the same essence as Christ. This principle is therefore that of community (*ecclesia*); that is, that which unifies beings. It provides the possibility and manner of the unison of the graded ranks of hierarchical beings. At this point, our thinking is faced with a still higher challenge— the challenge to think in "communities," to think "sophianically."[16]

In an article published in May 1931, Tomberg described the Divine Wisdom, or Sophia, as the "soul of the Church," who could only reveal herself in the community of believers. In a notebook entry of December 11, 1933, he described Sophia as an archangelic being who works on the level of the angels: "She is a pure grace for the world, who allows the *manas* to radiate in a bestowing way." Only through Sophia does one pass through the gates of the Father and of the Son and of the Holy Spirit. The Russian archangel, he said, is deeply connected to Sophia.[17]

---

14. Lecture of June 16, 1910, in *The Mission of Folk-Souls* (CW 121).

15. "The Gospel of St. John as a Way Toward Understanding the Spiritual Hierarchies," in *Russian Spirituality*, 1–12.

16. Ibid., "The Metamorphosis of Thinking through the Study of Spiritual Science," 20–21.

17. Transcriptions of notebooks made by Willi Seiss, Archive of the Freie Hermetisch-Christliche Studienstätte am Bodensee, Taisersdorf and Tomberg Archive in Steinbergkirche, both in Germany.

Valentin Tomberg and the *Ecclesia Universalis*

In an article on Bolshevism, Tomberg noted that the secret aim of Bolshevism was that the "metabolic man" should come to dominate culture. For the Bolshevists, all culture was to be understood as a function of economic life. To achieve this goal it was crucial to interrupt the rhythmic cultural life of the Church and religion, which mediated between metabolic and sensory life.[18]

Another important theme of this early period was the significance of guiltless suffering, through which the higher self can be developed. Tomberg approached this theme by reference to the legend of the City of Kitesh, and to the great importance of suffering as it lives in the Russian mentality. Suffering can be experienced as the breathing of the Christ spirit into human souls, he wrote.[19] Only once, on September 28, 1930, did the magazine *Das Goetheanum* (edited by Albert Steffen) publish an article by Tomberg. In this article he described how a group can arrive at living knowledge through working together "in the harmonious accordance of individual insights."[20]

During the years 1930 and 1931, Tomberg traveled twice a month to Riga, the capital of Latvia, to give public lectures. Between 1928 and 1932, Nikolai Belozvetov's mother led the anthroposophical work of a group of Russian emigrants there. During a stay in Dornach in September 1930, Tomberg was invited to Paris to give lectures for the Russian group. Here he again met Maria Belozvetov, who had been studying at the Conservatory in Paris since 1928.[21]

The Orthodox Church

For Russians, their national identity is strongly linked to the Orthodox Church. And so it was natural that Russian anthroposophists living as emigrés in the West still felt a strong connection with their Church. In a letter of April 11, 1931, Tomberg wrote to Marie Steiner

---

18. *Russian Spirituality*, "The Secret Motto of Bolshevism," 168–72.
19. Ibid., "The Saga of the Holy City of Kitesh as Revelation of the Essential Forces of the Russian Folk-Soul," 167–72, and "The East European Conception of Suffering," 111–15.
20. Ibid., "The Philosophy of Taking Counsel with Others," 43–47.
21. Heckmann and Frensch, *Valentin Tomberg*, Vol. I.2, 324.

Estonia (1918–1938)

(who at that time still very much appreciated him) that Nikolai and Maria Belozvetov, and the Russian anthroposophical circles in Tallinn, Riga, Berlin, and Paris, had for years been occupied with the issue of the relationship between Anthroposophy and Orthodox Christianity. They shared the view that a connection with Eastern Christianity was possible. Independently of each other, Tomberg and Belozvetov had taken the same position. On this question, they had entered into what Tomberg referred to as a "polemic" with the Christian Community (the movement for religious renewal that had been founded in 1922 with Steiner's collaboration) because it had come to their attention that some in the Christian Community had apparently expressed the view that, in effect, the cult of the Christian Community was to replace all other cults—indeed, that it conceived itself as the Church of the future for all humankind! In actual fact, with the wisdom of hindsight, we must interject that this radical position was not at all the general view in the Christian Community. It was the personal view of one or a few priests of the Christian Community, more specifically Kurt von Wistinghausen, who had written a brochure in Russian on the Christian Community in 1926. Belozvetov and Tomberg countered such claims by arguing that, although they did agree that the Russians benefited from the anthroposophical worldview, their cultic needs were fully met by the Orthodox Church.

Tomberg wrote to Marie Steiner as well that, in his work with Russian anthroposophists, he encouraged a connection with Orthodox Christianity, adding that he had done the same in prior years through his presentations on the work of the Russian philosopher Solovyov, and had recently been studying the Russian writer Dostoevsky in this same connection with a circle in Tallinn. He reported to her as well that he was engaged in a course of study on the dogmatic theology and liturgy of the Eastern Church, and was learning Greek in order to "get to the roots of Orthodox Christianity." He also asked Marie Steiner if she could report anything Rudolf Steiner might have said on this matter, and as well, how she herself viewed it. In his book *Wege und Worte*, the German anthroposophist Ludwig Kleeberg had quoted statements by Rudolf Steiner to the effect that the seeds of the future lay in Greek Catholicism, because everything was still fluid in it and "everything was Theosophy."[22] Pondering this question may have been a factor in Tomberg's decision to become a member of the Greek Orthodox Church in the early 1930s.

In July 1931, Tomberg met Marie Steiner in Helsinki, Finland at a conference where she read all the class lessons of the Free School of Spiritual Science.[23] These were nineteen meetings for members of the First Class of this School, at which the nineteen class lessons given by Rudolf Steiner were read aloud by a "class reader." During the class lessons Tomberg had a spiritual experience, about which he wrote to Marie Steiner on July 12, 1931:

> I experienced an awakening of the soul that I could hardly have expected. With my whole soul I have heard the meditation texts that you have spoken in the hall. And everything that they contained I was able to experience this time with all the inner movement of the soul, with all the radiance of the soul. Space disappeared from my consciousness, I lost myself, and instead of both the outside world and myself, a vibrating, radiant majestic experience descended like a mighty wedge of spirit that was both a piece of the world and a piece of man.[24]

Recalling that Tomberg began his studies of Anthroposophy in 1917, by now twice seven years had passed. He had been working for Anthroposophy in Estonia since 1924, and since 1931 had been actively involved in the International Anthroposophical Movement with lectures and articles.

The conference for Russian members of the School of Spiritual Science held in Dornach in August 1931 brought him his first criticism. Nikolai and Maria Belozvetov had taken the position that the Orthodox Church was a vessel for Anthroposophy. Tomberg had apparently supported this view with arguments of his own. On February 2, 1934, however, the German anthroposophist Hermann Poppelbaum wrote to Marie Steiner that Belozvetov had stated in a conversation with him that he had abandoned his view that

---

22. Letter to Marie Steiner, Rudolf Steiner Nachlassverwaltung, Dornach.

23. On this occasion, Tomberg himself gave a lecture on the Foundation Stone Meditation.

24. Heckmann and Frensch, *Valentin Tomberg*, Vol. I.1, 97.

Estonia (1918–1938)

Anthroposophy and the Russian Church could "go hand in hand."[25] Marie Steiner is said to have spoken negatively about Tomberg and Maria Belozvetov. Furthermore, Yekaterina Ilyina, a central figure among Russian anthroposophists, is reputed to have said in Dornach that Tomberg was still too young, and susceptible to the undesirable influence of Maria Belozvetov. The perception that Dornach was not satisfied with Tomberg soon spread back to those in Tallinn. It seemed that Tomberg was falling out of favor with Dornach.[26] Valentin and Maria found themselves in a field of antipathies that emanated from Dornach. (In Part II of the present book, this criticism from Dornach will be discussed in more detail.)

In April 1932, Tomberg was back in Berlin with Nikolai and Maria Belozvetov, whose marriage had ended earlier. On May 28, 1932, he wrote to Marie Steiner that he intended to marry Maria Belozvetov, and, after the summer, to study law in Berlin. He had already commenced such studies in St. Petersburg, but had been unable to complete them owing to the onset of the Russian Revolution. The present problem was that he lacked the financial means to study in Berlin. For this reason, on September 28, 1932, he wrote to Marie Steiner to say that he wished to remain in Estonia for another year and a half, and that during the past summer he had offered a course on Steiner's book *Knowledge of the Higher Worlds* as well as a study of some lectures from the series on *Karmic Relationships*.

On September 25, 1932, Tomberg was elected President of the Estonian Anthroposophical Society, succeeding Otto Sepp. He was also put in charge of the class lessons. Maria Belozvetov moved to Tallinn in the autumn of 1932. On January 19, 1933, Tomberg wrote to Marie Steiner asking for logistical support, as he hoped to live in Dornach over that year, working and studying with Maria Belozvetov for the purpose of writing a book on Eastern Europe. Further reasons were that the Estonian group now had a capable leader to take over his work, and that the group of Russian anthroposophists (which had numbered about thirty in the beginning) had dwindled

---

25. Ibid., 169.
26. Maja Hörschelmann, letter to Elisabeth Vreede, November 5, 1936, in Heckmann and Frensch, *Valentin Tomberg*, Vol. I.1, 511–22.

Valentin Tomberg and the *Ecclesia Universalis*

owing to their gradual emigration to the West, so that his task in their regard no longer had any future. In the letter, he described the extent to which he had become associated with the anthroposophical cause over the past sixteen years.[27] Marie Steiner replied: "In Dornach itself there is no need for speakers."[28] Moreover, she saw no possibility of helping him in the difficult economic situation prevailing at that time.

Marie Steiner, née von Sivers (1867–1948)

By the spring of 1933, Tomberg discovered that the articles he had sent to Albert Steffen had not been published in *Das Goetheanum*, with no reason having been given. Among these articles had been one entitled "Two contemporary Indian world teachers: Krishnamurti and Meher Baba."[29]

Tomberg was aware that Marie Steiner had accused Maria Belozvetov of not having a positive relationship with the Goetheanum (the center of the Anthroposophical Society in Dornach), and also of exerting a negative influence on him personally. He also noticed that some Estonian and German members of the Estonian Society had developed a certain antipathy towards Maria. It had come to his attention that in Dornach "absurd slander" was being spread about his wife-to-be, for example by the Russian Natalya Pozzo, against which Maria could not defend herself. A further problem was that Tomberg could do nothing to prevent his friend Nikolai Belozvetov, in his enthusiasm in Tallinn, and later in Riga, from honoring him as the "new initiate."

In the winter of 1932/33, Tomberg worked together with Maria in a group study on the Apocalypse of St. John. In February 1933, they

---

27. Letter to Marie Steiner, Rudolf Steiner Nachlassverwaltung, Dornach.
28. Ibid.
29. *Aufzeichnungen, Vortragsnachschriften*, 131–37.

Estonia (1918–1938)

came to understand they had a common task that would keep them in Estonia until at least the summer of 1934. During the Easter period of 1933, Tomberg gave three public lectures in Russian, each attended by two to three hundred people—the first lectures he had given to so large an audience. He also gave public lectures in Estonian.

The divorce proceedings of Nikolai and Maria Belozvetov in Berlin took some time to run their bureaucratic course. Only on March 1, 1933 was the divorce final. According to Estonian law, Valentin and Maria could only marry, at the earliest, six months later, on September 1, 1933. Their son Alex was born the day before this date, and so had to be officially "acknowledged" by Valentin as his son. All this was of course the subject of discussion in anthroposophical circles in Tallinn, and it was inevitable that in due course accounts of these events would reach Dornach. Alex was baptized in the Greek Orthodox Church in Tallinn. He would be their only child. Later, in England, Tomberg mentioned how he had enthusiastically played soccer with Alex until he himself had reached the age of 40.

In considering the decision taken by Tomberg and Maria to unite their destinies by marriage, Christopher Bamford writes:

> Both, of course, were [already] married. The Belozvetovs, however, had been estranged since at least 1928. On the other hand, for Elena Tomberg, her husband's decision was so unexpected and unwanted that she wrote about it to Marie Steiner, veiling her grief and shock. . . . Marie Steiner heard her cry of despair.

As it happens, at this same juncture Valentin also wrote to Marie Steiner about the situation:

> Naturally, I will never abandon Elena Eduardovna Tomberg, and will never leave her without the assistance and attention she needs and has earned. I will take her with me to Berlin. . . . I know that you cannot receive this news with any but mixed feelings. . . . But what can I do? I can say only one thing (and it is the truth): My conscience is absolutely clear. I know that I am acting correctly, that I cannot act otherwise than I am doing. Naturally, then, why conceal it? It would pain me deeply if you condemn us. You are the only person in the world whose condemnation would be a great blow to me. If you were to condemn me, which I would quite understand and am ready to accept, nothing will change in our

Valentin Tomberg and the *Ecclesia Universalis*

relationship to you and the work you are doing. We will remain your faithful coworkers.

Bamford continues:

> True to his word, Tomberg did not abandon Elena Eduardovna. Until he left Estonia in autumn 1938, she lived with the new couple, received about a third of Tomberg's meager income, and, when Alexis Tomberg was born, assumed the role of grandmother. In the eyes of the world, it must have appeared an odd arrangement that did little for Tomberg's reputation. Rumors circulated. Marie Steiner felt betrayed: "I liked Herr Tomberg very much, and I trusted him." Up to that point, she, who was the most powerful person in the Society, had supported him. They had been very close. Indeed, in a sense, Tomberg had been her protégé.[30]

On Maria Tomberg's initiative, a circle for the study of Christology was formed in the autumn of 1933. It met at their home twice a month, on Saturdays. Nikolai Belozvetov had already remarried in June 1933 and moved to Tallinn in August with his second wife, Anna Stockmar, to cooperate spiritually with the Tombergs. Being stateless, they could not stay in Estonia, and so they settled in Riga, Latvia, in December 1933. In the winter of 1933/34, Valentin came often to Riga to give lectures, in German and in Russian.

From left to right: Valentin Tomberg, Ludmilla Belozvetov, Nikolai Belozvetov (1892–1950), Anna Belozvetov-Stockmar (1896–1978), Maria Tomberg-Leitnecker-Demski, Alexis Tomberg.

---

30. *Christ and Sophia: Anthroposophic Meditations* (Gt Barrington, MA: SteinerBooks, 2006), xix; hereafter, *Christ and Sophia*.

Estonia (1918–1938)

One of Tomberg's notebooks covering the period from February 1933 to August 1934 shows that Maria was at that time in "spiritual communication" with Rudolf Steiner (who had died in 1925). The communications received by her from "Dr." (that is, Steiner), and from other spiritual beings, continued until October 1943 (and possibly beyond), and were written down by Valentin. Whether they are all reliable cannot be determined. A remark dated September 28, 1933, also mentions a communication Valentin himself received from "the angel." These communications included personal advice, temporal events, reincarnation matters, the occult activity of the Jesuits, Scottish Freemasons, and East Asian occultists, the human double, work on the chakras, the three forms of occultism, folk spirits, the spiritual leaders of humankind, and the second coming of Christ. The longer texts appear to have been edited by Tomberg.[31]

The Second Coming of Christ
The New Testament speaks of the second coming of Christ. Rudolf Steiner did not understand this as a rebirth of Christ in a physical body, but as a return to the sphere of life, the "etheric" world of the earth. He spoke about this from 1910 onwards, predicting that this second coming would be experienced in the early 1930s and extend over a period of about 2500 years.

For his part, on June 3, 1933, Tomberg recorded detailed messages on the mystery of the etheric Christ in his notebook, which may have been communicated from Steiner or a spiritual being. "Before the descent from the angelic hierarchy to the earth can take place, Christ unites with an angelic being, the Nathan-Jesus," he noted.[32] The Nathan Jesus was reported to have appeared on the "etheric

---

31. Transcription of notebooks of Tomberg (1933 and 1934). Tomberg Archive, Steinbergkirche.
32. According to Rudolf Steiner, the Nathan Jesus is the cosmic soul of Adam. It did not enter into the Fall, but incarnated later in the child Jesus from the Gospel of Luke, who descended from King David's son Nathan. Interested readers will need to research further in Steiner's works to acquire sufficient background in his understanding of the full nature of "Jesus of Nazareth." This will put in context not only the expression "Nathan Jesus" but "Solomon Jesus" as well.

Valentin Tomberg and the *Ecclesia Universalis*

plane" on December 26, 1932.[33] According to this communication, the second coming would take place in stages:

1. The descent of Christ through the heavenly hierarchies.
2. The horizontal movement of Christ over the surface of the earth.
3. The descent of Christ into the ninth sphere of the earth's interior.

Further material on this subject, drawn from the notes mentioned, was published in 1987 by Robert Powell.[34] He reports that these diary notes were written on June 3, 1933, and includes the following lengthy excerpt:

> The etheric return of Christ has its origin in a still higher world sphere than did the descent of Christ prior to the Mystery of Golgotha. . . . Just as the present descent of Christ is beginning in a higher sphere than at that time, so does it end correspondingly *deeper* than it could at that time. Nineteen centuries ago Christ descended as far as the sixth subearthly sphere; now he will descend to the ninth sphere. . . .
>
> The descent began with the commencement of the [Archangel] Michael Age (1879). In this period, it began with the passage of Christ through the Second Hierarchy. The Kyriotetes received him without hindrance. So did the Exusiai. But with the passage through the Dynameis he was held up by resistance which entered in with this hierarchy. This fact was mirrored on the earth in the Russo-Turkish war, which could easily have developed into a world war. In the Third Hierarchy, resistance occurred with the passage through the Archangels. This event was mirrored on the Earth as World War I (1914–1918). In the year 1920, Christ entered the sphere of the Angels. Since 1932 it is important that the necessary takes place in order that Christ is able to appear in the earthly realm. The line of his descent down to the earth is vertical. Then his horizontal movement across the earth's surface begins. This is the cross of his second coming. Then his descent down through the nine subearthly spheres begins. The occurrence (of the second

---

33. Transcription of notebooks of Tomberg (1933–1934), early February 1933. Tomberg Archive, Steinbergkirche.

34. Robert Powell, *Hermetic Astrology*, Vol. 1 (San Rafael, CA: Sophia Foundation Press, 2007), 325–27.

coming) in its various stages is as follows: Through Christ's etheric return, the Christ-Power is penetrating nature much more intensively than before (at the time of the Mystery of Golgotha). At that time it was up to mankind; this time it involves nature also. [...]

Usually the etheric return of Christ is imagined as signifying joy and happiness for mankind. But the reality will be quite different. Initially, it will not be joy and happiness which will be felt, but shame. A feeling of shame—in an elemental and powerful form—will take hold of human beings. The human being will become conscious of all his shortcomings, and no one else will be able to comfort him. Human beings will then go out to seek comfort from nature. [...]

And people will then be right in seeking comfort from dumb creatures, for creatures (the beings of nature) will be transformed through the presence of Christ. At present, nature has lost all hope of being redeemed, but will be filled anew with hope through the breath of the presence of Christ.... Wonderful changes will take place in nature. Springtimes will come which will be different from all other springtimes—with goodness which will be felt in air and in the breath, in the breathing of the ground, in the buds and green leaves. These springtimes will be filled with a blessing that nature has never experienced before.

Towards autumn, nature will bestow her fruits in generous abundance—the sap will be life-giving, seeds will be ripe and full. For Christ will be there for nature. [...]

Christ will move from the West to the East in wave-like lines: He will begin in America and will continue through Europe to the northeast of Europe. From there he will continue eastwards as far as China, where the resistance is strongest. His coming is not for all regions of the earth simultaneously, but progresses step by step. Thereby each further step of his movement will signify a stronger force, a growth in the transmission of the Christ-Power. Only after traversing the whole of the earth in this way he will appear to individuals in different parts of the world. Clairvoyants will see him earlier, where he will be present only in the kingdoms of nature, but for many others the first experience of him will be in the human kingdom, after his expansion through nature is accomplished.

Note added by Robert Powell: "The nine subearthly spheres are described by Steiner in his lecture series *At the Gates of Spiritual*

Valentin Tomberg and the *Ecclesia Universalis*

Science, lecture 14 (New York: The Anthroposophic Press, 1986). The nine subearthly spheres comprise that which is traditionally designated as "hell." Thus, according to [these notes], Christ's *descent into hell* was a descent through the first six of the nine subearthly spheres, and the descent into this realm at his second coming will extend right down to the ninth sphere.

At a conference in Rotterdam on August 19, 1939, Tomberg spoke in a lecture of the outward signs of the second coming of Christ in the etheric world.[35] He said there would be new springs that breathe warmth and healing, and summer seasons with two harvests. There would be three years in which nature would radiate goodness. Perhaps Tomberg was looking ahead to an altered experience of the seasons, and the appearance of a new realm of nature beings at the end of the twentieth century—which Rudolf Steiner had spoken of on September 19, 1911.[36] But according to Tomberg, before these three years would come, preparation was needed on the part of human beings: their conscience, their morality, must first be awakened and the meaning of the second coming understood before they could perceive Christ in His etheric form. Tomberg said in this regard that Rudolf Steiner

> experienced that meeting with the descending Christ on the intuitive level. Now it can be experienced on the level of inspiration. Eventually Christ will arrive on the stage of imagination. Then people shall surely perceive him in visions, as Rudolf Steiner has described.

By the beginning of the 1930s, such individuals as Steiner had anticipated (those born with a new, more "open" constitution after 1899, the end of the Kali Yuga or the Age of Darkness) were over thirty years old—as was Tomberg himself, of course. Had there been no unanticipated hindrances, this generation would have been the first to be able to use the new natural etheric clairvoyance, as well

---

35. "The Four Sacrifices of Christ," lecture 7, in *Christ and Sophia*.
36. Lecture of September 19, 1911, "The Christ Impulse in Historical Development," in *Esoteric Christianity and the Mission of Christian Rosenkreutz* (Forest Row, UK: Rudolf Steiner Press, 2005).

Estonia (1918–1938)

as clairvoyant abilities acquired through practice, to perceive the etheric Christ.

The new "descent into hell" of Christ into the interior of the earth—as a "repetition" of the event on Holy Saturday after the death on the cross on Good Friday—was not elaborated upon by Tomberg at this time. However, on January 7, 1940, he did speak from a new perspective about Christ's encounter with the Divine Mother in the depths of the earth, which took place after his crucifixion during his descent into hell, and had its part to play in his resurrection, as Tomberg described it.[37]

The Bible Studies

The spiritual cooperation between Valentin and Maria that had begun in the fall of 1932 led further into a thorough study of the Bible. The first fruits of this research were originally published as *Anthroposophical Studies of the Old Testament*, which appeared in installments from November 1933 onward.[38] In this first of the three volumes of Bible Studies (which were elaborations of lectures he had given in Tallinn), Tomberg wrote of the important role of the Jewish people in the formation of the body of Jesus.

It is vitally important to recall at this juncture that Tomberg was here describing the world-historical role of the Jewish people, thereby confronting the ominous maw of rising anti-Jewish agitation. This positive stance toward Judaism, and his later radical criticism of National Socialism, were shared only to a limited extent within the German Anthroposophical Movement at that most critical of times. In fact, leading figures such as Marie Steiner, Guenther Wachsmuth, and Roman Boos were, in the beginning, not unsym-

---

37. Robert Powell speaks of a Jupiter rhythm of 11.86 years, in which Christ will enter a deeper layer of the earth each cycle between 1933 and 2028, after which he will ascend again. According to Powell, when entering each of the nine layers, certain aspects of evil will begin to work on earth, and humanity will be confronted with these. In 2040, the union of Christ with the Mother will take place in the depths of the earth. See "Subnature and the Second Coming," in Paul V. O'Leary (ed.), *The Inner Life of the Earth* (Gt Barrington, MA: SteinerBooks 2008), 69–141.

38. Published in *Christ and Sophia*.

Valentin Tomberg and the *Ecclesia Universalis*

pathetic to the Nazi regime. By contrast, Ita Wegman, another leading figure, opposed it.[39]

In the author's note and the first chapter of the Old Testament Studies, Tomberg pointed out that his work was based on spiritual research, and that the Anthroposophical Society can only be kept alive by a constant inflow of such research. In particular, he stated that engagement with esoteric communications could only become authentic esotericism if and when the facts communicated in these teachings were also recognized by living esotericists. But let Tomberg speak for himself:

> The *Anthroposophical Studies of the Old Testament* are to be regarded as the beginning of a series of further writings whose publication the author takes upon himself to continue. The task of these publications, which are to appear regularly, is to meet the need existing among wide circles within the Anthroposophical Society for purely anthroposophical research. The contents of the *Studies* has come about neither by the method of speculation based on reasoning and the setting up of hypotheses, nor by the mere summarizing of factual material contained in the lecture cycles of Rudolf Steiner—but by means of anthroposophical research.[40]

These statements at the very outset of his Bible Studies could all too easily have been seen as thinly-veiled criticism, or even as an indictment of those then holding authoritative positions in the Anthroposophical Society—because these figures were for the most part not "authentic esotericists" capable of inwardly engaging esoteric communications and thus independently furthering *actual* spiritual research. In this sense, then, his words were provoking to them. In a letter of April 8, 1931 to Marie Steiner, Tomberg had been even more explicit:

---

39. Ansgar Martins (ed.), *Hans Büchenbacher: Erinnerungen 1933–1949. Zugleich eine Studie zur Geschichte der Anthroposophie im Nationalsozialismus* (Frankfurt: Info3, 2014).

40. Valentin Tomberg, *Anthroposophical Studies of the Old Testament* (Spring Valley, NY: Candeur Manuscripts, 1985), v; hereafter, Studies of the Old Testament.

Estonia (1918–1938)

For in the field of knowledge, anything that is simply presented as true—with no opportunity offered for individuals to assess that proposed truth by means of their independent judgment—is dishonest. I often feel pain when I hear or read anthroposophists who regard something (e.g., particular incarnations) as "fixed," that is, as in no need of further examination solely because "Dr. Steiner said so." Pretending to know something that one does not in fact know is dishonesty in the field of knowledge.[41]

Tomberg argued that for its healthy development Anthroposophy required a community of spiritual researchers whose results would be collaboratively examined and acknowledged. Otherwise, he said, such results would amount to nothing more than "anthroposophically-oriented religious, philosophical, scientific, and aesthetic convictions." With such words as these, Tomberg signaled a problem he would raise again in 1970, toward the end of his life. In 1933, however, there was as yet no forum where he could have presented his research findings collaboratively, even though the General Anthroposophical Section in the School of Spiritual Science was originally intended by Rudolf Steiner as *just such a forum*. Instead, Tomberg's research was rejected out of hand.

On January 7 1934, Roman Boos published in the Society's newsletter a short critique of the first chapter of Tomberg's Old Testament Studies, entitled "An Untrue Claim," without mentioning Tomberg by name. This publication could only have occurred with the agreement of Board members Albert Steffen, Marie Steiner, and Guenther Wachsmuth. Boos stated to Tomberg:

An "influx of spiritual knowledge" passes through every mind that immerses itself in Rudolf Steiner's work. Talk of "being initiated"' should be omitted.

A more complete account of the criticisms of Roman Boos and Marie Steiner will be presented in part two of this biography. For the present we need only add that, as a result of this criticism, Tomberg decided on January 21, 1934 to cease serving as a class reader in the First Class of the School of Spiritual Science.

---

41. Letter to Marie Steiner, Rudolf Steiner Nachlassverwaltung, Dornach.

Valentin Tomberg and the *Ecclesia Universalis*

Upon finishing his Studies of the Old Testament in June 1935, Tomberg immediately began its sequel, *Anthroposophical Studies of the New Testament*, which he completed at the time of his emigration to the Netherlands in October 1938. *Anthroposophical Studies of the Apocalypse* followed soon thereafter, but only three of the proposed twelve studies were ever published.[42] In these three works Tomberg opened up a highly original approach to the Bible—one informed not only by his study of Rudolf Steiner's published lectures on the subject and by his own long-term study of the Bible itself, but, even more significantly, by his own spiritual research. He drew broad lines of correspondence from the Old Testament to the New Testament, and then further to the Apocalypse. He came to results not to be found in Steiner's works, such as his description of the redemption of Lucifer at the event of the crucifixion (the Mystery of Golgotha). He also opened up a new perspective on the activity of Sophia—the Divine Wisdom—both in Old Testament history and in the event of Pentecost.

Tomberg did not often refer to individual lectures by Rudolf Steiner and apologized for this. In the preface to his Studies of the Old Testament he wrote:

> The author is not in the position to indicate all the cycles, books, and single lectures of Rudolf Steiner with which he has worked in order to come to the results presented in these *Studies*; it will suffice to say, once and for all, that the author is indebted to Rudolf Steiner for all that has come to him in the way of knowledge. Everything that he has to say has its roots in the life work of Rudolf Steiner, so that he was also led through Rudolf Steiner to the new sources of knowledge out of which he could then draw. As it is difficult to separate the air one has breathed in from that of the outside world, so it is difficult for the author to draw a dividing line between the results of his own endeavor and that which Rudolf Steiner communicated.
>
> Those who are well acquainted with the literature of Anthroposophy will themselves be able to differentiate between that which is new and that which has already been given. For others,

---

42. In *Christ and Sophia*. Hereafter, Studies of the New Testament, and Studies of the Apocalypse, respectively.

the question as to the truth of the content will have to suffice, independently from the question as to its source. It is also clearly a right approach, anthroposophically, when considering facts and ideas, to inquire first into their truth—instead of into the authority of the person conveying them.[43]

Readers of the three volumes of Biblical Studies were invited to examine their contents and inner coherence for themselves. They were soon translated into Czech and English. If considered on their own merits, absent any coloration by preconceptions, it may well be said that they quite literally fulfilled a demand—even a plea—made by Steiner *himself* in Stockholm on January 12, 1910, regarding the appearance of Christ in his etheric form, which was to take place from 1933 onwards:

> By 1933, the gospels must have been recognized in their spiritual sense in such a way that they have worked as a preparation for the Christ; otherwise a degree of psychic confusion beyond measure will ensue.[44]

The Crisis in the Anthroposophical Society

During these years the crisis in the leadership of the Anthroposophical Society that had arisen close upon Steiner's death came to a head. At Christmas 1933, Executive Council member Elisabeth Vreede was obliged for the first time to organize her own series of lectures separately from those of the official meeting; and only months later, at the General Meeting of the Society, March 27–28, 1934, both she and Ita Wegman were formally excluded from the Board. The remaining Board members then demanded solidarity with this exclusionary tactic from all the National Societies, including Estonia. Tomberg, however, could concede support only to the Board as instituted by Rudolf Steiner himself, and refused to choose between the two groups. In April 1934, therefore, he took the step of resigning as President of the Estonian Anthroposophical Society.

---

43. Studies of the Old Testament, v.
44. Harald Giersch, *Rudolf Steiner über die Wiederkunft Christi* (Dornach: Verlag am Goetheanum, 1991), 108 (notes of Marie Steiner).

Valentin Tomberg and the *Ecclesia Universalis*

Tomberg's refusal to opt for either Board faction in Dornach underscores his awareness of the need for actual, authentic spiritual collaboration. Steiner had *unequivocally* impressed upon the Board his intention that a bond of togetherness should be the decisive criterion for its relationship to the truth. Indeed, he indicated that if this unity and cooperation were not constantly renewed, *it would be better never to have come together*. Again, if considered without prejudice, it is evident that in adopting the stance he did, Tomberg was only acting in accordance with Steiner's own wishes.

In consequence of these unfolding events, the Estonian Society split into those remaining loyal to the leadership in Dornach and those continuing to take part in Tomberg's group work. Tomberg himself continued for another year to lecture on the Society's premises. In a series of Sunday lectures, which began in October 1933 and continued through May 1934, he spoke about the angels.[45] Notes of six Monday evening lectures on the spiritual hierarchies, given in the autumn of 1934, were later published.[46]

The conflicts in the Society continued unabated; in fact, they escalated. On July 4, 1934, three months after Vreede and Wegman had been excluded from the work of the Executive Council, independent groups of anthroposophists who did not agree with the Dornach policy banded together to form what were called Free Anthroposophical Groups. These included, in particular, young people from the Youth Circle founded in 1922 and from the Free Anthroposophical Society founded in 1923, which existed until 1931.

In March 1935, twelve supporters of the Executive Council published a pamphlet called the *Denkschrift*, in which they aggressively attacked their opponents. In an even more poisoned atmosphere, Vreede and Wegman were expelled from the Executive Council at the General Assembly in Dornach on April 14, 1935. The members present on this occasion also took the decision to expel the members of the United Free Anthroposophical Groups and of the Dutch

---

45. Notes (in Estonian) of participants of these lectures are kept in the Tomberg Archive, Steinbergkirche.
46. *Aufzeichnungen, Vortragsnachschriften*, 195–222.

and British National Societies. In all, about two thousand persons were expelled as a result of these authoritarian actions—some ten percent of the total world membership. Those expelled represented the Youth Movement, but also those countries more characterized by what Steiner called the "consciousness soul" (the aspect of the soul in which modern self-consciousness has been developing ever since the end of the Middle Ages). Symptomatically, as we shall see, this latter circumstance is very telling when viewed in broader perspective, for by taking these drastic actions, the Society in effect dissociated itself from the people of the West, on whom Rudolf Steiner had pinned his hopes after the downfall of Germany in the First World War.

Tomberg was not among the excluded members at that time. Then, only six months later, on November 1, 1935, the Anthroposophical Society in Germany was banned by the Nazi regime.

The United Free Anthroposophical Groups

In these difficult years, various new friends came into Tomberg's life. On June 18, 1934, Elisabeth Vreede (1879–1943) wrote a letter to him. Now, according to Steiner's usage of the term, Vreede can be seen as a forerunner of the individuals from the "Platonic" movement whom he had expected to appear later in the twentieth century. According to this view, the Anthroposophical Society in its first beginnings was considered by most to have been comprised largely of people with esoteric Christian interests; then, from 1920 on, by an additional grouping of more scientifically oriented "Aristotelians." In the summer of 1924, Steiner had spoken to the members of the Society more particularly of the need for collaboration at the end of the century with the great "Platonic individualities" of the School of Chartres.

Tomberg had first met Elisabeth Vreede in July 1927 at the Danzig Conference. In late 1933 he sent her the first installments of his Studies of the Old Testament. Vreede's reply contained some constructive criticism. Tomberg was delighted with the tone of her letter, and replied on July 21, 1934, that he had found her letter an "expression of sincere anthroposophical friendship." An intensive correspondence ensued, of which twenty-six letters dating from 1934 to 1938 have

Valentin Tomberg and the *Ecclesia Universalis*

been preserved.[47] Tomberg was also very appreciative when the German anthroposophical historian Karl Heyer visited him in Tallinn in 1931. Vreede did much to support Tomberg by bringing his work to the attention of those expelled members now active in the circle of the Free Anthroposophical Groups. She herself was the leading figure in this circle, of which Tomberg also became a member in July 1935.

Elisabeth Vreede (1879–1943)

That same year, Tomberg contributed three articles on "The Spiritual Basis for the East European Tragedy" to the *Correspondence of the Anthroposophical Working Groups*, edited by Jürgen von Grone.[48] In this venue appeared also articles by Karl Heyer, Sigismund von Gleich, Maria Krück von Poturzyn, Maria Röschl, Ernst Lehrs, Herbert Hahn, Walter Johannes Stein, Karl König, Elisabeth Vreede, Emil Leinhas, Caroline von Heydebrand, and others who, having likewise been expelled from the Anthroposophical Society on April 14, 1935, now belonged to the Free Anthroposophical Groups.

After the collapse of the General Anthroposophical Society, Tomberg brought his work for the three language groups within the Estonian Society to an end. It was shortly thereafter, in June 1935, that the first installment of his *Studies of the New Testament* appeared. That same autumn, Tomberg traveled to Riga three times to give lectures on the Michael impulse, on the baptism of Jesus by John and the Nicodemus initiation, and on the angelic hierarchies. A new series of Russian lectures commenced in December 1935 in

---

47. Correspondence of Valentin Tomberg with Elisabeth Vreede. Archive of the Goetheanum, Dornach.
48. See "The Spiritual Basis of the East European Tragedy," *Russian Spirituality*, 178–95.

Estonia (1918–1938)

Tallinn, with associated public lectures on "The Foundations of Spiritual Life in Europe" and "Raskolniki [Dissenters] and Orthodoxy in the Middle Ages." At Easter 1936, Tomberg was back in Riga with his wife and child. In the spring of 1936 he gave public lectures in Tallinn on Goethe and his drama *Faust*.

At this time, Tomberg's Sunday evening circle consisted of ten people: Valentin and Maria, Elena Tomberg (Tomberg's first wife), Jeanette Heinrichsen, Maja Hörschelmann, Heinrich Walter, Elmar Müller, Sinaide Sepp, Margrit Schneider, and Regina von Dumpff. Because the participants were not allowed to attend the class lessons of the Estonian Society, Tomberg himself withdrew from the first class. From then on, the circle met under Maria's leadership on the premises of the Society. She also led a study group at their home.

A particularly enthusiastic reader of Tomberg's writings and articles was the Polish Count Stefan Lubienski (1893–1976), who since 1927 had lived in the Netherlands, where he worked as a commercial attaché at the Polish consulate, first in Rotterdam, later in Amsterdam. When speaking in his memoirs of meeting the "greatest friend of his life," Lubienski wrote that he read Tomberg's writings "with increasing astonishment," and came to the conclusion:

> At last there is someone who, after the death of Rudolf Steiner, has the courage and capacity to further explore spiritual-scientific questions independently—not only intellectually, but with a penetrating, keen spiritual intuition, avoiding all superficiality.[49]

Stefan Lubienski (1893–1976)

In the summer of 1936 Lubienski traveled to Estonia, where he spent five days as a guest of Valentin and Maria in their small summer cottage in Hiiu, not far from Tallinn. This meeting led to a lifelong friendship.

---

49. *Vor der Schwelle* (Rendsburg: Lohengrin Verlag, 1987), 192–95.

Valentin Tomberg and the *Ecclesia Universalis*

That October, Professor Ernst von Hippel (1895–1984), a legal scholar from Königsberg (now Kaliningrad, in Russia) came to Tallinn. He was not a member of the Anthroposophical Society, but was connected with the Christian Community movement. A profound friendship developed between von Hippel and Tomberg that lasted until the latter's death thirty-seven years later. Through this connection, as early as December 1936, Tomberg was invited to Königsberg to give several lectures on the Apocalypse for the Christian Community. At the home of von Hippel and his wife Gertrud, the service of consecration (the worship service of the Christian Community) was regularly celebrated.[50]

Ernst von Hippel (1895–1984) and Valentin Tomberg

In the autumn of 1936, Tomberg had commenced two new series of public lectures in Tallinn, held twice a month until the spring of 1937: one series, given in German, was on Goethe's *Faust*; the other series, given in Russian, took as its theme the work of Dostoevsky and Solovyov. Early in 1937, Tomberg wrote two articles on the subject of "Suggestion and Will" for an Estonian magazine.

Since 1925, Tomberg had regarded Rudolf Steiner's Foundation Stone Meditation as the cornerstone of all anthroposophical studies

---

50. Communication from Wolfgang Gädeke.

Estonia (1918–1938)

and had made it the basis of all his work. He spoke of this remarkable meditation as his guide in the preface to the first part of his book *The Foundation Stone*,[51] which circulated among the Free Anthroposophical Groups in November 1936. Elisabeth Vreede had inspired him to write it. Here, Tomberg emphasized the cosmic-spiritual aspect of the Foundation Stone Meditation. At Christmas 1937, a second part appeared, in which he emphasized the aspect of the human soul. And in the third part, written in Rotterdam in 1939, he focused on the "true relationship between man and nature."

Meanwhile, tensions in the Estonian Anthroposophical Society had become unbearable. In July 1937, Maria and a few others resigned their membership of the Dornach Society. In October 1937, Valentin also formally left the Society. He made preparations to found a Free Anthroposophical Society, which he intended to register under the name "Christological Society," but the Estonian authorities did not grant the necessary authorization. Because they also wanted to distance themselves from the members of the Dornach Society, some other anthroposophists decided to withdraw and become members of the Free Anthroposophical Groups, as described above. At Christmas 1937, these free anthroposophists met at Valentin and Maria's home for a celebration. It was a circle of ten people, which over time grew larger. Elisabeth Vreede made the journey to Tallinn to be present at the Whitsun meeting of this circle on June 5, 1938. Other participants came from Latvia, where a similar split had taken place.

From a long letter which the Latvian mathematics teacher Valerian Schmaeling wrote to Elisabeth Vreede at the end of 1937, we are well informed regarding Tomberg's work in Latvia and the problems that had also arisen there within the Anthroposophical Society. Schmaeling was part of a circle of about ten who, under the inspiration of Tomberg's lectures and writings, had come together in October 1933 around Nikolai Yablokov in Riga. Schmaeling described this group as a "small brotherhood" that studied the writings of Tomberg and Belozvetov (who also lectured in their circle)

---

51. *Studies on the Foundation Stone Meditation* (San Rafael, CA: LogoSophia, 2010).

and focused primarily on the revelation of Christ in the etheric world and the activity of the bodhisattva. They directed their attention to two powerful currents of the spiritual world—those of the "Archangel Michael–Yahweh" being and of the "Nathan-Jesus–Sophia" being—and their common grounding in Christ; furthermore, they investigated how these currents played into the karma of the Anthroposophical Movement. According to Schmaeling, it was in Estonia and Latvia that the expectation of, and longing for, the revelation of Sophia was first awakened—earlier than elsewhere in the Anthroposophical Movement.[52]

In a letter of January 5, 1938, to Elisabeth Vreede, Schmaeling called Yablokov's circle a "resurrection circle," which was also a "renewal circle" in that it sought to contribute to "the stream of renewal, that should revivify and gradually advance the Michaelic esotericism founded by Rudolf Steiner, but now in the spirit of the 1930s—that is, in the mild light of the Nathan-Jesus being." On the basis of these two letters, we can place Tomberg's work in Tallinn and Riga in the context of the development of an Anthroposophy inspired in particular by the Nathan-Jesus and Sophia.

The Lecture Tours to Western Europe

In the autumn of 1936, Elisabeth Vreede made a proposal to Tomberg that altered his destiny. She wanted to organize a lecture tour for him. In a letter dated November 17, 1936, he replied:

> I would be delighted to undertake a lecture tour to Holland, England, and Switzerland. In Holland I will meet quite a few friends—I have several letters from there from readers of the Meditations [Biblical Studies]. Mr. Lubienski visited us in the summer, and with Mr. von Gleich I have corresponded already for some time. Dr. Hahn also lives there, and Dr. Zeylmans has been with us.

Tomberg wrote further that he had come into contact with a Mr. W. B. Paton from London, and had old connections in Czechoslovakia with the group of Colonel G. Dohnal as well. He mentioned that

---

52. Valerian Schmaeling, letter to Elisabeth Vreede, October/November 1937, Archive at the Goetheanum, Dornach, and at Tomberg Archive in Steinbergkirche. See also Heckmann and Frensch, *Valentin Tomberg*, Vol. I.1, 293–95.

he could speak English, although not well enough to deliver a public lecture. In the Netherlands he would like to speak about Rudolf Steiner's *Mystery Dramas* and Goethe's *Faust*, and in England he could speak about the Apocalypse.

Stefan Lubienski heard directly from Elisabeth Vreede about her offer to Valentin, and wrote to his friend, inviting him to be his guest in Amsterdam. In January 1937, he referred to Tomberg's new writing on the Foundation Stone Meditation in the newsletter of the Anthroposophical Society in the Netherlands. He also wrote that Tomberg was "spiritually strongly connected with anthroposophical work in the Netherlands and England and with everything that happens in our circles."

On March 7, 1937, Tomberg informed Elisabeth Vreede that a connection had also come about with a circle in Vienna, but that an extension of the trip to Prague and Vienna was out of the question. For this trip, Tomberg asked for a leave of absence from his employer for a further two weeks without pay, after his one-month holiday. We note here as a possible point of interest to some readers that mid-May 1937 was the time of Tomberg's second lunar node.

The First Tour (Summer 1937)

On August 1, 1937 Tomberg left on his tour together with Ernst and Gertrud von Hippel, who had spent the month of July with him in Tallinn. The first destination was Königsberg. In a letter to Vreede dated July 5, 1937, he described his plans for the rest of the journey. He would first visit some friends in Frankfurt, Germany. From August 5th to 7th he would be in Stuttgart, where he hoped to meet Emil Leinhas (the former editor of the journal *Anthroposophie*) and some others, including Jürgen von Grone. Then he would visit Karl Heyer and his wife in Kressbronn on Lake Constance in southern Germany. On August 10th he hoped to arrive at Elisabeth Vreede's house in Arlesheim near Dornach. This plan was subsequently realized.

From Arlesheim, Tomberg traveled on to England to take part in the International Summer School of the British Anthroposophical Society, which was held in Swanwick (Derbyshire) August 21–30, 1937. At these meetings the most important representatives of those

Valentin Tomberg and the *Ecclesia Universalis*

Passport photo of Valentin Tomberg (1937)

members of the Anthroposophic Society who had been excluded by Dornach had been gathering for some years.[53] Prior to this meeting, George Adams had introduced Tomberg in an article as the author of "some of the most remarkable works that the Anthroposophical Movement has produced in recent years." Adams later edited the English version of Tomberg's book *The Foundation Stone Meditation* and provided an introduction. At the meeting in Swanwick, which was attended by more than two hundred people,

Tomberg spoke on "The Trial of Man and Mankind by Fire, Water and Air, in Connection with the Christ Impulse." There are notes of this talk made by the leader of the membership group in Liverpool, Hannah Shatwell.[54] The painter Liane Collot d'Herbois, who attended this meeting, told the author of this book shortly before her death that Tomberg had made a great impression on all participants, and that nobody had spoken with as much inspiration as he had. On September 16, 1937, Tomberg reported to Vreede on his subsequent stay in the Netherlands:

> I spoke in four cities: Rotterdam, The Hague, Amsterdam, and Zeist. In Rotterdam, my contact was already present with the group. All went well in The Hague, and also in Amsterdam and Zeist, with the help of others. In Rotterdam the event was so well received that it went on from ten o'clock in the morning until half past three at night; the attendees were able to talk together undisturbed. I also gave three lectures there, including a public one.

---

53. Charles Lawrie, "Valentin Tomberg," in Ramsteiner Kreis, *Valentin Tomberg*, Vol. II, 384.

54. Lecture notes of Hannah Shatwell, published as "Feuer-, Wasser- und Luftprobe," in *Aufzeichnungen, Vortragsnachschriften*, 139–42.

Estonia (1918–1938)

Daniskas and von Gleich, who met me in Rotterdam, were also the last ones to say goodbye to me in Zeist.

John Daniskas (1907–2002) was the leader of the anthroposophical group in Rotterdam and a teacher at a private music school. The writer and lecturer Sigismund von Gleich (1896–1953) had left Germany in 1934 and lived for two years as a guest of Elisabeth Vreede in Arlesheim before moving to the Netherlands in 1936, where he was helped by a circle of friends. His book *Geesteswetenschap, openbaring van de kunsten en religieuze levensbeschouwing*, published in 1937, was "kindly dedicated" to Valentin Tomberg.

In a letter of September 29, 1937 to Elisabeth Vreede, Tomberg returned to the subject of his summer travel. He had decided to leave Estonia within the next two years. He hoped to earn as much in Holland with his literary work as he had in Estonia on a fixed salary. He wrote to Vreede:

> We had already talked about it in Arlesheim, but this intention became concrete after my visit to Holland. When I came to the Netherlands, I knew: you are in the right place. But that is not the decisive factor for me, for in the end I do not much care personally where I am. I mean, it is not that important to me. But as regards my loved ones, the matter is quite otherwise. There are only two, as you know, who make up my whole personal life—my wife and child. Now, every year it is more difficult for my wife to endure the climate, the land, and the atmosphere here—both from a health and from a spiritual point of view. On the other hand, it is not possible to send my son, who is growing up and being educated here, to a school other than a Free Rudolf Steiner school. This is simply a necessity of life.

Elisabeth Vreede reacted positively to this plan and asked if she should go ahead and speak to some others about it, such as Willem Zeylmans van Emmichoven, the General Secretary of the Dutch Anthroposophical Society. On October 30, 1937, Tomberg replied that he had already approached the people concerned: Fritzanton and Maria Krück von Poturzyn in Stuttgart, John Daniskas in Rotterdam, Sigismund von Gleich in Zeist, and F.W. Zeylmans in The Hague—and that he had received replies from Daniskas and Von Gleich. Their letters exuded radiant joy and active readiness to do everything [...] to assist in the realization of this intention. With this, the most important thing for the realization has already happened: There are people there who want us.

On November 17, 1937, he wrote to Ernst von Hippel that he hoped to move to the Netherlands.[55] It was also a prudent decision from a political point of view, because at the time the independence of Estonia, on the border of the Soviet Union, was increasingly under threat.

In January 1938, Tomberg's article "Meaning and Significance of a Free Anthroposophical Group" appeared in the Dutch *Reports of Anthroposophical Endeavors*,[56] and also in the first (and only) issue of *Anthroposophical Working Papers*, published by the Free Groups in Czechoslovakia. In this article, Tomberg makes clear that a working group, through the interaction of head and heart, can be an organ for receiving insights from a spiritual being—insights that would otherwise not be accessible to individuals separately. He wrote about conversations leading to insights in the sense of what Steiner had called the "reverse cult." The aim of such a group, he wrote, was to become a "council of friends."

The Second Tour (Summer 1938)

On December 6, 1937, Tomberg wrote to Elisabeth Vreede regarding his plan for the coming summer. Maria would travel with their son Alex via Stuttgart to Lake Constance to spend a holiday with the Heyer family in the better climate there. (As Tomberg's work file shows, an Estonian doctor had recommended such a cure to them, especially for Maria, to improve the condition of their lungs and heart.) Tomberg would follow after them and travel with Maria via Arlesheim to Holland. She wanted to see for herself in Holland how and where they could settle, and what possibilities for work might be open to her as a "musician and craftswoman."

On July 13, 1938, Tomberg informed Ernst von Hippel of his travel

---

55. Correspondence of Valentin Tomberg with Ernst von Hippel. Tomberg Archive, Steinbergkirche.
56. *Russian Spirituality*, 48–51.

plans. The traveling party would consist of Maria and Alex Tomberg, Jeanette Heinrichsen, and Miss Taft. Tomberg and Jeanette Heinrichsen were to travel directly to Bangor in North Wales to attend a conference; Maria and Alex would travel via Stuttgart to the Heyer family in Kressbronn; and Miss Taft would go to Arlesheim. After his lectures in Bangor and Rotterdam, Tomberg would also come to Arlesheim and rejoin his family.

The journey began on July 28, 1938. Willem Zeylmans had already invited Tomberg in September 1937 to attend the upcoming summer conference in the Netherlands. This took place in Zeist in July 1938, but unfortunately Tomberg had no time for it. Most of the speakers who took the floor there traveled on afterward to Bangor.

From August 2 to 12, 1938, another Summer School of the British Anthroposophical Society was held in Bangor. Elisabeth Vreede and Ita Wegman were among the nearly two hundred participants. During this meeting they climbed the nearby hill above Penmaenmawr upon which stood the large Druid stone circles that Rudolf Steiner had also visited in July 1923. A report by Dorothy Lenn shows that at the opening meeting Tomberg "pointed out the fate of the Russian anthroposophists, who, he said, had been completely forgotten. He then pleaded that the anthroposophists in Central Europe not now suffer the same fate."[57] Tomberg gave four lectures here on "The Spiritual Hierarchies and Their Working in the Twentieth Century," notes of which have been published.[58]

In her report, Dorothy Lenn wrote: "We took great pains to follow him as he led us to esoteric heights, to ever loftier realms of the spiritual world." At the end of the meeting "Tomberg spoke appreciatively of this place as having enriched him inwardly, as evoking in him old memories, as a place where it was good to say profound things. He spoke of the ancient Druid mysteries and of how important it was to him that he was here, and to build on what had so long ago been wrought on the hills of Penmaenmawr."[59]

---

57. Lawrie, 387.
58. *Starlight*, Vol. 8, Fall 2008, 3–13, downloadable at https://sophiafoundation.org/portfolio/starlight-journal/.
59. Lawrie, 387–88.

Valentin Tomberg and the *Ecclesia Universalis*

Tomberg then moved on to Rotterdam, where an anthroposophical conference was held August 14–21, 1938, at which he was the sole lecturer. He gave two series of seven lectures each. One was intended for members of the Society and took as its theme "The Inner Development of Man." The other was open to the public. In the announcement for the public lectures, the leadership of the Rotterdam Group of the Society wrote: "As Mr. Tomberg is one of the most distinguished continuators of Rudolf Steiner's work, his lectures will provide an excellent opportunity to become acquainted with Anthroposophy through one of its most important representatives."[60] The texts of the lectures for the members were copied and distributed.[61] This conference in Rotterdam was very well received. About fifty people attended the lectures for members, and about seventy attended the public lectures. John Daniskas, the organizer of this conference, spoke of "a new, strong impulse for anthroposophical life" in the September 1938 issue of the newsletter of the Anthroposophical Society in the Netherlands.

After the conference, Tomberg left for Arlesheim, whither Maria and Alex were also traveling from Kressbronn. On his return journey, stops were planned in Kressbronn, Stuttgart, Frankfurt, Berlin, and Königsberg. He did not return to his workplace in Tallinn until September 15.

---

60. Announcement of Tomberg's public lectures. Archive of the Library of the Dutch Anthroposophical Society, Den Haag.
61. *Inner Development*.

3

The Netherlands

(1938–1944)

O N OCTOBER 1, 1938, AT HIS REQUEST, TOMBERG WAS DIS- missed from his position at the main post office in Tallinn, where he was then head of the department for international connections. It was now thrice seven years since he had discovered Anthroposophy. In the first seven years he had studied Anthroposophy intensively. In the second seven years he had worked actively for Anthroposophy in Estonia. In the third seven years he had extended his anthroposophical work abroad. Now, in the Netherlands, he was commencing his work anew. This new biographical phase would not endure another seven years, however, but be cut short at five and a half years.

On October 4, 1938, Valentin and Maria, together with their son Alex, left Tallinn for their new home in the Netherlands. On the way, they visited Nikolai Belozvetov and his wife in Riga and the von Hippel family in Königsberg. On October 12, 1938, they were registered as new residents of the city of Rotterdam. John Daniskas and Jan van der Most had arranged for the Tombergs to live in a boarding house at 118 's-Gravendijkwal in the city, and to be supported financially by a circle of friends.

Tomberg was aware that in July 1938 the Estonian Ministry of Foreign Affairs in Tallinn had appointed an honorary consul in Amsterdam. This was Jan Roth, director of a trading company in Amsterdam. He also knew that another consulate had recently been established in Rotterdam. Planning ahead, Tomberg had informed the Ministry in Tallinn already at the end of September of his intention to apply for the position of secretary to the new consul. His

Valentin Tomberg and the *Ecclesia Universalis*

The Tomberg family in the Netherlands

friend Lubienski (himself a commercial attaché at the Polish consulate) had undoubtedly advised him on this matter. After an interview with Jan Roth at the end of October, Tomberg wrote a formal letter of application, in which he stated that he could speak and write five languages (Estonian, French, English, German, and Russian) fluently, and had partial command of three others (Dutch, Italian, and Spanish). He mentioned further that, as a correspondent-translator at the international post office, he had had occasion to apply these languages daily for more than fifteen years. He pointed out as well that in June 1938 he had extemporaneously

The Netherlands (1938–1944)

translated a speech of the Estonian President into French, and in the same year had translated all the speeches at an international meeting in Tallinn from German into English, and vice versa. He noted that he was currently taking classes in Dutch, and expected to master it sufficiently within six months. Furthermore, he emphasized, he was well familiar with all aspects of office work generally and had passed an exam in administrative law in Estonia in December 1937. On January 17, 1939, he was officially appointed secretary to the honorary consul at a salary of 100 guilders per month. He was to begin work a few months later.[1]

Anthroposophical Activities until May 1940

On December 19, 1938, Tomberg wrote to Ernst von Hippel about the kindness and warmth his family felt in Holland: "We are really enveloped by an atmosphere of human warmth, a warmth not of mere passing enthusiasm, but of many deeds both great and small—and without an excess of words." In the same letter, Tomberg wrote that he had five ongoing activities, by which he meant working groups in Rotterdam, Hilversum, Eindhoven, and Zeist, to which would soon be added groups in The Hague and Amsterdam. When he wrote this letter, he had just been ill for five days with an attack of colitis, as Maria reported to Gertrud von Hippel in a letter dated December 19, 1938. Maria herself had had a heart attack and been ill for most of her stay in Holland. Both Tombergs had sensitive constitutions and were repeatedly afflicted by illness throughout the rest of their lives.

By this time, Tomberg had already completed three written works in Holland. Published first, at the end of 1938, was the initial installment of Studies of the Apocalypse. The second work, published in early 1939, was the third and final part of the *Foundation Stone Meditation*. The third work was published in February 1939 in the Dutch (non-anthroposophical) monthly *Mensch en Kosmos*. This was to be

---

1. Personal files of Valentin Tomberg, secretary of the honorary consul in Amsterdam, Estonian State Archives, Tartu, archive file 957 (Ministry of Foreign Affairs, inventory 3, file 507, 1–16).

Valentin Tomberg and the *Ecclesia Universalis*

Tomberg's only article written in the Netherlands, namely "Indian Yoga and Christian Occultism."[2]

In 1939, the Studies of the Old and New Testaments appeared in English. Elisabeth Vreede wrote an introduction to these in which she pointed out "the many deeply spiritual and sublime reflections" they contained. The Studies of the Old Testament had been published in Prague in a Czech translation at the end of 1936 in an edition of two hundred copies. Czech translations of Tomberg's *Foundation Stone Meditation* and the Studies of the New Testament were in preparation at that time. There was considerable interest in his writings in Czechoslovakia: three early articles had appeared in the Czech magazine *Anthroposophické Rozhledy* in these years (1936 and 1937).

In the above-mentioned letter to Ernst von Hippel of December 19, 1938, Tomberg wrote that he was working on a book about Goethe's *Faust*, a subject he had already lectured on in Tallinn. We learn of this same intention from a letter to Elisabeth Vreede of September 29, 1937, with the further information that publication in Germany was already "quite certain." However, the book was not completed.

Between 1938 and 1940, the newsletter of the Anthroposophical Society in the Netherlands reported on Tomberg's lectures and study groups. All told, he had given about sixty lectures and participated in fourteen study groups and courses in the Netherlands since 1937. Already by the autumn of 1938 he had established study groups in Rotterdam, including one on Rudolf Steiner's *Mystery Dramas*. A second group on Steiner's *Outline of Occult Science* met fortnightly until at least February 1939. He also worked on Steiner's *Anthroposophical Leading Thoughts* together with Daniskas and Van der Most. This work continued until the autumn of 1939. On January 29 and February 19, 1939, he held lectures in Rotterdam on the "Inner Development of Man."

Tomberg's study groups in other places soon found mention in the newsletter: in Hilversum, Eindhoven, Amsterdam, and The Hague. In these places (as well as in Bergen, Zwolle, and Voorthui-

---

2. Tomberg, "Indische Yoga en christelijk occultisme" in *Mensch en Kosmos* (February 1939). Published in *Aufzeichnungen, Vortragsnachschriften*, 125–30.

The Netherlands (1938–1944)

zen) he gave lectures also. Tomberg could understand and speak Dutch, but gave his lectures in German.

In August 1938, Tomberg had a conversation with Maria Louise van Rijnberk from Blaricum near Hilversum, which led in the autumn of 1938 to a study group in her circle on the *Anthroposophical Leading Thoughts*. Her husband, Gérard van Rijnberk, was a professor of physiology at the medical faculty of the University of Amsterdam. A close friendship developed between the two families. Valentin and Maria visited them often. Van Rijnberk was a great connoisseur of the Tarot, and people from many spiritual currents met in his house. He was the leading figure of French Martinism in the Netherlands. This is how Tomberg, twenty-one years after having read Shmakov's Tarot book in 1917, came again into contact with the Hermetic tradition. It was another twenty-one years later, in 1959, that he would commence his own masterpiece on this theme.

Gérard van Rijnberk (1875–1953)

In Eindhoven, Tomberg had a small fortnightly study group at the home of Mr and Mrs Jurriaanse on Rudolf Steiner's lecture series *From Jesus to Christ*. The group itself had chosen the subject, and because aspects of Jesuit esotericism were dealt with in the series of lectures, Tomberg had advised them to delve into the history of the Jesuit order as well. For this purpose, the book *The Power and Secret of the Jesuits*, by René Fülöp-Miller, was read.[3] In Eindhoven, Tomberg gave several lectures.

In Amsterdam as well as in The Hague and in Utrecht there was a School for Spiritual Science, which had been organizing public lectures on Anthroposophy since 1936. Such Schools had been

---

3. New York: George Braziller, Inc., 1956.

Valentin Tomberg and the *Ecclesia Universalis*

established on the initiative of Willem Zeylmans. In Amsterdam, the School's activities took place in the home of the secretary of the Anthroposophical Group, Mrs Van Houten-Wegerif. Tomberg gave many lectures here, the first two in February 1939 on "Life after Death." From September 1939 he also participated in the study of the *Anthroposophical Leading Thoughts* in Amsterdam together with Sigismund von Gleich. On March 16, 1939 (the very day he moved to Amsterdam) he started his study group on the gospels.

On March 30, 1939, Tomberg gave a lecture in Amsterdam on the occasion of the anniversary of Rudolf Steiner's death. Two days later, on the first of April, the Estonian consulate was officially opened, so he could start his work as its secretary. The Tomberg family now lived in their own sunny three-room apartment with a small garden at 17 Berkelstraat in Amsterdam. On May 7, 1939, their friend, the nurse Maja Hörschelmann, came from Tallinn to live with them as housekeeper.

At that time the Anthroposophical Society in the Netherlands had about six hundred members. In Amsterdam, the members' group was small, with only twenty-five members. Here Valentin Tomberg found a circle that supported him, and from which, together with people from other places, a core group was formed for his further work, which focused on deepening the Christian content of Anthroposophy. The work on the Old and New Testaments that had already begun in Tallinn could develop further here. The public study group on the gospels, which first took place on March 16, 1939 at the School of Spiritual Science in Amsterdam, was continued on April 27 and concluded on June 8. It was supplemented by a new group on the gospels for members, now jointly led by Valentin and Maria in their home. This group met biweekly, commencing May 18, 1939.

From Amsterdam, Tomberg traveled to Hilversum for an introductory course in Anthroposophy that was held on Friday evenings at the home of the Wertheim Aymès family. This led, as early as April 1939, to a study circle for those interested in John's gospel. On Easter Monday, April 10, 1939, Tomberg gave a lecture in Bergen on "The Mystery of Golgotha." For the following Easter he gave two lectures on Ascension and Pentecost in The Hague on May 19th and

The Netherlands (1938–1944)

22nd. On June 18th he gave the St. John's lecture at the annual members' meeting of the Dutch Anthroposophical Society in Zeist, and on June 22th he gave another lecture on the Feast of St John at the home of Stefan Lubienski in Amsterdam.

In 1939, the Rotterdam members' group again prepared a summer conference with Tomberg. The theme this time was "The Four Sacrifices of Christ and the Appearance of the Christ in the Etheric World." During the period August 13–20, 1939, nineteen lectures and four study sections took place. Mornings, presentations were made to members on various aspects of Christianity, offered by six speakers: Elisabeth Vreede, Sigismund von Gleich, Maja Hörschelmann, Nikolai Belozvetov, John Daniskas, and Maria Tomberg (her topic was "The Future of Christianity"). On the final morning, general secretary of the Society, Willem Zeylmans, read the ninth class lesson. During the afternoon study groups, Maria gave an introduction to group work. In the early evenings, seven lectures by Valentin on the theme of the conference were held for the members. The texts of these lectures have been published.[4] In the later evenings, public lectures were offered on "Spiritual-Scientific Foundations for a Modern Christianity." The speakers in this evening program were Elisabeth Vreede, Sigismund

Valentin and Maria Tomberg in Rotterdam (1939) at the entrance to the conference center

---

4. Published in English translation most recently as the Appendix, "The Four Sacrifices of Christ and the Reappearance of Christ in the Etheric," to *Christ and Sophia*, 357–401.

Valentin Tomberg and the *Ecclesia Universalis*

von Gleich, Henri Zagwijn, Valentin Tomberg (on "Rudolf Steiner's Life's Work as a Form of Modern Christianity"), and Willem Zeylmans.[5]

In his assigned lectures, Tomberg spoke of the decisive help that Christ, in his cosmic activity, gave to the development of humankind. In accord with the spiritual vista first presented in part by Steiner, but which is too complex a subject to adequately summarize here, Tomberg described how in the greater scheme of things the death of Christ Jesus on the cross on Golgotha had been his *fourth* sacrifice (of seven in total, and of which the fifth is the second coming or etheric "return in the clouds" spoken of in the gospel), which brought with it five specific karmic consequences that would take place in the etheric, or life, sphere of the earth at his second coming. An excerpt from the text of his lecture on the karmic consequences of the Mystery of Golgotha was for some time mistakenly considered to be Rudolf Steiner's words from 1910. As late as 1980, this text was read out by Rudolf Grosse, then President of the General Anthroposophical Society, at a conference at the Goetheanum. It is instructive to note that when the fact that Tomberg had writ-

Rotterdam (1939), l to r: Martha Poldermans, Stefan Lubienski, Jan van der Most, J. Mackenzie

---

5. Program of the conference. Archive of the Library of the Dutch Anthroposophical Society, The Hague.

The Netherlands (1938–1944)

ten the text became known, it was suddenly considered irrelevant, and not mentioned again.

Tomberg's intentions in these pivotal lectures (as in all of his work) was to deepen the understanding of this central event of our time, which, for him, was the main task of Anthroposophy. They culminated in the presentation of the second coming of Christ: "The Pentecost of our time is the beginning; it is the arising warmth of awakened moral conscience; it is the dawn of understanding the meaning of the etheric return of Christ."[6]

As at the first summer meeting, about fifty members were present. The public lectures were also attended by some non-members. Ingeborg Zeylmans van Emmichoven, the wife of the General Secretary of the Society, wrote in her report of the meeting in the Society's newsletter of September 1939 that Tomberg's reflections had made a deep impression on all. To which we may add that they were also of great importance in the context of world events, for they took place on September 1, 1939, shortly before the outbreak of the Second World War was set in motion by the German attack on Poland. Shortly before this, Ernst von Hippel and his wife Gertrud had come to the Netherlands for a two-week visit.

At the end of his first year in the Netherlands, Tomberg gave lectures for the feast of the Archangel Michael (September 29) in Rotterdam, Amsterdam, and Eindhoven. On October 17, a new introductory course in Anthroposophy began, held every two weeks at the School of Spiritual Science in Amsterdam until December. In this course Tomberg gave five lectures.[7] On October 19, the gospel lectures by both Valentin and Maria recommenced, held twice a month at their home, as before. During these autumn lectures, both the two lines of descent converging in Jesus of Nazareth and the twelve bodhisattvas were discussed.[8] In Hilversum, the Friday evening group on John's gospel was continued, now once a month.

---

6. *Christ and Sophia*, Appendix, "The Four Sacrifices of Christ," 401.
7. Tomberg, Lecture notes published in *Starlight*, Vol. 9/1, Spring 2009, 2–6, *Starlight*, Vol. 9/2, Fall 2009, 3–6, *Starlight*, Vol. 10/1, Spring 2010, 3–6 and *Starlight*, Vol. 10/2, Fall 2010, 3–5. These volumes can be downloaded at https://sophiafoundation.org/portfolio/starlight-journal/.
8. Notes of M.L. van Rijnberk, in *Starlight*, Vol. 5/2, Fall 2005, 6–9.

Valentin Tomberg and the *Ecclesia Universalis*

The participants of the conference in Rotterdam, 1939 (Elisabeth Vreede, far right, seated)

The Netherlands (1938–1944)

Over the period October 27–29, 1939, a members' meeting was held in The Hague, with six speakers presenting on the spiritual condition of the time. Tomberg's lecture dealt with the Russian people. In the November issue of the newsletter a report of this lecture was given:

> What in the Polish soul still appears as tension becomes in the soul of the Russian people an infinite emptiness that nothing can overcome. This inner emptiness is connected with the task of the soul of the Russian people, which lies in the distant future. Using legends with powerful images, Mr Tomberg depicted how the Russians must again and again live through the three temptations of Christ as an actual reality in its history.

During these autumn months of 1939 in Amsterdam, Tomberg gave several other lectures. On November 21st he spoke about the appearance of the "three tribulations" in modern culture, and on December 19th about conscience. There are also notes of two lectures he gave at this time on "Matter, Force, and Chance."[9] For Tomberg, these three—matter, force, and chance—made up the "materialistic trinity," which he had earlier described in June 1935 in the first chapter of his Studies of the New Testament.

In the autumn of 1939, Tomberg spoke with his friends about Hitler and the occult foundations of National Socialism. Anna de Groot, the widow of Jan van der Most, later recalled that Tomberg had denounced and condemned National Socialism at a special meeting in Amsterdam.

In Amsterdam, Eindhoven, and Zwolle, Tomberg held Christmas speeches in which he described in some detail how members of the English, French, Russian, German, Italian, Polish, and Dutch nations were connected with their archangels.[10] Regarding the lecture in Zwolle, the newsletter of January 1940 reported "This lecture, which made a very deep impression on those present, dealt, among other things, with the connection all human beings can

---

9. *Aufzeichnungen, Vortragsnachschriften*, 42–46.
10. For an elaboration of these thoughts, see Our Father Course, week 30.

Valentin Tomberg and the *Ecclesia Universalis*

experience at Christmastime with the archangel of their particular people." On January 11, 1940, the fortnightly gospel reflections at Tomberg's home resumed. On February 22nd, a presentation on the Buddha lineage was given by Valentin, and later continued by Maria. On March 7th, Maria spoke about Maria-Sophia, and on April 4th, about the two Madonnas.[11] On April 18, Valentin spoke about Elijah, and on May 2nd about John the Baptist.[12]

Besides this course, Valentin offered a Tuesday evening course in The Hague at the Lievegoed home, and an introductory course in Anthroposophy on seven Friday evenings in Eindhoven, starting on January 26, 1940 and ending on May 10, 1940. The introductory courses in Amsterdam continued fortnightly until at least May 9th on "The Human Being as Trinity of Body, Soul and Spirit," "Soul Life," "Macrocosm and Microcosm," "The Divine Plan," "Concerning Karma," and "The Law of the Narrow Way."[13] Tomberg offered lectures (in connection with the nine beatitudes) on "Inner Development," "Functions of the Nine Angelic Hierarchies," "The Three Temptations in the Wilderness," and "The Seven Petitions of the Our Father." This remarkable tapestry of themes, which had been adumbrated already in his Studies of the New Testament, would within a mere matter of months blossom into his extended Our Father Course, a work of astonishing breadth and depth.

On March 8, 1940, shortly before the end of the Soviet Union's Winter War against Finland, Tomberg spoke in Amsterdam on the subject of "Finland and Russia." At the Easter Conference of the Anthroposophical Society in Rotterdam, March 22–24, 1940, he delivered three lectures on "The Battle between Good and Evil." On

---

11. Notes of M.L. van Rijnberk, in *Karmische Zusammenhänge bei Gestalten des Alten Testaments* (Taiserdorf, Bodensee, Germany: Achamoth Verlag, 2003), 152–65.

12. Notes of M. Hörschelmann and R. Ritsema, ibid., 68–84.

13. Lecture notes published in *Starlight*, Vol. 11/1, Easter 2011, 5–11, *Starlight*, Vol. 11/2 Advent 2011, 20–24, *Starlight*, Vol. 12/1, Easter 2012, 8–12 and *Starlight*, Vol. 12/2, Advent 2012, 5–9. "Concerning Human Karma," *Starlight*, Vol. 13/1 Pentecost 2013, 6–12. "The New Law on Karma," *Starlight*, Vol. 13/2, Advent 2013, 4–9. "The Law of the Narrow Way," *Starlight* 2014/1, Easter 2014, 7–10. These volumes can be downloaded at https://sophiafoundation.org/portfolio/starlight-journal/.

the following April 3rd and 10th, two lectures on Death and Resurrection were given in Amsterdam. On May 1st, he spoke about the Ascension, and a week later on "Pentecost as the Seed of the True Community of Nations."

On May 10, 1940, the Friday before Pentecost, the German army invaded the Netherlands. Tomberg's planned lecture in Eindhoven could not take place. Five days later, the country was occupied. On May 24, 1940, Willem Zeylmans informed the members that the Anthroposophical Society had to be considered as dissolved. He wanted to prevent the German authorities from banning it, as had happened in Germany in 1935.

Owing to this situation, Tomberg's work at the Estonian consulate in Amsterdam came to an end. In June 1940, the honorary consul resigned, because Estonia had lost its independence. On August 6, 1940, Estonia was incorporated into the Soviet Union as a Soviet republic.

Tomberg was now unemployed. As an Estonian citizen, he had previously applied for a name change, as had many Estonians who did not bear an Estonian surname. As secretary of the Estonian consulate in the Netherlands, this may also have been of particular importance to him. On July 19, 1940, the name Tomberg was officially changed to "Alguste," so that from then on he was actually called Valentin Alguste. At the registration office in Tallinn, his old family name was put in brackets and replaced by Alguste. In the Estonian language, the word *algus* means "beginning." A background for this new surname (which did not exist, as such, in Estonian) could be that the John gospel, so beloved of the Tombergs, opens in Estonian with: "Alguses oli sõna" (In the beginning was the Word). Valentin never used his new name, but perhaps it symbolized for him a new beginning in his life story.

The Our Mother Prayer

On January 7, 1940, Tomberg's group came together to celebrate the Orthodox Christmas feast. This feast was celebrated thirteen days after the Western Christmas, because its timing was based on the Julian calendar used by the Orthodox Church. According to Maria Louise van Rijnberk's report of this meeting, Tomberg read out in

Valentin Tomberg and the *Ecclesia Universalis*

German what he called the Our Mother prayer. He had received this prayer in his meditation and written it down in Russian (in which original form it has unfortunately been lost). The German translation was his own:

Unser Sophia. 7 Jan. 1940 V.T.

Verfasst mit Russisch. V.T.

Unsere Mutter die du als Schatten in der Unter-Welt bist.

Es leuchte auf in der Erinnerung die Heiligkeit deines Namens

Es durchwärme das Erwachens deines Reiches

Alle Wandrer in der Heimatlosigkeit.

Es beleben die Auferstehung deines Willens

Die ewige Treue bis in die Tiefen der Stofflichkeit

Heute aber empfange lebendige Gedanken deiner, aus Menschenherzen

Die dich flehen zu vergeben die Schuld des Vergessens deiner

Und wollen gegen die Versuchung kämpfen in der Welt

Die dich zum Schattendasein geführt hat,

Um durch das Sohnes Werk

Den unendlichen Vaterschmerz zu stillen

Indem alle Wesen erlöst sein werden

Von dem Übel deines Entschwindens

Denn dein ist die Heimat und das Schenken und das All-Erbarmen

Aller und Allen für Alle

Im Kreisen des Alls

(Kreis O anstatt Amen)

The Netherlands (1938–1944)

Below is a transcription of the handwritten German text, which will be followed by one effort at translation. An adequate treatment of this prayer would of course require a separate work.[14]

⊕

Over Sophia   7 Jan. 1940 V.T.
Vertaald uit Russisch. V.T.

Unsere Mutter die du als Schatten in der Finsternis der Unterwelt bist,
Es leuchte auf in der Erinnerung die Heiligkeit deines Namens,
Es durchwärme das Erwachen deines Reiches alle Wanderer
 in der Heimatlosigkeit.
Es belebe die Auferstehung deines Willens die ewige Treue
 bis in die Tiefen der Stofflichkeit.
Heute aber empfange das lebendige Gedenken deiner, aus
 Menschenherzen
Die dich flehen zu vergeben die Schuld des Vergessens deiner,
Und wollen gegen die Versuchung kämpfen in der Welt, die
 dich zum Schattendasein geführt hat,
Um durch des Sohnes Werk den unendlichen Vaterschmerz
 zu stillen,
Indem alle Wesen erlöst sein werden von dem Übel deines
 Entschwindens.
Denn dein ist die Heimat und das Schenken und das All-Erbarmen
Aller und allen für Alle
In Kreisen des Alls.

(Kreis O anstatt Amen)

---

14. See *Karmische Zusammenhänge*, 11. It needs saying that, in the presence of so profound a text as this, with its rich implications, exacting symmetry with the Our Father prayer, and promise for the future, all that can be offered here is an early effort at putting this prayer into words at least adequate to its sense. As with all great prayers, its content, which lies beyond any particular formulation in words, comes to light only in the devoted praying of it.

Valentin Tomberg and the *Ecclesia Universalis*

On Sophia 7 Jan. 1940 V.T.

translated from Russian. V.T.

Our Mother, Who art as a shadow in the underworld,
May the holiness of Thy name shine forth in our remembering.
May the awakening of Thy kingdom warm those wandering
   in homelessness.
May the resurrection of Thy will renew eternal faith unto
   the depths of materiality.[15]
But this day receive the living memory of Thee from human hearts,
   who implore Thee to forgive the fault of forgetting Thee.
And would fight against the world's temptation,
   which brought Thee to exist in shadow,
That through the work[16] of the Son,
The infinite pain of the Father be stilled[17]
By liberating[18] all beings from the misfortune of Thy
   disappearance.[19]
For Thine is the homeland, bounty, and universal mercy
For all and everything in the rounds of the Universe.[20]

   (A circle instead of amen)

Until his death more than thirty years later, Tomberg continued to include the Our Mother in his evening prayers. For this purpose, toward the end of his life, he prayed the following version, after which, again, an English translation is offered:

Unsere Mutter die Du bist in der Finsternis der Unterwelt.
Es leuchte auf die Erinnerung an die Heiligkeit Deines Namens.
Es erwärme der Hauch des Erwachens Deines Reiches alle Wanderer
   ohne Heimat.

---

15. *Stofflichkeit.*
16. *Werk.*
17. *Stillen* [also satisfy, quench, assuage, allay, staunch].
18. *Erlösen* [also deliver, redeem, save, release, rescue]. In German, Christ is usually called the *Erlöser* (Savior).
19. *Deines Entschwindens* [also Thy vanishing]
20. *All-Erbarmen aller und allen für Alle in Kreisen des Alls.*

The Netherlands (1938–1944)

Es belebe die Auferstehung Deines Willens ewige Treue bis in die
   Tiefen der Leiblichkeit.
Heute empfange das lebendige Gedenken Deiner von menschlichen
   Herzen,
Die Dich um Vergebung flehen für die Schuld des Vergessens Deiner
Und bereit sind zu kämpfen gegen die Versuchung in der Welt,
   die Dich zum Sein in der Finsternis geführt hat,
Um durch die Tat des Sohnes den maßlosen Schmerz des Vaters zu
   beschwichtigen[21]
Durch die Erlösung alles Seienden vom Unglück des Zurückziehens
   Deiner.
Denn Dein ist die Heimat, die Freigiebigkeit und All-Barmherzigkeit
Für alle und Alles im Kreise des Seins. Amen.

Our Mother, Who art in the darkness of the underworld,
May the holiness of Thy name shine anew in our remembering.
May the breath of Thy awakening kingdom warm the hearts
   of all who wander homeless.
May the resurrection of Thy will renew eternal faith even unto
   the depths of corporeality.[22]
Receive this day the living memory of Thee from human hearts,
   who implore Thee to forgive the fault of forgetting Thee,
And are ready to fight against the world's temptation,
   which has led Thee to existence in the darkness,
That through the deed[23] of the Son,
The immeasurable pain of the Father be appeased
By the liberation of all that exists from the misfortune[24]
   of Thy withdrawal.
For Thine is the homeland, the bounty and the all-mercy,
For all and everything in the round of Existence.[25] Amen.

---

21. *Beschwichtigen* [also placate, assuage, console, conciliate, still, mollify].
22. *Leiblichkeit*.
23. *Tat*.
24. *Unglück* [also accident, disaster, tragedy, adversity].
25. *All-Barmherzigkeit für alle und Alles im Kreise des Seins.*

Valentin Tomberg and the *Ecclesia Universalis*

Tomberg gave an explanation of this prayer.[26] Because of its fundamental importance, we cite this explanation in full, to better situate how it forms a complement with the Our Father prayer:

> Christmas this year was a "spiritual Easter," namely, the resurrection of the World Soul as memory. Until this time, humanity still lived according to the Ten Commandments which, however, have an infinitely greater content, and need to be understood ever more deeply.[27] For example, we may take "Thou shalt not take my name in vain" to mean as well that we ought not acknowledge anyone else in life as "Führer."[28] "Thou shalt not make any graven image" appeals to moral intuition, so that we find our way freely and inwardly, connecting with our God without the intermediation of any image. Or again, "Honor your Father and Mother" refers not simply to our physical parents, but to our Heavenly Father and our Earth Mother.
>
> But the Earth Mother is not to be found; She has been blotted entirely from consciousness.[29] Where can one find Her? One comes to the Father through the seven stages of death.[30] In each sphere through which we ascend to the Father we leave part of ourselves behind, peeling something away. Finally we ascend as purely spiritual beings into the realm of the Father, where we lose consciousness. The way to the Earth Mother leads through the subearthly spheres.[31] It is there that we find Her and eternal life.

---

26. *Karmische Zusammenhänge bei Gestalten des Alten Testaments* (Taiserdorf, Bodensee, Germany: Achamoth Verlag, 2003), 8–10.

27. Tomberg's last finished work consists of a profound meditation on the Ten Commandments in the spirit of the brief indications given here into the introductory explanation of the Our Mother prayer. See *The Proclamation on Sinai: Covenant and Commandments* (Brooklyn, NY: Angelico Press, 2022).

28. *Führer* ("leader"): most likely referring to Hitler, whose armies had only recently invaded and occupied the Netherlands, where Tomberg was then living.

29. This may be taken as referring more specifically to the Western world at the time this presentation was made: Christmas 1940. Tomberg offers further insights into the mystery of the "Mother" from a broader cosmological perspective in the Our Father Course, in *Meditations on the Tarot*, and in *The Proclamation on Sinai*.

30. Based not only on references to this subject by Rudolf Steiner, but also references by Tomberg, "coming to the Father through the seven stages of death" may be taken to mean the soul's passage in the life after death through the seven planetary spheres: Moon, Mercury, Venus, Sun, Mars, Jupiter, and Saturn.

31. See Robert Powell's "Sub-Nature and the Second Coming" in *The Inner Life of the Earth*, ed. by Paul V. O'Leary (Gt Barrington, MA: SteinerBooks, 2008).

The Netherlands (1938–1944)

After having encountered the Mother, we can be resurrected. Christ, the Son, reunited the Father and the Mother, who had been separated by evil, by the belt of lies, and by matter. Human beings also have the task, in due time, of restoring this union. Through Christ's descent into hell, whereby he encountered the Mother, the Resurrection and the Ascension were made possible; by virtue of thus uniting the above and the below, a magic arose. Matter cannot be controlled; it can only be subdued from within.

The Mother hid Herself; She fled to the interior of the Earth, and so, for a span, was forgotten. And now, in this our present Christmas-time there has reappeared a first indicator to guide us step-by-step in our renewed search for and understanding of the Earth Mother: that indicator is the remembrance of Her name.

On Earth, the human soul has no place. Neither has it any place in the spiritual world—for that is the place of spirit, not of soul. The soul's real place was that of Paradise, which disappeared with the Mother into the interior of the Earth. Paradise, Shambhala, is our homeland; without it, we are homeless wanderers. But after his death, Christ encountered the Tree of Life.[32] Thus, we may hope that Shambhala[33] may reappear on Earth. It is not to be conceived of in a spatial sense, as a place of any kind, but rather as a state of consciousness always and everywhere present. It is the Earth's ether-body, permeated with the breath of buddhi.[34] In the coming kingdom[35] we will experience how the Mother warms our homeless souls, and how through this experience we are enabled, organically from within, to become truly faithful. At present, we are not faithful in this organic sense, but, rather, unfaithful. Then the stream of our daily bread will consist of the commemoration of the heart of the Mother, of the name of the Mother.

One day we will experience the guilt of forgetting the name of the Mother. We will take up the struggle against the evil in the world and against the temptation that led Paradise to disappear, leaving the Mother in darkness. The interminable suffering of the Father on account of His separation from the Mother will be

---

32. In the fallen Paradise in the interior of the Earth.
33. Or the fallen Paradise.
34. The breath of the spiritualized etheric, or life, body.
35. Of the return of the fallen Paradise.

stilled through the Son. To Sophia belongs the homeland and the bounty and the mercy for all things and all beings in the round of existence.

As far as we know, this was the first time Tomberg expressed the idea that the Earth Mother had fled to the interior of the earth. In his subsequent Our Father Course, which commenced shortly thereafter in May or June of 1940, he spoke of the Mother within the earth as Sophia-Eve.[36] It is an old mythological theme that the Creator-Father abides in the heavenly realms and the Cosmic-Mother in the earth. Greek mythology, for example, spoke of the three Cosmic-Mothers Rhea, Demeter, and Persephone. Gnostic writings from the time of early Christianity speak of the fallen Sophia (Achamoth), who is redeemed by Christ. According to Tomberg, Achamoth is not the Mother, but the Holy Soul.[37]

According to Tomberg it is not known when the Earth Mother disappeared. Possibly this was already at the Fall, but her disappearance was a lengthy process for both humanity and nature. The spiritual experience of nature only disappeared in Western culture beginning from the seventeenth century, when nature came to be regarded by "natural" science as a vast, inanimate mechanism. Rudolf Steiner did not speak of the Earth Mother and of her stay in the depths of the earth. This was Tomberg's vision.

In a conversation with Maria Louise van Rijnberk on October 28, 1941, Tomberg called Sophia's Mother Prayer "the second Our Father." According to him, it originated on Holy Thursday when Christ decided in the night of Gethsemane to descend to the Mother.[38] The descent itself followed on Holy Saturday, in the interval between his death on the cross on Good Friday and his resurrection on Easter Sunday morning. The Christian confession of faith refers to this as "the descent into hell." For Tomberg, the Mother was one of the *three* aspects of Sophia, alongside those of the Daughter and of the Holy Soul. Furthermore, as we have seen, he

---

36. Our Father Course, weeks 33, 92, and 93.
37. The Holy Soul represents for Tomberg the third aspect of Sophia, the second aspect being the Daughter.
38. *Karmische Zusammenhänge,* 110.

said that when the Mother disappeared into the interior of the earth, so also did Paradise, the original world of the soul. What had thus come into the center of the earth's interior he called Shambhala, a mythical kingdom spoken of in the Buddhist tradition. For Tomberg, this mythical kingdom was both a *state of consciousness* and the *life-body* of the earth. It is said that in times to come this kingdom will reappear on earth and again become accessible to humankind. When this time comes, the homeless souls spoken of in the Our Mother prayer will be warmed again by the Mother, who will care for them and for all creation.

When Steiner laid the foundation stone of the underground Rosicrucian temple in Malsch, Germany, on the night of April 5, 1909, he spoke of Mother Earth and how she has been hardened by pain and suffering. He said that it is our mission to spiritualize her again, to redeem her.[39] The following year, on March 9, 1910, he spoke about Shambhala, saying that in consequence of the natural etheric clairvoyance that would in due course accompany the returning Christ, humankind will again be able to enter this etheric kingdom (which otherwise would only have been accessible to initiates over the span of the next 2,500 years).[40] It is not known whether Tomberg was aware of this lecture. On October 12, 1923, Steiner called the Spirit, "Father" and the Earth, "Mother" when he presented the St. John Imagination.[41] Only later did it become known that on June 16, 1924, Steiner had said to Countess Johanna von Keyserlingk in a personal conversation that the "golden fairyland of Shambhala"[42] can be found in the interior of the earth, in its golden core:

> Spiritual science teaches us that when the blood flowed to earth from the cross on Golgotha, a new Sun-globe was born in the interior of the earth. And it is there that the Christ...has, since His

---

39. *Rosicrucianism Renewed* (Gt Barrington, MA: SteinerBooks, 2007) (CW 284).
40. *The Christ Impulse and the Development of Ego Consciousness* (Forest Row, UK: Rudolf Steiner Press, 2014) (CW 116).
41. Lecture of October 12, 1923, in *The Four Seasons and the Archangels* (Forest Row, UK: Rudolf Steiner Press, 2002) (CW 229).
42. Johanna and Adalbert von Keyserlingk, *The Birth of a New Agriculture* (London: Temple Lodge Press, 1999), 87.

descent, made His throne as Regent of the earth. If we take this seriously it can become a fact to us that golden rays ascend from this center [...] I do not know if Rudolf Steiner has referred to this so concretely anywhere else. His words [...] telling us that this golden earth-center is the legendary land of Shambhala, sunk away from humanity and to be rediscovered by the seeking, Christ-guided soul, are of great importance.[43]

According to Tomberg's notes from 1933, Christ descended as far as the sixth subearthly sphere prior to his resurrection; and furthermore, that with his second coming, Christ will descend to the ninth and final sphere—the earth's core. In 1933, however, when those notes were written, Tomberg did not yet speak (as he would later) of Christ's meeting with the Earth Mother.

Tomberg prayed this Our Mother prayer until his death. When, around 1943, he became acquainted with the Catholic rosary, which he later prayed every evening, he included with it the Our Mother prayer.[44] The rosary itself comprises five Our Father prayers and fifty Hail Mary prayers.

The Conversation with Willem Zeylmans van Emmichoven

Tomberg had already met Willem Zeylmans van Emmichoven in Tallinn in October 1929, when the latter was in the Baltic States on a lecture tour. He did not know then that Marie Steiner regarded Willem Zeylmans as one of the "Macedonian generals" with whom she would soon have problems. This term she reserved for those associated with Ita Wegman, in an allusion to the time of Alexander the Great. In a letter of March 10, 1931, to Marie Steiner about what was then called the "Zeylmans affair," Tomberg wrote that, after a conversation with Zeylmans in Tallinn, he had "a burning feeling of pity for him." The "Zeylmans affair" was the result of a conflict between the Executive Board of the Anthroposophical Society in Dornach (which wanted to keep central control of the Society) and

---

43. Ibid., 17–18.
44. See pages 152–54.

The Netherlands (1938–1944)

the group around Zeylmans, Ita Wegman, and Daniel Nicol Dunlop (which strove rather to ensure that Anthroposophy could develop freely in the wider world).[45] For these reasons, great resistance had arisen on the part of the Board against the latter group's activities at that time, including a large pedagogical congress in the Netherlands (1926), a world conference on Anthroposophy in London (1928), and the youth camp Stakenberg in the Netherlands (August 1930), which had a thousand participants.

In a letter to Elisabeth Vreede some years later, on August 24, 1935, Tomberg wrote that his meeting with Zeylmans had been "one of the few deep, friendly, and open conversations that have been possible for me in the Anthroposophical Society over the past several years."

When Tomberg had decided to move to the Netherlands, he also contacted Zeylmans (October 1937). At that time, Zeylmans would have had no reservations about Tomberg, who had, like him, become a member of the Free Anthroposophical Groups upon leaving the Anthroposophical Society of Dornach in October 1937.

It is not known whether Tomberg took the step of formally becoming a member of the Anthroposophical Society led by Zeylmans after settling in the Netherlands in the autumn of 1938. He was in any case afforded plenty of room in this Society. And yet, it was also in this context that resistance to him first appeared.

Leendert Holleman, a relative of Maria Louise van Rijnberk (who introduced him to Tomberg after the Second World War), described in a letter of January 15, 1985 to the Dutch Tomberg researcher Jan Evert de Groot how, already before the beginning of the war, opposition to Valentin Tomberg and his group had begun to take form in the Dutch Anthroposophical Society. In a conversation with De Groot on March 8, 1985, Holleman described how the tension between the two groups manifested. Among Tomberg's circle, that of Zeylmans was characterized as one of "cool light," although Tomberg himself, he reported, spoke rather of "cool elegance" with respect to that group. By contrast, among Zeylmans' circle,

---

45. Conclusion of Emanuel Zeylmans van Emmichoven in his book *Wer war Ita Wegman?*, Vol. 3 (Spring Valley, NY: Mercury Press, 2005), chapter 3.

Valentin Tomberg and the *Ecclesia Universalis*

Willem Zeylmans van Emmichoven (1893–1961)

Tomberg's group was characterized as "intensely warm." According to Holleman, however, not all members of the Society subscribed to such general views.[46]

Nevertheless, such phraseology does help point to a contrast that had arisen between the more practical approach around Zeylmans and the more Christological approach around Tomberg (to which Lubienski also belonged); or to put it another way, between a "circumferential" Anthroposophy of practical work and a "central" Anthroposophy focused on the Christian path of inner schooling. The two paths are, of course, not mutually exclusive. On another level, one might also speak of a general polarity of "types" as between Western and Eastern Europeans—or, in a nomenclature introduced by Steiner late in his life, between an "Aristotelian" stream of *intellectual* knowledge and a "Platonic" stream of *revelatory* knowledge. But lying beyond this polarity, according to Tomberg, is another level, which he takes up as a theme in his 1938 article "The Meaning and Significance of a Free Anthroposophical Working Group." The aim of such a group, he said, was to form what he called a "council of friends." If we take this theme to be characteristic of Tomberg's own "type," we may well imagine how such a "council of friends" might initially have been perceived by others of the "cooler" type as one of intensely warm (or perhaps even overly fervent) human relationships. But these are, after all, only complementary "types," not opposing factions!

In the natural course of events, an intimate circle or "council of friends" did in fact gather around Tomberg. It seems that he needed

---

46. Letter of L.J.W. Holleman to J.E. de Groot (January 15, 1985) and notes of the latter during a conversation with Holleman (March 8, 1985).

The Netherlands (1938–1944)

such an unreservedly warm and sincere setting to feel he could speak of presumed previous incarnations of some of the circle's members and of the results of his esoteric research. In due course, this matter came to be discussed outside Tomberg's immediate circle, and understandably gave rise to unrest among some members of the Anthroposophical Society more generally. In view of this element of tension, Zeylmans invited Tomberg for a clarifying discussion. It is not known when this meeting took place. We do know that until the last issue of the newsletter in April 1940, Tomberg's study groups and courses were still being announced, so it would appear that the meeting could only have taken place in April or May. Emanuel Zeylmans, who gave an account of this conversation between his father and Tomberg to the Russian anthroposophist Sergei Prokofieff, believed the meeting took place before May 10, 1940, the day of the German attack on the Netherlands.[47] From Emanuel's account, it appears that Willem Zeylmans told Tomberg that he did not feel such revelations of earlier incarnations, even in Tomberg's intimate circle, were hygienic, and that he should curtail broaching this topic. In expressing himself this way, Zeylmans was taking his lead from the fact that when Rudolf Steiner appointed him General Secretary of the Dutch Society in 1923, he had impressed upon him that in accepting this office he now bore "the entire esoteric and exoteric responsibility for all aspects of anthroposophical activity in the Netherlands." Viewed in this light, Zeylmans had legitimate grounds to censure Tomberg, given that speculation about incarnations was at that time quite widespread in various anthroposophical circles, and in most cases had led to unfortunate consequences.

There is, however, another version of this conversation that complements the account given by Emanuel Zeylmans. After the death of Willem Zeylmans in 1961, Eva Cliteur (1912–1996) of Amsterdam, who had been a friend of the Tomberg family since 1964 and visited them several times in England, lamented in a conversation with Val-

---

47. Sergei Prokofieff, *The Case of Valentin Tomberg* (London: Temple Lodge Press, 1997).

entin that the conflict with Zeylmans had not been fully resolved. He contradicted her on this point, however, saying that they had had an objective conversation at the 1940 meeting, and that as a result the situation had been clarified. According to Tomberg, Zeylmans had pointed out his particular responsibility for anthroposophical work, emphasizing that he represented education, psychology, art, and medicine (which he considered more appropriate in the Netherlands), whereas Tomberg emphasized Christology and moral development. In effect, they had reached an agreement regarding the different emphases of their respective work. Tomberg was said to have asked whether he was hindering Zeylmans in his development of anthroposophical work in the Society, to which the latter answered in the affirmative.[48] It was on this apparently genial basis, then, that Tomberg took the decision to withdraw and continue his anthroposophical work in a small circle more on the periphery of things.

In conversation with Robert Powell, Eva Cliteur recalled that when asked by Tomberg whether he had understood correctly (i.e., that it would be best if he withdrew from the Society), Zeylmans affirmed that yes, he had correctly understood what he was trying to say.[49]

The Our Father Course (1940–1943)

Valentin Tomberg, now forty years old, had gathered around him in Amsterdam a small circle of people who considered him their spiritual teacher. National Socialism held oppressive sway in the Netherlands, and it had became dangerous to meet together for common spiritual work. We know that already in 1939 Tomberg had quite openly described National Socialism as a coming-together of a "triple evil." In personal conversations he was even more candid, referring to Hitler as "the man with the evil ego." In fact, this designation appears in his notebook as early as August 1934:

---

48. Eva Cliteur, written communication to Karl Bitterwolf (June 23, 1977) and notes on Tomberg's biography (April 18, 1985). Tomberg Archive, Steinbergkirche.
49. Communication from Robert Powell.

The Netherlands (1938–1944)

H. [Hitler] is an evil Mars-type. He is the man with the evil ego; and so the fourth Fall has come upon humanity in this age:

1st Fall in Lemuria (expulsion from Paradise)—physical body.

2nd Fall at the beginning of Atlantis (the gods found pleasure in the daughters of the earth)—etheric body.

3rd Fall at the end of Atlantis (the Babylonian confusion of tongues)—astral body.

4th Fall at present—now there is an evil ego.

It is not a matter of the ego being seduced by the evil in the other bodies, as was the case before; now the source of evil is the ego itself.[50]

Participants of the Our Father Course: Maja Hörschelmann *, Maria Louise van Rijnberk **, Jan van der Most †, Ans Waterreus ††, John Daniskas ‡, Rie Ritsema ◊. (1939 photo)

---

50. *Karmische Zusammenhänge*, 158.

Valentin Tomberg and the *Ecclesia Universalis*

With these words, Tomberg communicated that an "evil ego" had been incarnated in Hitler, thereby uniting the three preceding Falls into a fourth Fall—just as Christ Jesus had united the three aspects of the Trinity into a fourth aspect, the "Persona," which, ever since the earthly life of Christ, has been present as the conjunction in a human being of the Trinity as a Unity.[51]

Meanwhile, in Amsterdam on Ascension Day, May 18, 1939, a new group had emerged out of the circle that had begun studying the gospels together. This group met for ninety-seven evenings around Tomberg for an esoteric course on the Our Father prayer. The Saturday evenings were devoted to spiritual work and the following Sunday mornings to socializing. The eight primary attendees of the Our Father Course were:

Valentin Tomberg (1900–1973)
Maria Tomberg-Leitnecker Demski (1893–1973)
Maja Hörschelmann (1890–1946)
Rie Ritsema (1891–1967) from Amsterdam
Maria Louise van Rijnberk-Holleman (1894–1980) from Blaricum
Ans Waterreus (1905–2001) from The Hague
John Daniskas (1907–2002) from Rotterdam
Jan van der Most (1908–1992) from Rotterdam

The Our Father Course started at the end of May or early June 1940 and ended on Tuesday evening, February 2, 1943 (Candlemas). Thus, it extended over about thirty-three months. The first confirmed dates of the Course notes taken by Maria Louise van Rijnberk are from autumn 1940. She was allowed to copy Tomberg's own notes. Notes by Maja Hörschelmann have also been preserved. In the winter of 1943, the Course could no longer be continued owing to increasing difficulty associated with traveling by train in the war situation.

On the one hand, the Our Father Course was still very much rooted in Tomberg's anthroposophical research. In presenting bibli-

---

51. *The Four Sacrifices of Christ*, lecture 1.

The Netherlands (1938–1944)

cal lessons and exercises along the lines of his Studies of the Bible, he employed anthroposophical terminology familiar to the participants. But he supplemented these Studies of the Bible with new results drawn from his own, continuing, inner research. On the other hand, the emphasis in the Course on praying the Our Father presaged his later work, in which the practice of prayer was given at least as much emphasis as meditation. We may say, then, that this Course stands as a bridge between Tomberg's earlier work, in which he made use of anthroposophical terminology, and his later work, written more in the terminology of Christian Hermeticism, and later in ecclesiastical terminology.

As it unfolded, the Course led the participants through active meditation on the seven petitions of the Our Father prayer to an ever deeper experience of Christ's activity. It progressed through the cycle of the seven petitions of the Our Father in this way four times. In the first passage through the prayer, essential themes of Christianity were linked with the seven petitions to form an introductory panorama. In the second passage, each petition served as a focus for about one week. In the third passage, each petition became the central theme for about seven weeks. In the fourth passage, the petitions were further explored in prayer and meditation. Unfortunately, after about four months of this fourth passage through the petitions, the course had to be broken off. As the Course unfolded and deepened, the petitions were brought into connection with the nine beatitudes, the seven I AM sayings, the seven stages of the Passion, the seven miracles from John's gospel, and the seven sayings of Christ Jesus on the cross. The interweaving of these archetypal Christian themes resulted in a stunning, intricate tapestry of spiritual insight. Correlative texts and themes from the Old and New Testaments and the Apocalypse were interlaced layer upon layer and illuminated with an astonishing wealth of detail. Of all these riches, only a small part was based on the work of Rudolf Steiner. The Course described the whole path of humankind—from the Fall, to the gradual overcoming of its consequences, through the saving acts of Christ, and on to the final transformation of the earth into the heavenly Jerusalem. The second coming of Christ was dealt with only incidentally in the Course (in weeks 34 and 36).

Valentin Tomberg and the *Ecclesia Universalis*

The thrust of the Course was aimed at rekindling the original image of God which human beings bear within themselves. This gave it a deeply Christian character that amounted to nothing less than a full-blown esoteric path for Christian-minded souls. As one example, at a certain stage Tomberg elaborates how the three "feminine" vows of the monks (obedience, chastity, and poverty) and the three "masculine" virtues of the knights (courage, loyalty, and justice) can each be exercised in our thinking, feeling, and willing in the service of the development of a Christ-connected "consciousness soul."

Tomberg called special attention to the seven "lotus flowers" (chakras), offering a much-needed, detailed, teaching on the nature and development of these spiritual organs of perception in a Christian context.[52] He described not only the opening of these seven organs of spiritual perception, but especially how each can be purified by being meditatively linked to one of the seven I Am sayings. In this, he was in fact continuing, in what may in some ways be considered its "second volume," the spiritual schooling Rudolf Steiner had earlier presented in his book *Knowledge of the Higher Worlds*—a sequel Steiner himself may not have undertaken because he felt that anthroposophists had not yet worked sufficiently with the contents of his "first volume."

The final meeting of the Our Father Course, on February 2, 1943, began with the theme of "building a spiritual ark." This ark was meant to contain all essential cultural values and truths. It needed to be constructed as an ark *within* our consciousness in order save all such values and truths from a new deluge pouring through the floodgates in a rising tide of evil:

> In the present day we are experiencing the rise of overpowering evil, a kind of biblical flood. This inundation of awakening evil works directly within our waking day-consciousness. In the wake

---

52. Tomberg, lecture notes: "The Lotus Flowers," *Starlight*, Vol. 7/1, Spring 2007, 6–9, *Starlight*, Vol. 7/2, Fall 2007, 3–8 and *Starlight*, Vol. 8/1, Spring 2008, 3–8. These volumes can be downloaded at https://sophiafoundation.org/portfolio/starlight-journal/. See also Tryge Olaf Lindvig, "Die Chakra-Lehre Valentin Tombergs," in Frensch a.o., *Valentin Tomberg*, Vol. III, 112–23.

The Netherlands (1938–1944)

of such a deluge, it is a matter of sink or swim. This is the trial that consciousness is undergoing in our time. Rescue from this state of affairs, then, is a matter of what we may call the "law of the ark." What does it mean to build an ark? It means to build in our consciousness a four-square edifice, whose height, breadth, and length are such as to contain everything essential in the whole expanse of life. All cultural values and truths are to be gathered and preserved therein as an extract comprised of unextinguished memories of all that is essential, which means to say of all that is true and good. We might call this essentialized extract the life-raft that will keep us from drowning. Given that we are presently engulfed in darkness, it is needful that we bear the ark just spoken of inwardly, that we recall to memory in this way all essential cultural values. If we accomplish this, the *life* of our soul—our "life body"—will not wither away but, together with our soul, remain engaged in life. Bearing the ark of memory within ourselves makes it possible for faith, love, and hope to arise within us. It may be said that when a truth has grown so strong within us that it is experienced "right down to the life body," it becomes thereby faith, love, and hope. For although the Platonic virtue of justice or righteousness represented the purification of the *astral* body, Christ took this purification further, right down to the *life* body, giving rise to faith, love, and hope. If we have *faith*, we will never suffer aridity in our head-organization, that is, become sclerotic. If we have *love*, we will never be empty or arid, because the life of our heart (that is, our "etheric" heart) will never shrivel away but remain ever radiant and life-filled. If we have *hope*, the weakness we are otherwise prone to simply does not arise—failing which, we are either "galvanized" by the forces of evil or we grow feeble and apathetic. The life body is dependent upon the streams of faith, love, and hope; but these can only be present for so long as the life body dwells in the "ark," that is, in the memory of all that is true, beautiful, and good.[53]

Tomberg concluded this last evening of the Course with the words:

The mission of esoteric Christianity (symbolized by the Rose Cross) is to experience these things ever more deeply, whereas

---

53. Our Father Course, week 97.

Valentin Tomberg and the *Ecclesia Universalis*

exoteric Christianity sets limits for itself, as we see in the case of the Church.[54]

According to Michael Frensch, we may see in this program of building an ark the source for Tomberg's further work, in which he examined the tradition of law, the tradition of Christianity, and the tradition of Hermeticism. It was about, he wrote, "not letting the thread of tradition break, but nevertheless giving it a new impulse by building the ark."[55]

Thanks to Maria Louise van Rijnberk, who summarized her conversations with Valentin Tomberg and some of his reflections, we are also familiar with the group work that took place alongside the Our Father Course. For example, we know of an Easter meditation that Tomberg held in 1941, in which he spoke of the apocalyptic nature of our times, during which wars, earthquakes, and epidemics occur, and Christ comes near... is already here. All this misery in the present is necessary, he said, to dispel the clouds that prevent us from recognizing Christ, who is already waiting:

> But it is also true that Christ is here already. There he stands in the south of the earth, and waves are going out from him. All of us can now join together with him. But we ourselves must undertake to do this, for Christ is not yet in motion, but only stands there. For this, only two things are needed: knowledge of Christ and of Antichrist; and standing up as advocate for Christ. In choosing one of these two currents—that of Christ or that of Antichrist—which flow through the world like light blue and black streams, we thereby implicate ourselves already in the one we have chosen. We are strengthened beyond all measure by the power of Christ. With him we can make our way in deepest calm through any horrors we may face. Through his power we may bear up under unimaginable burdens; for yes, his strength suffices even for this.[56]

Maria Louise van Rijnberk also recorded the following passage from Tomberg's notebook:

---

54. Ibid.
55. Michael Frensch, "Valentin Tombergs geistiger Weg nach dem Zweiten Weltkrieg," in Ramsteiner Kreis, *Valentin Tomberg*, Vol. II, 79.
56. *Karmische Zusammenhänge*, 12–13.

The Netherlands (1938–1944)

In the Anthroposophical Society it is now the case that what Rudolf Steiner said is simply being repeated. Thereby the 10-petal lotus flower rotates only mechanically instead of working creatively. From here a stream goes to the 16-petal lotus flower, whence the stream circles back [to the 10-petal lotus flower]. Thus arises a purely mechanical *circulus vitiosus*. In consequence of this, the system of lotus flowers as a whole becomes mummified, ossified. At the present time this is the same as what the cult of Baal was in the past.[57]

In addition to the Our Father circle, there was a second circle of four people meeting during the same period: Valentin and Maria Tomberg, John Daniskas, and Jan van der Most. According to a statement by John Daniskas, Tomberg held thirty-six esoteric lessons in this circle, for which he wrote the meditation texts himself.[58] These meetings were probably held monthly on Saturday afternoons, immediately preceding the Our Father Course.[59] In addition, in the summer of 1941, a study group was formed on the Old Testament, which continued at least until the spring of 1942. In this group, which met bi-weekly, the books of Daniel and Ezekiel, the figure of Solomon, and the patriarchs Abraham and Isaac were studied.[60]

During this time, Tomberg also expressed essential thoughts on Rudolf Steiner.[61] On March 30, 1942, the anniversary of Steiner's passing, Tomberg said that already before his death Steiner had foreseen that his work would come to ruin. He had considered making some arrangements, or leaving a will, but in a spiritual encounter, the Archangel Michael had pointed out to him that his

---

57. Maria Louise van Rijnberk, "Allgemeines über die Lotusblumen," 24. Tomberg Archive, Steinbergkirche. Also, "The Lotus Flowers: Part III," *Starlight*, Vol. 8/1, Spring 2008.
58. Daniskas later passed these texts on to Martin Kriele.
59. There is no unequivocal indication that the Our Father Course, and these esoteric lessons, were intended as contents of the School of Spiritual Science. However, on the basis of fragments present, Michael Frensch believes that Tomberg, who had been a class reader himself, actually conducted class work in the Netherlands with three classes. See also: "Valentin Tombergs Beziehung zur Freien Hochschule," in Wutte/Röschert, *Perspektiven freier Hochschularbeit*, 100ff.
60. *Karmische Zusammenhänge*, 14–67.
61. Ibid., 120–21, 123–25, 134–36, 139–40.

Valentin Tomberg and the *Ecclesia Universalis*

entire life-work was dedicated to human freedom, and that for precisely this reason he should leave his work exposed to this human freedom—even were it to perish as a result.[62]

A Reorientation in the Christian Tradition

Tomberg was a deeply religious man from northeastern Europe. During his youth in St. Petersburg he had been raised Protestant, but his mother had introduced him to other Christian traditions as well, especially the Russian Orthodox Church. Tomberg's wife Maria, a Polish countess, had been baptized Roman Catholic. Their son Alex was baptized in the Greek Orthodox Church in Tallinn on December 8, 1933. According to an entry in the 1943 baptismal register of the Thomas Aquinas parish in Amsterdam, made when Alex was admitted to the Roman Catholic Church, Nikolai Belozvetov and Maja Hörschelmann were his godparents.

Officially, this Church in Tallinn was called the Estonian Orthodox Apostolic Church. It did not belong to the Patriarchate of Moscow, but to that of Constantinople, and included Russian believers living in Estonia. Valentin and Maria had therefore been members of the Orthodox Church at least since 1933.[63] It is also quite possible that Maria had joined the Russian Orthodox Church already in 1920, at her first marriage to the Russian Orthodox Nikolai Belozvetov.

Tomberg and Belozvetov thought that a connection with the Orthodox Church was important for Russian anthroposophists—that they did not need the Christian Community, because the Orthodox Church could meet their liturgical needs. As already mentioned, Tomberg had written a letter to Marie Steiner on April 11, 1931, to ascertain whether it was in fact true what the German anthroposophist Ludwig Kleeberg had said about Rudolf Steiner's statements regarding the Orthodox Church. According to Kleeberg,

---

62. Ibid., 123–24.
63. The Orthodox Church comprises several patriarchates, among them the Greek and Russian. The Estonian Orthodox Church was founded because the Russians who fled to Estonia from Russia quite naturally wanted nothing to do with the Russian Orthodox patriarchate.

The Netherlands (1938–1944)

Steiner told him on February 22, 1908 that only Greek Orthodoxy contained seeds for the future.[64] Belozvetov for some time advocated the idea of a fusion of Anthroposophy with the faith of the Russian Orthodox Church.

Ans Waterreus, who belonged to the Our Father circle, recalled that Tomberg felt the lack of piety and of the religious, sacramental element in Anthroposophy. Although the practice of humility and devotion is considered a prerequisite of the anthroposophical path of development as described in *Knowledge of the Higher Worlds*, this necessary phase of the path seems all too often to have been neglected in practice.

Now, there was a small Russian Orthodox congregation in the Netherlands, and according to Ans Waterreus, Tomberg met its priest, Father Dionisi, in Amsterdam in the autumn of 1941. Father Dionisi was thirty-one years old at the time, and his congregation was linked to the Moscow Patriarchate. His home church was at 9 Obrechtstraat in The Hague, but he regularly came to Amsterdam, where there was a chapel in Gerard Brandtstraat. Father Dionisi often visited the Tombergs and had intensive conversations with them in Russian. Within his congregation, Father Dionisi spoke openly against National Socialism.

Jan van der Most and Anna de Groot, who had married shortly before Easter 1941, were encouraged by Valentin and Maria to attend the Easter service of the Russian Orthodox Church in The Hague, and in the autumn of 1941 they became members of this church. Their baptism took place by immersion in a pool. Valentin stood as godfather at the baptism of Jan van der Most, and Maria as godmother of Anna de Groot. As a Greek, John Daniskas was already Orthodox. Several other members of Tomberg's circle also became Russian Orthodox. Ans Waterreus became a member of the Orthodox Church at the end of March 1942 and received the *Confessions* of the Church Father St Augustine at her baptism as a gift from the Tombergs. Anna de Groot reports that Valentin and Maria came to The Hague to celebrate the Russian Orthodox Easter of 1942 together with the Van der Most family.

---

64. Ludwig Kleeberg, *Wege und Worte* (Stuttgart: Mellinger Verlag, 1993), 195.

Valentin Tomberg and the *Ecclesia Universalis*

As matters turned out, however, Valentin and Maria's connection with the Russian Orthodox congregation soon came to an end. In a conversation between Ans Waterreus and Father Dionisi, the subject of reincarnation came up. The priest told her that if she believed in reincarnation, he would have to exclude her from communion—because, so he said, in the Orthodox Church one is not a "true believer" in this case. Now, in the Orthodox and Catholic Churches there is in fact no "dogma" properly speaking on the question of reincarnation. However, at the Council of Constantinople in AD 553, the doctrine of the theologian Origen that the soul exists before it is born was condemned. This is what gave rise to the Church's "teaching" that there is no such thing as reincarnation. In this regard, the practice in the Orthodox Church is that the individual priest decides how to treat those members who believe in reincarnation (or for whom it is an inner experience), and determines whether or not they may receive communion.

Father Dionisi

In this conversation, Ans Waterreus mentioned that, from personal experience, Tomberg held to the reincarnationist view. In consequence, a few weeks after Easter 1942, a conversation took place between Tomberg and Fr Dionisi, with the result that Valentin and Maria, Jan van der Most, Anna de Groot (and a few others) left Fr Dionisi's congregation.

Ans Waterreus recounts that Fr Dionisi was very upset after he spoke to Tomberg, and said to her: "They are all leaving!" Only she herself remained in his congregation, which at that time was probably the only Orthodox congregation in the Netherlands. The fact that Tomberg withdrew from this congregation did not mean he "left" the Orthodox Church. As we shall see, there are good reasons to assume that he remained a member of the Church.

After withdrawing from Fr Dionisi's Orthodox congregation in

The Netherlands (1938–1944)

the spring of 1942, Tomberg began to reorient himself in the Christian tradition—more specifically, in the Catholic Church. This came as a surprise to the Russian Orthodox Nikolai Belozvetov, who had moved from Riga to Stuttgart with his family in 1941. Johanna Thylmann, an acquaintance of the Belozvetov family, who also lived in Stuttgart, mentioned in a letter of March 21, 1947 to the young Wolfgang Garvelmann that Belozvetov was quite upset when "on a Pentecost Sunday" he heard of Tomberg's move towards Catholicism.[65] This must have been on May 24, 1942.

Ernst von Hippel, who was a member of the Christian Community, at first saw in this situation an opportunity to link the Tombergs' further path with the Christian Community. It seems quite likely that he suggested to Valentin that he meet Emil Bock, the leader of the Christian Community at that time, in Stuttgart. Bock had visited Ernst von Hippel several times in the 1930s in Königsberg, and so it would have been quite natural for von Hippel to arrange a meeting between Tomberg and Bock. The Christian Community was banned in Nazi Germany in 1941, and Bock was soon arrested; but in February 1942 he was released and returned to Stuttgart.

Von Hippel had been appointed professor of public law, international law, and philosophy of law at the University of Cologne in 1940. Beginning in April 1941, he had contrived to visit the Tomberg family in Amsterdam, and also supported them financially. To facilitate the visits, he wrote articles of a cultural nature for the German newspaper *Das Reich*, which qualified him to obtain permits to travel to the Netherlands.

In the available letters from this period nothing is said about a trip by Tomberg to Stuttgart; and in the archives of the Christian Community nothing can be found about conversations between Bock and Tomberg.[66] However, in her recollections of the friendship between her godfather Valentin Tomberg and her father Nikolai,

---

65. Joanna Thylmann, *Briefe an einen jungen Freund* (Basel: Verlag Die Pforte, 1992), 133.
66. Communication from Wolfgang Gädeke.

Valentin Tomberg and the *Ecclesia Universalis*

Emil Bock (1895–1959)

Ludmilla Belozvetov recorded that when she was six years old the Tombergs visited her parents in Stuttgart during the war: "We were often together in 1942 [with Valentin and Maria Tomberg] in Stuttgart, during which visits there were also serious discussions with various anthroposophists and priests from the Christian Community."[67]

Among the priests alluded to, one may have been Luba Husemann, an acquaintance of the Belozvetov family who had a Russian mother and had spent part of her childhood in Kiev. According to Ludmilla Belozvetov, Dora Krück von Poturzyn also took part in these conversations. Johanna Thylmann possibly participated as well, because on January 3, 1943, she wrote to Wolfgang Garvelmann that she had met Valentin Tomberg in person.[68]

It seems quite certain, therefore, that a meeting took place in the autumn of 1942 between Tomberg and Emil Bock, who lived close by the Belozvetov family. Von Hippel most likely arranged this meeting. It is even possible that he was present. What was discussed is not known. Von Hippel had had a separate conversation with Bock shortly before, or perhaps on, December 9, 1942. This did not end well, for in a note bearing this date, von Hippel wrote to his wife that he had informed Emil Bock of his withdrawal from the Christian Community.[69] In view of later events, it seems likely that this was directly related to the presumptive unsatisfactory meeting between Tomberg and Bock.

Tomberg's further spiritual path worried his friends. Nikolai

---

67. Ludmilla Zimmermann-Belozvetov, "Eine große Freundschaft—Valentin Tomberg und Nikolai Belozvetov," in Heckmann and Frensch, *Valentin Tomberg*, Vol. I.2, 652.
68. Thylmann, *Briefe an einen jungen Freund*, 47.
69. Heckmann and Frensch, *Valentin Tomberg*, Vol. I.1, 372–73.

The Netherlands (1938–1944)

Belozvetov nevertheless wrote to Ernst von Hippel on November 25, 1942 that he could understood his friend's decision:

> In conversation, Frau von Hippel told us about Valentin's important steps in a direction [toward the Catholic Church] that some wish he had not taken. Although I did not expect this from Valentin, I can understand and approve of it very well. I suspect that behind this decision lies a very serious and deep issue, which we can explore together another time.[70]

In a later letter to Ernst von Hippel of December 5, 1942, Belozvetov wrote that he intended to visit Tomberg in Amsterdam after Christmas (apparently to talk to him about the Catholic Church). If a visit was not possible, he would come to Ernst von Hippel for a week. On December 13, he wrote again to von Hippel, reporting that he would not be going to see the Tombergs after all, "for reasons I will explain when we meet." He wanted to visit Ernst von Hippel before Christmas, prior to his departure for Amsterdam. On December 20, Belozvetov and his wife did indeed go for two weeks to Bad Godesberg near Bonn, where the von Hippel family lived.

Eva Cliteur's notes from 1985 on the subject of Tomberg's inclination towards the Catholic Church have been preserved. There she reports that he was very impressed by the attitude of the Dutch Catholics towards the Nazis. Archbishop De Jong deserves special mention in this regard.[71] Eva also referred to a statement Tomberg made in the 1950s to Elisabeth Einberg, according to which he felt the need to join an organization that resisted National Socialism.[72] The Anthroposophical Society had offered no resistance, and had been banned in Germany.

During the war years, Tomberg immersed himself in the Christian tradition. In a conversation in March 1942, he compared the Greek Orthodox with the Roman Catholic Church. Their union, he

---

70. Tomberg Archive, Steinbergkirche.

71. Johannes de Jong (1885–1955) was a Dutch Cardinal of the Roman Catholic Church. He served as Archbishop of Utrecht from 1936 until his death. During the Second World War he was one of the major leaders against the Nazi occupation of the Netherlands.

72. Eva Cliteur, notes on Tomberg's biography (April 18, 1985). Tomberg Archive, Steinbergkirche.

said, could be difficult. The Roman Catholic Church was all "head-culture" and had developed thinking to a high degree. The Greek Orthodox Church on the other hand was all "heart-culture," living deeply in rituals and prayer. In a general way, then, the Roman Church missed the pure heart experience. It works in a "cooler," dogmatic fashion. On the other hand, the Greek Orthodox Church lacked a strong center, and in consequence had disintegrated into many patriarchates.[73]

Around Christmas 1942, Tomberg spoke in the Our Father Course about another division of the community of all Christians: the exoteric Church of Peter, or the "fighting" church, and the esoteric Church of John, the "waiting" church. The task of the Church of Peter, he said, is to hold humanity together, to preserve the unity of tradition, and to fight the battle between good and evil in the *present*. The task of the Church of John is to unite the "initiated," to nurture, preserve, and transmit spiritual experience, and to prepare for the *future* struggle between good and evil.[74]

In Holland, Tomberg experienced first-hand how spiritually impoverished Calvinist Christianity was, and how devastating the consequences of the Reformation had been for people in the West. Holy places had been desecrated, shrines and their relics had been razed, and the "network" of healing forces that had existed on the

---

73. Notes of M.L. van Rijnberk, in Tomberg, *Karmische Zusammenhänge*, 122.

74. In Catholicism, the "fighting" Church Militant comprises Christians who are living; the Church Suffering, those in Purgatory; the Church Triumphant, those who enjoy the beatific vision in Heaven. The Church Suffering stands between the Church Militant (those still living upon the Earth) and the Church Triumphant (those who by individual effort and/or grace achieve during that life a moral state worthy of admittance to Heaven). Since the Church Suffering represents souls "waiting" as they pass through Purgatory, we might be tempted to consider it the "waiting" Church here spoken of; but the sense of this difficult passage found in the Our Father Course (week 83) seems to imply something more (or at least an enhanced Johannine understanding of Purgatory), whereby the threshold alluded to may not be simply that between the usual conception of human life as spanning only one birth and death (that is, between Purgatory and Heaven in the commonly understood sense), but rather the threshold between multiple earthly births and deaths of our eternal entelechy on the one hand, and on the other hand the spiritual world wherein that entelechy subsists during the periods separating each death and the subsequent birth.

The Netherlands (1938–1944)

face of nature in the Middle Ages had withdrawn underground. According to Tomberg, it was Bernadette de Soubirous (1844–1879) who, in Lourdes in the south of France, had sparked the reappearance on the surface of the earth of these accumulated healing forces and reunited them with the spiritual world.[75]

As has been said, the Our Father Course broke off on February 2, 1943. Tomberg's personal notes from the spring of 1943 show that he was then investigating the schooling paths of the monastic orders.[76] This turn to the Catholic tradition had already been announced within his family. In the autumn of 1939, the young Alex Tomberg first attended the Waldorf School in Amsterdam, which had its classrooms in the Montessori school on Quinten Massijsstraat. Because it was officially called the "Geert Groote school," it was not closed by the German authorities during the war. After a year, however, Alex at his own request was placed in a Catholic school. Eva Cliteur recalled that Valentin Tomberg was not happy with the Waldorf school, which may have had something to do with his withdrawal from the Anthroposophical Society in the spring of 1940.

The new school, St. Joseph's, was located close to the Tomberg home. It belonged to the parish of the Thomas Aquinas Church (on the Rijnstraat) and was run by friars. When children in his class were being prepared for their First Communion, Alex wished to participate also, and told his parents that he wanted to become a Roman Catholic. This must have been in the course of 1942. He made his *professio fidei* to the Dominican Father Diekman in the first week of May 1943, when he was nine years old. According to an entry in the church register, this was done formally with the permission of the bishop.[77]

In Germany, two years later (1945), Tomberg entered the Catholic Church. Eva Cliteur wrote in a letter from 1975 that this took place after a life-threatening illness and a convalescent stay in a monastery.[78] According to Martin Kriele, the administrator of Tomberg's

---

75. Notes of M.L. van Rijnberk, *Karmische Zusammenhänge*, 141–42.
76. Tomberg Archive, Steinbergkirche.
77. Written communication from the parish secretariat (January 25, 2001).
78. Tomberg Archive, Steinbergkirche.

Valentin Tomberg and the *Ecclesia Universalis*

literary estate (who died in 2020), this event took place shortly after the end of the war in a camp where Tomberg was then working as an interpreter. No official registration has been found.

As a child, Maria Tomberg had been baptized Catholic. As a member of the Orthodox Church, Valentin did not have to be baptized. Eva Cliteur wrote on April 18, 1985, that Ernst von Hippel had told her: "Tomberg was permitted to receive communion in both Churches," i.e., in both the Greek Orthodox Church and the Roman Catholic Church.[79] This extremely important note was not known of previously, and throws a special light on Tomberg's connection with the Catholic Church, for it establishes that this came about without his having had to officially withdraw from the Orthodox Church. Furthermore, as a child he had been baptized Protestant. He thus united the three Churches in his own person and in so doing linked himself,

The Thomas Aquinas Church, Amsterdam (now demolished)

we could say, with the original, "undivided" Church, what we might call the *Ecclesia universalis*. In Tomberg's case, then, we cannot really speak of "conversion."

This same connection with the original, "undivided" Christianity is also visible in the life of the Russian philosopher Vladimir Solovyov (1853–1900), for whom Tomberg had great respect. Solovyov professed the "religion of the Holy Spirit," which in his view will bring the disintegrated parts of the original united Christianity together again in one universal Church. Solovyov was familiar with the idea of the "Three Ages" in the historical development

---

79. Notes of Eva Cliteur. Tomberg Archive, Steinbergkirche. It is not known whether Tomberg later received communion in the Orthodox Church.

The Netherlands (1938–1944)

of Christianity put forward by the medieval abbot Joachim of Fiore (c. 1135–1202): the Age of the Father (the Old Testament), the Age of the Son (the New Testament), and the Age of the Holy Spirit (the Apocalypse). In 1896, Solovyov received communion from a priest of the Uniate Church (united with Rome) and recognized the leading role of the office of Peter in the communion of the Christian Churches. This is also clear from his *Short Narrative on the Antichrist*. Solovyov remained Russian Orthodox and believed that the sacraments of the Orthodox Church were valid. Thus he tried in his own way to overcome the schism in the Church. "Solovyov," wrote the philosopher Nikolai Berdyaev, "wanted to be Catholic and Orthodox at the same time, wanted to belong to the universal Church, in which there was one fullness."[80] Tomberg apparently wanted the same.

As far as we know, Tomberg never gave a written reason for his affiliation with the Catholic Church. After 1948, when he was already living in England, the leader of an anthroposophical group in London, Eugenia Gurwitsch, asked him why he had become a Catholic. He is said to have replied, "Rudolf Steiner wanted me to do it."[81] According to Oliver Mathews, priest of the Christian Community in England, Tomberg had hoped to speak about this at the Steiner House in London. Whether this happened, and what he may have said there, is not known. Mathews also obtained information from the British philosopher and anthroposophist Owen Barfield, who knew Tomberg personally and had visited him in order to discuss his transition to the Catholic Church. Barfield wrote to Mathews that, according to Tomberg, the difference between the Catholic Church and Anthroposophy was exaggerated.[82]

As mentioned earlier, this step taken by Tomberg was incompre-

---

80. Leonid and Tatjana Sytenko, *Wladimir Solowjow in der Kontinuität philosophischen Denkens* (Schaffhausen: Novalis Verlag, 1997), 80–82 and 233–34; Wladimir Szylkarski, *Solowjew und Dostojewskij* (Bonn: Götz Schwippert Verlag, 1948), 68–72.

81. Quoted in Lawrie, "Valentin Tomberg," in Ramsteiner Kreis, *Valentin Tomberg*, Vol. II, 392–93.

82. *Priesterrundbrief* nr. 328 (December 1977). Archive of the Christian Community, Berlin. File 6.1.

Valentin Tomberg and the *Ecclesia Universalis*

hensible to many of his anthroposophical friends, who only found out about it later. Most anthroposophists in the Netherlands at that time had a Calvinist background. For them, Catholics were representatives of the "medieval" religion, toward which many Protestants harbored a negative attitude. The fact that Rudolf Steiner, who himself was a baptized Catholic and never formally left the Catholic Church, criticized this Church for various reasons, no doubt contributed further to this lack of understanding. It is worth noting in passing, however, that according to its constitution, people of all faiths can become members of the Anthroposophical Society.

In short, Tomberg's move was ultimately and entirely a private matter. In the course of time, some of Tomberg's friends took a similar step. As early as June 1943, Jan van der Most and his wife converted on his advice to the Catholic Church. Later, Maria Louise van Rijnberk, Maja Hörschelmann (1944), Nikolai Belozvetov and his wife (1947), and Ernst and Gertrud von Hippel, also joined the Catholic Church.

The Last Year in Amsterdam

After the Our Father Course came to an end, things became quiet around Valentin and Maria. It was more difficult to get together, and the food supply in the winter became increasingly difficult in the cities. The couple often had little to eat in those years and, as Eva Cliteur noted in a letter, would try to satisfy their hunger by smoking cigarettes. Before the war, Tomberg could still earn a modest income with his lectures and writings, in addition to his salary as secretary of the Estonian consulate. But from the beginning of the war he had became dependent on the help of his friends to supplement his own efforts. Ernst von Hippel often came to Amsterdam in 1941 and helped them financially.

Tomberg did manage to earn something during the war years by giving private lessons. A note by Eva Cliteur mentions that he gave "countless lessons in languages, history, and religion, both to young people and adults." Gemma van Rijnberk, a daughter of Gérard van Rijnberk, also received religion lessons from Tomberg. He was quite familiar with such work, for the same note also states that for years he had organized and led courses in modern languages for state

The Netherlands (1938–1944)

officials in Estonia, where he had himself acted as a teacher. Maria taught Russian during the war years. Valentin was active in the Dutch resistance during the war years, helping hide downed English pilots so that they could return to England.[83]

In a letter dated January 3, 1943, Ernst von Hippel wrote that Tomberg had the prospect of an assistantship at the university's Russian chair. At the end of that year, in a letter dated November 14, 1943, Tomberg wrote to von Hippel that he was preparing for exams that would entitle him to teach languages at Dutch secondary schools. Shortly before this, on October 28, 1943, von Hippel had informed Tomberg that he could matriculate to work toward a doctorate in law at the University of Cologne, where von Hippel himself taught in the Faculty of Law. Immediately afterwards, he sent his friend some study books. Tomberg took this opportunity, agreed to write a dissertation under his supervision, and began preparing to start his studies in mid-December 1943.

Tomberg had been stateless since Estonia's annexation by the Soviet Union in August 1940. One year later, the German army conquered the Baltic States. Estonia was abolished as a state and incorporated into the new province of Ostland. His situation in Amsterdam offered little prospect, and so the idea was born to move to Cologne. Ernst von Hippel saw an opportunity to get Tomberg a job with the city administration there. He also organized the logistics for the departure of the family Tomberg from Holland. For this purpose he traveled to Amsterdam on December 12, 1943. According to a note, he was most likely there for the last time on February 5, 1944. On the 18th of the month, the Tombergs arrived in Bad Godesberg, where the von Hippels lived. The timing of the move was also quite providential in that it saved the Tombergs from having to endure the well-known "Dutch Hunger Winter" of 1944/45. Before his departure, Tomberg is reputed to have given Van der Most a manuscript about the occult foundations of National Socialism. Unfortunately, this has been lost. There was also a manuscript on

---

83. Wolfgang Garvelmann, "Valentin Tomberg—Ein Versuch ihm gerecht zu werden," in *Info3* (1988/5).

Valentin Tomberg and the *Ecclesia Universalis*

"the doubles," which Tomberg himself destroyed because "there were no people for whom it could have been useful."[84]

Officially, the Tomberg family was de-registered from the Amsterdam population register on April 18, 1944. Maja Hörschelmann accompanied them to Germany. She is said to have worked in a hospital there and to have died of tuberculosis in 1946.

Valentin Tomberg in the Memory of His Friends

In the late 1990s, memories of Valentin Tomberg were still very much alive among people who had last seen him 55 or 60 years earlier. John Daniskas, who had done a great deal for Tomberg, remembered that he was excellent at drawing, especially portraits. Although Wil van Houwelingen from Heemstede had seen him only once at a lecture around 1939, she still spoke sixty years later in 1999 with great awe about his "luminous spiritual being." While reading Tomberg's final book, *Lazarus: The Miracle of Resurrection in World History*, this vision came to her again.

The piano teacher Ans Waterreus, who in the early 1940s often spent weekends with the Tomberg family (staying overnight with them as well), had had no further contact with them since 1942/43. Yet still in the 1990s she remembered clearly how, during the conference in Rotterdam in August 1939, she had played a piano piece before one of Tomberg's lectures and how he had come up to her afterward and said: "You are drawing from the same source I draw from when I give my lectures." When staying with them, she heard Valentin read chapters from the John's gospel in Greek to Maria on Saturday evenings before falling asleep. She also recalled that, in the early years of the war, Tomberg had spoken about the division and later reunification of Germany.

Anna de Groot, the widow of Jan van der Most, remembered her conversations with Tomberg vividly. She recalled that he could look at someone very seriously and make spiritual observations, but then, suddenly, be quite normal again, telling some new tale about

---

84. Eva Cliteur, in a letter to Mr W. de Jongh (September 6, 1973). Tomberg Archive, Steinbergkirche. "Doubles" refers to psycho-spiritual aspects of the personality or else independent entities more commonly called "shadows" in our day.

The Netherlands (1938–1944)

his "uncle" Eben-Ezer with much humor. She was deeply impressed by his humility.

Eva Cliteur, a pharmacist who had a laboratory in Amsterdam for preparing and researching medicines, attended Tomberg's lectures between 1938 and 1940 and got to know the Tomberg family personally. In November 1948 she visited them in England. From 1964 to 1973 she maintained a close relationship with them, and also helped them financially. In the Netherlands and Germany, she introduced many people to his writings. After the death of Valentin and Maria (shortly after each other) in 1973, she wrote an *In Memoriam*, which was not published. There she describes her personal impression of Valentin during a lecture at the School of Spiritual Science in Amsterdam in 1939. The speaker, she said:

Eva Cliteur (1912–1996)

> was of medium stature, with thin blond hair and blue eyes that were usually directed slightly downward. He was very serious, extremely polite and modest (I only got to know his particular humor later). In fact, when he was silent, he looked more like a servant than the honored guest of the evening. But when he spoke, people listened with fascination to his crystal-clear explanations, which he did not impose, but simply offered like fruit on a tray. Even when dealing with very difficult subjects [...] one felt the warm undertone of the person who could undertake to explain them, because he obviously had the requisite experience at his disposal, and was in any case accustomed to being in this position. [...] Tomberg was very taciturn. He managed to distance himself by good-natured humor, without being rude. At times he could even play the fool, which went down well with the English. His loneliness and piety were kept within.[85]

85. Ibid.

Valentin Tomberg and the *Ecclesia Universalis*

At the beginning of the war, Stefan Lubienski was head of the Polish consulate in Strasbourg. Later he became the civilian head of the secret resistance in the French Dordogne, of which many Poles were part. In this capacity he gave shelter to Polish and English paratroopers. After his return from France, he sought renewed contact with Valentin and Maria. He often visited them in England, maintained a correspondence with Valentin, and distributed his anthroposophical writings in the Netherlands and Germany (which was not actually Tomberg's intention). He also assisted Tomberg with his Tarot book, the manuscript of which he typed. In his lectures and writings he often mentioned Tomberg, and his work shows that he had learned much from him in the field of inner development. In a letter to his friends dated January 23, 1956, Lubienski wrote about the "Tomberg problem."[86] He could not follow Valentin and Maria on their way to the Catholic Church, but nevertheless tried to understand them. If only we want to experience the Christ impulse in others, this "problem" can be solved, he intimated in this letter. Some quotes:

Stefan Lubienski in 1973

> Until 1941, Tomberg was spiritually the richest man in Europe; he knew an incredible amount. He has given up this wealth: He no longer knows anything, but he can pray like no one else, and the spiritual world is so needful that someone prays—not in his own, personal name, but in the name of humanity—in the manner of the Our Father, very piously and humbly. Tomberg did not find true piety in Anthroposophy. [...] His life-experience in West Germany immediately after the war [as an interpreter in camps for

---

86. Ibid.

The Netherlands (1938–1944)

forced laborers and prisoners of war] taught him solidarity with the "poor" (yes, also the spiritually poor), with ordinary people. He also saw how important the Church was for these uprooted people.

In the year of Valentin Tomberg's death (1973), the eighty-year-old Stefan Lubienski (1893–1976) dedicated to his deceased friend a series of lectures on the seven petitions of the Our Father. The texts of the lectures were first published as a book in 2000, one hundred years after Tomberg's birth. In the introduction, Lubienski writes:

> The relationship between Valentin Tomberg and myself was one of great friendship. If someone were to ask me who my greatest friend was, I would have no hesitation in naming Valentin Tomberg. I met him for the first time in 1936. A year earlier I had read his Studies on the Old Testament with astonishment. It was quite an experience to encounter someone capable of writing in so simple and yet deeply knowledgeable a way on spiritual matters of the greatest possible importance for humanity. [...] In his work, Valentin Tomberg was quiet and withdrawn. He connected himself in a sacrificial way with the Catholic Church in order to investigate whether new esoteric impulses could be given there. This has been only partially successful.[87]

Lubienski pointed out what radiant traces "the silent work of Valentin Tomberg, which was entirely devoted to the Christ," has left in the spiritual sphere of the earth. Shortly before his own death, Lubienski spoke with his friend Dieter Brüll about Tomberg's turn toward Catholicism. Lubienski felt that Tomberg had completed the work of purification, except for that of pride, so that "it could have been that the spiritual world closed in on him, that he lost his visionary consciousness, except for an opening to the Christ—who remained present for him to the last."[88] Just when, according to Lubienski, the spiritual world may have "closed in" on Tomberg, is not known.

---

87. Stefan Lubienski, *De evolutie van de materie* (Eemnes: Stichting Stefan Lubienski, 2000), 12–13.

88. Written communication from Dieter Brüll (November 7, 1995).

4

Germany

(1944–1948)

AFTER THEIR ARRIVAL IN GERMANY, THE FAMILY TOMBERG moved, on February 18, 1944, into the house in Bad Godesberg where the von Hippel family lived. Having worked for a short time at the War Damage Office of the Cologne city council, Tomberg (in July 1944) became an assistant at the Institute for International Law in Cologne. During this period he worked on his dissertation on the topic "The Degeneration and Regeneration of Law,"[1] which was completed in October. On November 25, 1944, he was awarded his doctoral degree.

During these months, bombs were dropping over nearby Bonn and Cologne. Tomberg had already begun working on his new book, *The Fundamental Principles of International Law as a Law of Humanity*, which was completed in January 1945. These two books were published in 1946 and 1947, in print runs of 15,000 and 5,000 copies respectively.

In February 1945, Tomberg began working in the basement of the von Hippel house on a second dissertation intended as his *habilitation* (the prerequisite for a future academic career in Germany). This new book on international law was to be his contribution to the discussion of the new post-war German Constitution. It was completed in November 1948, but by that time he had abandoned his *habilitation* plans and moved to England with his family. It was never published. Tomberg destroyed the manuscript in 1950 because

---

1. Recently published in English as *The Art of the Good: On the Regeneration of Fallen Justice* (Brooklyn, NY: Angelico Press, 2021).

Valentin Tomberg and the *Ecclesia Universalis*

Valentin Tomberg and Ernst von Hippel

in his opinion it was no longer relevant.

In 1949, Fritz von Hippel, a brother of his friend Ernst, and a law professor also, suggested to Tomberg that he write something more on the subject of international law. The German publishing house Herder, he said, would be interested in such a book. This resulted in a substantial manuscript, completed toward the end of 1952, which Tomberg entitled *Die Problemgeschichte der Völkerrechtswissenschaft.* Owing to its length, however, it was not accepted by Herder, which had apparently assumed Tomberg would be contributing to an anthology on the subject. Tomberg seems to have misunderstood this.[2] These writings in the field of law were the fruit of a creative period that lasted from 1944 to 1952. In them we no longer find Tomberg the spiritual researcher, but Tomberg the jurist.

In June 1944, Tomberg met the anthroposophist Bernhard Martin, and they became good friends. In the notes of seven conversations with Tomberg between 1944 and 1948, Martin remarked that, according to Tomberg, the Anthroposophical Movement had failed. Tomberg, he said, referred him to the Catholic faith, to which Martin converted in 1946. In these conversations, Tomberg was reported to have emphasized devotion to Mary and recommended that Martin pray the Rosary.[3]

The young Wolfgang Garvelmann also had several conversations

---

2. This book, with the new title *Vom Völkerrecht zur Weltfriedensordnung: Die Problemgeschichte der Völkerrechtswissenschaft*, has just been published by Novalis Verlag. An English translation (in process) will be entitled *From International Law to Peace on Earth: A History of the Problem of the Jurisprudence of International Law.*

3. Heckmann and Frensch, *Valentin Tomberg*, Vol. I.2., 48 and 121ff.

Germany (1944–1948)

with Tomberg between 1944 and 1948, in the course of which he was advised to get to know the Catholic Mass, because, as Tomberg said to him, Christ is present in the sacrament of the altar. Garvelmann joined the Catholic Church in 1950. In an article written in 1988, he said that according to Tomberg the anthroposophical impulse had derailed and become ineffective—and that the second coming of Christ had not yet taken place.[4] By this he meant that the three-year movement of Christ across the earth (which he had predicted in 1939) had not yet occurred. In the second part of this book we will return to these conversations with Martin and Garvelmann.

In the post-war period, the British occupation forces organized the repatriation of forced laborers and prisoners of war, as well as a re-education program for the population of the former Nazi state. Tomberg became involved in these activities, which gave him the opportunity to help people from Eastern Europe and contribute to the re-education of the German population.

A "Second Incarnation"

"The distance that now separates me from the Valentin Tomberg of the 1930s is as great as that between two incarnations," Tomberg wrote in a letter from 1970. It makes sense, then, to compare the anthroposophist Tomberg with (as he put it in 1970) his "inner successor": the jurist and Christian Hermetic philosopher Tomberg. However, we are not concerned here with two different personalities, but with *one* spiritual researcher who, beginning around 1943, was looking for a new field of activity. It has been suggested by some that the difference between the latter and the former Tomberg could lie in the fact that the earlier "anthroposophist" Tomberg may have been inspired by a spiritual being who in some sense left him in 1943. As will be discussed in the second part of this book, there are those who hold the view that this being inspiring Tomberg during the period in question was the "Maitreya bodhisattva." This at least opens up the possibility that in his ensuing activity as Christian Hermetic philosopher he may have been inspired by a different spiritual being.

---

4. Wolfgang Garvelmann, "Valentin Tomberg," *Info3* (1988/5).

Valentin Tomberg and the *Ecclesia Universalis*

However that may be, it was at this time that Tomberg became convinced that Rudolf Steiner's attempt to renew culture spiritually through the Anthroposophical Society had failed. As he saw it, this Society had proven unable to resist the forces of apocalyptic evil that had so terrorized Europe in the form of Bolshevism and National Socialism. The development that should have led to a free and self-conscious human being had stalled.

The "ark" Tomberg built in Amsterdam came to rest for him now on the "Ararat rock" of the Catholic Church. Ideally, for him, the "catholicity" of this Church could stand in for the *Ecclesia universalis*, or Universal Church (the Greek *katholikos* means "universal"), the Church that would recognize the primacy of the pope but also include the Orthodox Church in which Tomberg was still allowed to receive communion. For Tomberg, this Universal Church represented the rock that could withstand the struggle against evil— the evil so horrifically manifest in World War II. As a spiritual researcher, he wanted to revive the "dimension of depth," as he called it, in this Church. He was convinced that Christians who were intrinsically, even irrevocably, esoteric in orientation, also had a responsibility towards the more institutional "church" or ecclesiastical Christianity. For him, the all-embracing Church of Christ was not only the Church of Peter, but also the Church of John. Speaking broadly, such a Church would include both exoteric and esoteric Christianity.

When Tomberg emigrated to Germany in 1944, he was a man with a wealth of spiritual experience and knowledge, although, for the most part, this wealth remained in the background during this phase of his life, until he took up again his Tarot studies. Clearly, he had suffered deep shocks in the first half of his life. First there was the Russian Revolution, which drove his family as refugees to Estonia, where his mother was assassinated by the Red Guards. The failure of the anthroposophical impulse, as he experienced it after the death of Rudolf Steiner, must have shaken him to the core. He suffered immensely under the Nazis during their occupation of the Netherlands, and subsequently experienced firsthand in the Allied bombing of Cologne their final, violent demise. After all this, there followed his "second incarnation" (c. 1943), after which he followed

Germany (1944–1948)

inner directives that led him to the law and later to Hermeticism. In his new life, he drew on the medieval philosophy of law, Catholic theology, the monastic tradition, and the Hermetic philosophy of Egyptian antiquity. His activities in these fields are described in this and the following chapter.

The Regeneration of Law and Re-Education

As a young man in the autumn of 1917, Tomberg had begun studying law at St. Petersburg University, and in due course continued these studies in Estonia. In 1932 he had hoped to take up the study of law again in Berlin, but lacked the means to do so. Not until the end of the war was he able to realize this ambition. By this time in his eventful life he had witnessed at close hand and great personal cost the emergence of criminal states in Russia and Germany, where evil rather than law determined the functioning of the state.

In his doctoral thesis, "Degeneration and Regeneration of Law," Tomberg investigated the degeneration of law. He developed a model in which he distinguished three levels: the *concept* of law, the *idea* of law, and the *ideal* of law. According to this view, so-called positive law (which determines the actual practice of law) must be based on a *concept* of law. This in turn must originate in a legal *idea*, which in turn stems from a legal *ideal*. Actual positive law degenerates if its links with the idea of law and the ideal of law are broken. This process of degeneration had already begun in the late Middle Ages, when the stability of the legal edifice that had been raised by the philosopher and theologian Thomas Aquinas began to crumble. For Thomas, this edifice comprised four storeys:

Eternal law, anchored in God
Divine law, governing the hierarchies of angels
Natural law, governing the cosmos
Human law, governing the earth

This overall articulation of the nature of law was structured on the Platonic model of knowledge. If this edifice collapses, only human law remains, and it soon becomes the instrument of evil. Such "law" descends in fact into the subhuman sphere.

According to Tomberg, the regeneration of law depends upon

Valentin Tomberg and the *Ecclesia Universalis*

establishing a renewed connection with both its idea and its ideal. Once this is achieved, higher forms of law will reappear. In his doctoral thesis, Tomberg described the Catholic Church as a prime example of a community of law that had not undergone such degeneration.

Tomberg's book on international law, *The Fundamental Principles of International Law as a Law of Humanity* (written as a sequel to his doctoral dissertation, as we have said), broadened Tomberg's idea of a regeneration of law. International law (which he conceived of as the law of humanity as a whole) had to stand above the law of states. Yet it still had to be subordinated to natural law. Divine law stood above it. When international law is violated, external intervention is justified. The Nuremberg trials that took place at that time followed this principle. Tomberg argued also for an international court.[5]

At the beginning of March 1945, British-American troops took Cologne. The foreign forced laborers were soon gathered together for repatriation. The British army set up a camp in Cologne-Ossendorf, where in mid-July 1945 Tomberg took on a new task in connection with this work of repatriation. He moved there with his family, working as an interpreter in the British service and dressed in an officer's uniform. Maria was also involved in this work. It was here, according to Martin Kriele, that a camp priest received Tomberg into the Catholic Church.[6] At the end of December 1945, the family

---

5. In his article "Ein Freund von jenseits des Grabes" (in Frensch a.o., *Valentin Tomberg*, Vol. III, 74–76), Michael Frensch explains in anthroposophical terms (which cannot be adequately expounded here) that the degeneration of the law can be seen in the context of the fate of the "Nathan soul" of Jesus (the unfallen "sistersoul" of Adam, who was incarnated in the Jesus-child of the Luke gospel). Rudolf Steiner had pointed out that, from the beginning of modern times, due to the rise of materialism, the Nathan soul had "fallen into a faint" in the angelic world, until finally its consciousness was extinguished in the middle of the nineteenth century. Only when people would awaken in their own conscience could this Nathan angelic-being reawaken in their souls. Steiner indicated that this would become possible from about 1933 onwards. In and through the Nathan soul, Christ could then reveal himself to souls in his "etheric" form. On earth, the impotence of this soul was accompanied by the degeneration of the law, which will not regenerate on a social level as long as the moral consciousness of the people is not awakened.

6. Martin Kriele, *Anthroposophie und Kirche* (Freiburg: Herder Verlag, 1996), 173.

Germany (1944–1948)

moved to Mülheim on the Ruhr, where they worked under difficult conditions in a camp set up for Russian prisoners of war. There, in the summer of 1946, Valentin met the English officer Francis Collin, with whose help his family was able to settle in London later, in 1948.

In February 1946, Tomberg became involved in the British re-education programs that aimed to bring democracy back to political life in Germany. To this end, he was asked to set up and run a center for adult education in Mülheim. Here he organized and led evening courses for adults, for which he invited his friend Ernst von Hippel and other speakers. He himself gave about twenty-five lectures. Even amid all these demands, however, he still found time for the articles "On Inner Work" and "The Work on the Road to the Jordan," both written in Russian in October 1946. In 1947 he also gave lectures in ecclesial and related contexts, at an international summer conference on international relations for the military government in Bad Godesberg, and at the annual conference of the Catholic Academy in Bonn.

In October 1946, Tomberg received a lectureship in ethics and law at the Technical University in Aachen, where he taught four hours a week. This modest academic activity might have been the beginning of a university career, but he did not feel at home in post-war Germany. Although he had made many contacts (in addition to which, his friend Nikolai Belozvetov had moved to Mülheim with his family in the summer of 1947), he felt oppressed by the shadow of the Soviet army (which had, after all, assassinated his own mother). Until the establishment of NATO in 1949, the danger of Stalin's occupation of Western Europe loomed large.

In 1948, to the great surprise of his friends, Tomberg emigrated with his family to England. He resigned from both the adult education center in Mülheim and the university in Aachen, and left Germany on July 22, 1948. In further explanation, he later wrote (February 1, 1950) to Ernst von Hippel that he could no longer stay in Mülheim because he felt there was no place for him there, and he knew now that he would always remain a foreigner in Germany. The following day he also wrote to Bernhard Martin that he could not accept the proposal of some friends that he take over a lectureship in Germany. One sign for him of the rightness of his decision was that

Valentin Tomberg and the *Ecclesia Universalis*

Bernhard Martin, 1965

his work in Mülheim could just as well be done by a German, and another was that his second treatise on international law would not be published.[7] Years later (November 27, 1958), Tomberg wrote again to Bernhard Martin, regarding his turning away from Germany, that in truth it involved "the painful experience that in the past I have not worked on the proper soil, that I have deluded myself into believing that my work was needed on soil which in truth was not destined for it. I mistook that I was needed there, whereas it has turned out—God forgive me, so late!—that all those years of work in Germany, and for Germany, were lost to the work awaiting me elsewhere."

For Joanna Thylmann from Stuttgart, who had met Tomberg personally, there was another side to this. On December 30, 1947, she wrote to a young friend that she found it very painful that Tomberg had so completely given up on Germany: "He does not see the Central European man, he does not count on him, he does not want him; he sees only his darkness, he hates him."[8] This sharp personal sentiment of Joanna Thylmann ignores the fact, however, that Tomberg continued to write texts in the German language until the end of his life, and that he visited the von Hippel family in Germany several times during his later years. Furthermore, he maintained contacts with Bernard Martin, and later with the German jurist Martin Kriele, who became the administrator of his literary estate.

Valentin and Maria had suffered a great deal, first from the Russians, later from the Germans. The spiritual Russia and the spiritual Central Europe with which they had felt themselves so connected had perished. It was only in England that they would come to find their place as displaced persons.

---

7. Tomberg, letter from February 6, 1950 to Bernhard Martin, Archive of Christiane Martin and Tomberg Archive, Steinbergkirche.
8. Joanna Thylmann, *Briefe an einen jungen Freund*, 146.

5

England
(1948–1973)

FRANCIS COLLIN HAD ORGANIZED THE EMIGRATION OF THE Tomberg family and arranged for their residence permit in Britain. He did this (at the end of July 1948) by registering the couple as his domestic servants. He also arranged for their accommodation at 11 Eaton Rise in Ealing, a suburb of London. However, it was not easy for Tomberg to find work. He was even less needed here than he had been in Germany. In August 1948 he applied in vain for a job in the Department of International Relations at the London School of Economics and at the Royal Institute of International Affairs. In his letters of application he stated that he knew twelve languages: six of which he spoke fluently (English, Russian, Estonian, French, Dutch, and German). In addition, he stated, he could read Spanish, understand Polish and Ukrainian, and also knew three "dead" languages (Latin, Greek, and Church Slavonic).

It was not until early May of 1949 that he found a job at the BBC in Reading, west of London, where his task was to monitor news reports from the Soviet Union, mainly Russian and Estonian. Important radio broadcasts had to be translated and dictated simultaneously so that their contents could be typed out promptly. Other news items had to be summarized.

Tomberg was immersed in this work eight hours a day, in day and night shifts, until December 1965. In his last years there he served as assistant monitor. The nature of this occupation exposed him to what he described as an incessant "stream of lies and hatred." The work exhausted him. His colleagues, who, like him, were mostly intelligent immigrants, were "collegial, friendly, and fair," as he

Valentin Tomberg and the *Ecclesia Universalis*

wrote to Nikolai Belozvetov in 1950; but even in their company he felt utterly alone. They knew nothing of his spiritual activity. He had fled from Russia in 1918—and now, here he was, during his working hours, back again in the "hell" of the Soviet Union.

Before long, friends from the continent began coming to visit. In March 1949, Stefan Lubienski and Maria Louise van Rijnberk arrived for a stay. A year later, the news that his friend Nikolai Belozvetov had died (on May 12, 1950) caused a great shock. In August 1951, the Tombergs traveled to the Netherlands to visit the Van Rijnberk family. There they also met other anthroposophical friends, with whom they talked about the Anthroposophical Society. "If Steiner's followers had really taken his method seriously and worked on themselves accordingly, they would all have become Christians and come to a living experience of Christ," Tomberg said. As he put it, "the real purpose of Anthroposophy was to be an expedient for people to follow the way to Christ."[1] In the summer of 1952, Valentin and Maria were in the Netherlands again.

Maria Louise van Rijnberk (1894–1980)

Occasionally, Tomberg found time and peace to write articles, some of them still on quite esoteric anthroposophical themes. At the end of December 1952 he wrote three short texts on the chakras. His article "The Philosophy of Darkness—a Study of Marxian Ideology" dates from this period, and may be related to his daily confrontation with the lies of Soviet propaganda in his work for the BBC.[2] These texts were not published at the time.

As mentioned before, Tomberg had learned as early as 1949 that his book *From International Law to Peace on Earth*, on which he was

---

1. Heckmann and Frensch, *Valentin Tomberg*, Vol. I.2, 212.
2. "Philosophie der Finsternis," in *Aufzeichnungen, Vortragsnachschriften*, 167–83.

working at the time, would not be published. Nevertheless, he continued to work on it and completed it at the end of 1952. Ideas from his doctoral thesis (written in 1944) played a role in this legal work also. Here Tomberg argued that the peaceful coexistence of all states should be based on reason, justice, and humanity. To achieve this, however, requires a higher law—the *divine* law. Divine law is the rock on which the legal edifice rests, as he had first set forth in his earlier thesis.[3]

By contrast, when in fact the new Constitution of the Federal Republic of Germany came into force (on May 23, 1949) it made no reference whatsoever to divine law. Nevertheless, its first article does open with a principle that can be understood as at least an *ideal* of law: "Human dignity is inviolable. It is the duty of all state authorities to respect and protect it. Therefore, the German people accept the inviolable and inalienable rights of man as the basis of every human community, and of peace and justice in the world."

Now, as Tomberg points out, ever since the end of the Middle Ages the traditional worldview, in which the individual human being was subordinate to the whole, had gradually collapsed. In this former world, people had lived together in a hierarchically-ordered social structure (of clergy, nobility, and peasants) that rested upon a moral-religious basis. For Tomberg, the loss of this basis constituted in fact the "fall of the law." However, this same loss had also made possible the freedom of the individual person.

In modern society, the free individual has, in principle, become the source of the law itself. But this situation carries with it the risk that economic interest groups, or even anti-human ideologies, may seize control of the law. This is precisely what happened in Bolshevism and National Socialism. These movements led many Russians and Germans to commit unscrupulous acts, just at a time when a deep awakening of *conscience* was meant to be preparing them to perceive Christ in the etheric world. Here, Tomberg was confronted with the dramatic crisis of the development of the "I" in which the whole of humanity now finds itself entangled, and which, he was

---

3. Heckmann and Frensch, *Valentin Tomberg*, Vol. I.2, 222–27.

convinced, could only be solved by forging a renewed connection with God. To this end, he envisaged a constitutional state in which Christian ethics would form the basis of law.

In the field of law, then, Tomberg represented a conservative position, one far removed from Rudolf Steiner's radical (but in the end unsuccessful) commitment to a "threefold social order"—a program for the reform of society that he had proposed thirty-three years earlier. Tomberg's position becomes more comprehensible if we bear in mind that from his point of view the development of the "I" (or the higher self) had originally been the special vocation of the German people, and as such was meant to have been brought forward above all in Germany. Unfortunately, however, this intended development had been compromised on account of the two World Wars.

Von Hippel and Tomberg took this conservative position in July 1953 at a conference of the *Abendländische Akademie* in Eichstätt, southern Germany. This academy was a conservative Christian training facility founded in 1951 for the recovery and renewal of the Christian West. The theme of the conference was "Man and Freedom." Von Hippel spoke on the subject of freedom and order. He maintained that all order is based "on the unity of humankind with God," which is also the basis for "the true unity of humankind among themselves." Tomberg, who shared this view, spoke on "The Destruction of Freedom in Totalitarianism."[4]

In the post-war years, von Hippel and Tomberg, together with some other jurists, were regarded as leading representatives of the idea of *natural law* in the medieval Catholic tradition. They were of the opinion that an objective standard could be found in conscience, and that the human sense of justice is always directed towards objective justice. The problem they faced was how to justify judgments about the law, because an appeal to conscience can all too easily lead to subjectivism.[5] In England, Tomberg wrestled for some time with this problem of the objective validity of personal judgments on spiritual matters.

---

4. Ibid. 236–42.
5. Lena Foljanty, *Recht und Gesetz* (Tübingen: Mohr Siebeck, 2012), 98, 294–97.

England (1948–1973)

While in Germany in July 1953, Tomberg would have liked to visit the stigmatized Catholic mystic Therese Neumann in Konnersreuth (in Bavaria), but this did not prove possible.

The Search for Personal Certainty

After concluding his studies in law, Tomberg entered a new phase in his life, lasting from the end of 1952 until 1959. During this period he lived through a crisis arising out of the question of how one finds personal, inner certainty. After all, the derivation of practical (or "positive") law from divine law requires divine revelation. But this in turn raises the question of whether there are universally valid criteria for testing the truthfulness of revelation. This can be further extended to the question: what is truth? Inspired by his collaboration in the course of 1955 with the physician Erich Ledermann, who developed a "holistic" medicine, Tomberg engaged in a holism or integral "synthesis" of the methods of knowledge. This search gave him the idea for a book that would summarize his forty-year quest for truth. The projected work was to be entitled *Science, Philosophy, Religion—and Truth*.[6] He commenced work on this book around the time of his third moon node, which occurred at the end of December 1955.

In November 1955, Maria Tomberg visited Maria Louise van Rijnberk (a widow since 1953) in the Netherlands, and then traveled on to Belgium. She had special spiritual experiences in the Chapel of the Holy Blood in Bruges and in Beauraing, where Our Lady had appeared in 1932/33.

During this period, Valentin had begun to study modern psychology (Freud, Adler, and Jung). The psychology of C.G. Jung made a deep impression on him. In a letter to Ernst von Hippel dated May 19, 1956 he wrote:

> As compared to Anthroposophy, in my opinion Jung's work has some advantage—for, whereas in Anthroposophy "mystical facts" are converted into terms of ordinary day-consciousness, in the

---

6. Only the preface and introduction to this planned book came about. They were written in English and published in German translation in Tomberg, *Aufzeichnungen, Vortragsnachschriften*, 183–94.

Valentin Tomberg and the *Ecclesia Universalis*

Jungian school the terms of day-consciousness are converted into "mystical facts" (symbols).

In a letter to his friend Bernhard Martin written in July 1956, Tomberg elaborated his view of Anthroposophy at that juncture in his life. "In Anthroposophy," he wrote:

> spirituality is intellectualized into a conceptual system. Such is the belief in the authority of Rudolf Steiner that he is made out to be an infallible "antipope." Anthroposophists regard themselves as members of a chosen "community of the archangel Michael," and, in so doing, risk delusions of grandeur. Making their start armed in advance with a whole panoply of ready-made concepts, only *then* do they actually set about trying to actually *experience* them—but it does not work that way!⁷

By contrast, in Tomberg's view, concepts are best understood as symbols open to multiple interpretations. In fairness, however, it should be noted that such tendencies as these, which Tomberg was destined to observe (and also suffer from) among many anthroposophists, were *not* intended by Steiner, and were totally at odds with his own approach.

"The spiritual world speaks to us," Tomberg wrote, "in a language of mystery, in symbols that stimulate us to learn from them." Such learning was to take place, as he put it, "in silent, unpretentious mysteries." To some degree, at least, he believed he could discern the "beginning of the rebirth of the mysteries" in psychotherapy, for the "language of symbols is the language of mystery." He called attention to the tradition of the mystery schools of antiquity, where priests who had been initiated into those mysteries learned to communicate with spiritual beings, and then received from the spiritual world (among other things) symbolic images, which it was their task to interpret.

However, Tomberg did not get beyond the initial phase in his effort to write this book on personal certainty. The following month (August 1956) he made a renewed attempt, choosing as the title for this new iteration of the book *The Seed, the Seed-Power, the Tree: A Contribution to the Question of the Way, the Truth, and the Life*. He

---

7. Heckmann and Frensch, *Valentin Tomberg*, Vol. 1.2, 272–83.

worked on this until 1958, but then broke it off also. This unfinished book was published in 2012 under the title *Innere Gewissheit: Über den Weg, die Wahrheit und das Leben* ("On Inner Certainty: Regarding the Way, the Truth, and the Life"). In this text, Tomberg had tried to develop a "synthetic" or "total" method sufficient to encompass such diverse domains as life experience, observation, study, conscience, thinking, etc. His purpose was to establish a method capable of leading one to a condition of personal certainty, to a certainty that, although necessarily a "wisdom," must at the same time be a process of growth and development. After commencing a section on the Kabbalah, however, he broke off this undertaking for good. We have no further information on his reasons.[8]

In the summer of 1958, the Tombergs paid another visit to Maria Louise van Rijnberk in Amsterdam, where they also investigated the apparitions of Mary in the Thomas Aquinas Church. It was in this church on the Rijnstraat that their son Alex had been received into the Catholic Church in 1943. Between 1945 and 1959, the visionary Ida Peerdeman received (at home, in this church, and elsewhere) fifty-six messages from Mary. The Tombergs established to their satisfaction that these messages from the "Lady of All Nations" (as the Mary of these visions called herself) were authentic.[9] They included a prayer for the healing of the diseases of the nations and a request to the pope to proclaim Mary the Co-Redemptrix (signifying her subordinate but essential participation in the redemption of humanity). In Letter XI of *Meditations* Tomberg mentions that his research on the authenticity of these visions was later confirmed by experiences of a personal nature.[10]

---

8. This book is scheduled for publication by Angelico Press in 2022 under the title *Personal Certainty: On the Way, the Truth, and the Life*.

9. Prayer to Our Lady of All Nations: Lord Jesus Christ, Son of the Father, send now Your Holy Spirit over the earth. Let the Holy Spirit live in the hearts of all Nations, that they may be preserved from degeneration, disaster, and war. May the Lady of All Nations, who once was Mary, be our Advocate! Amen!

10. On the back cover of the first English-language collection of Tomberg's last writings, *Covenant of the Heart*, these experiences are interpreted as "a personal experience of Sophia in a cathedral in Holland." There are no indications, however, for this interpretation.

Valentin Tomberg and the *Ecclesia Universalis*

In October of 1958, Valentin and Maria took another trip, this time to the south of France, which proved pivotal for his project of presenting Christian mystery wisdom, not as a science but as personal experience. In Lyon he visited the publisher Paul Derain, a friend of Gérard von Rijnberk, whose book *Le Tarot* had been published by Derain in 1947. In France, Tomberg rediscovered the living Hermetic tradition, which he had first encountered in St. Petersburg in 1917.

The Renewal of the Hermetic Tradition

By the time he returned from France, it had become clear to Tomberg just how he should proceed. In effect, from 1959 to 1967 he worked as a spiritual teacher in the service of the Hermetic tradition. As mentioned before, this tradition has its origins in the teaching of Hermes Trismegistus, whose name first appears in Egyptian literature at the beginning of the second century. A fundamental principle of this teaching concerns the relationship between the microcosm and the macrocosm: "That which is below is like that which is above, and that which is above is like that which is below, to accomplish the wonders of the One." So says the *Emerald Tablet*, of which Hermes Trismegistus is said to be the author. Hermes Trismegistus (the man, that is, not the god Hermes) is reputed to have lived as a guiding initiate who laid the foundation for the culture of Ancient Egypt.

The Egyptian name of the Greek god Hermes was Thoth. He was revered as the god of writing, magic, science, and wisdom, and was considered to have been the inspirer of the so-called Hermetic writings dating back to the first centuries AD. These writings include religious and philosophical treatises on the world and on the salvation of the soul, as well as on magic, astrology, alchemy, and medicine. They combine ancient Egyptian knowledge with the philosophy of Plato. The early Church Fathers differed on the question whether or not these writings were compatible with Christian doctrine. Seventeen of these writings, or treatises, which came to be known as the *Corpus Hermeticum*, were brought to Italy from the Byzantine Empire in the fifteenth century. They became widely known in Western Europe after the Italian humanist and neo-Platonic philosopher Marsilio Ficino translated them from Greek into Latin in 1463.

For Tomberg, Hermeticism was a philosophy based on mysticism, gnosis, and magic. In his 22 Letters to the "Unknown Friend" about the Greater Arcana of Tarot in *Meditations*, he developed a Christian Hermeticism of which the "mother" was the Jewish Kabbalah and the "father" Egyptian Hermeticism (Letter XII). He regarded Hermeticists as "guardians of the life and of the common soul of religion, science, and art" (Letter I). He described the mission of Hermeticism as promoting the "union of spirituality and intellectuality" (Letter XXI). It is worth noting that, according to Rudolf Steiner, such a union is also the goal of the joint work of what he characterized as the enduring streams he denominated as "Platonists" and "Aristotelians." Tomberg was of the view that, in addition to Hermeticists properly speaking, other thinkers had also often contributed to the progress of the Hermetic work. In this connection he made special mention of Christian existentialism (Berdyaev), Christian gnosis (Solovyov), Christian evolutionism (Teilhard de Chardin), and the depth psychology of revelation (C.G. Jung).

For Tomberg, Christian Hermeticism represents the "dimensions of depth and height" that have all too often been lost to view in "institutional" or ecclesial Christianity. Therefore, alongside those who are active in the more institutional forms, there is always need of individuals in the service of esoteric Christianity to keep bringing these dimensions back to light, so that exoteric, ecclesial Christianity may ever and again be revivified. One must not forget, he wrote, "that Christian Hermeticism is not a religion apart, nor a Church apart, nor even a science apart, which would compete with religion, the Church, or with science" (Letter VI).[11] Christian Hermeticism is, rather, an aspect of the universal Church of Christ, the *Ecclesia universalis*. Therefore, for Tomberg, "all Church Doctors who teach the way of spiritual experience beyond theoretical theology, and all the saints and mystics of the Church who have had this experi-

---

11. *Meditations*, 135.

ence—that is, representatives of the depth and loftiness of Christianity—are at the same time Hermeticists." In this view, the Church is the "mystical body of Christ," which, as such, includes the exoteric Church of Peter and the esoteric Church of John.

It was because a living Hermetic tradition still existed in France that Tomberg linked up with it and elected to write his own Hermetic work in French. For his purposes, he limited his discussion to the French Hermetic tradition and left unconsidered the well-known English Hermetic Order of the Golden Dawn, which was founded in London in 1888 by three Freemasons, and practiced the ceremonial magic that Tomberg specifically rejected.

Louis Claude de Saint-Martin
(1743–1803)

French Hermeticism can be traced back to Martinez de Pasqually, who around 1740 founded a mystical tradition that came to life in lodges with a Masonic character. These lodges had no connection with either the Catholic Church or Renaissance Hermeticism properly understood. On the other hand, Louis Claude de Saint-Martin, Pasqually's secretary from 1768 to 1771, *was* an adherent of what came to be known as Christian Hermeticism. In general terms, this was a Christian "theosophy," inspired by the German mystic Jakob Boehme, which took on the name "Martinism" in the circle of Saint-Martin's disciples. Its path or practice was one of meditation and inner alchemy. The later "Masonic Martinism" of Papus centered on ceremonial magic, and was not connected with it.

In Letter VIII of *Meditations*, Tomberg explains that in the Hermetic movement there was a "Greek," or knowledge-oriented tendency (represented by Fabre d'Olivet and St.-Yves d'Alveydre), a "Jewish" tendency (represented by Eliphas Lévi and other writers on practical magic and kabbalah), and a "Christian" tendency, connected with Saint-Martin, who came to be known as the "Unknown Philosopher." Parallel with these developments, the French Freemason Antoine Court de Gébelin founded in 1773 the Divine Order of Philaletics, which was dedicated to the rediscovery of ancient wisdom and study of kabbalah. After coming across Tarot cards in 1781 in a Parisian salon, Court de Gébelin published his opinion that the Tarot had its origins in Egypt and was designed to transmit in symbolic language the secret knowledge of the ancient Egyptians.

This set the stage for a twofold development. On the one hand, the "layout" of Tarot cards to predict the future was popularized by Jean-Baptist Alliette in 1785. On the other, Hermeticism proper sought to study and interpret the arcana (secrets) of the cards according to their symbolic meaning. This latter study is called "arcanology." The Major Arcana consist of twenty-two images; the Minor Arcana of fifty-six images. Court de Gébelin believed, furthermore, that the twenty-two cards of the Major Arcana stood in correspondence with the twenty-two letters of the Hebrew alphabet.

The French occultist Eliphas Lévi may be considered the founder of the tradition of arcanology, in which the Major Arcana are regarded as carriers of occult and magical knowledge. His book *Dogma and Ritual of High Magic* (1854–1856) forms the basis of the nineteenth century French tradition of arcanology (which included, as well, Stanislav de Guaita, Joseph Péladan, and Papus), on which the Russian arcanologists built further.

Let us recall that as early as 1917, Valentin Tomberg had become acquainted with the arcanology of the Rosicrucian school of Shmakov of Moscow, which included also gnostic and kabbalistic elements. Shortly thereafter in Estonia, in 1919/20, he was studying the arcanology of the school of Mebes from St. Petersburg, which for its part went back to Papus, and had a magical character. There he met Nina Roudnikova and several other distinguished students of Mebes, who told him about the work in his lodge. Roudnikova developed her own arcanology, *The Sacred Mysticism of Egypt*, which was published in Estonia in 1936. The linguist Vsevolod Belyustin, who taught in Shmakov's school, published his *Arcanology of Light* in Moscow in 1925. His pupil Maria Dorogova, born Baroness von Mengden, who had studied medicine, continued the Moscow tradition of arcanology with her book *The Secret Doctrine of Jesus*.

Valentin Tomberg and the *Ecclesia Universalis*

Both Belyustin and Dorogova were familiar with Anthroposophy. They were twice arrested by the secret service during the Stalin regime. Belyustin died in prison. Shmakov himself was able to emigrate from Russia in 1924 and died in Argentina in 1929. Mebes died in a Gulag camp in 1930. As a matter of the unfolding of destiny, it is interesting to note that had Tomberg still been living in Estonia in 1940, he would most likely also have been deported to Siberia, along with many other Estonians. Dorogova and others passed the tradition of arcanology on to Vladimir Stepanov, who then founded a Hermetic school for esoteric Christianity in Moscow under the name "The Ship of Fools." During seminars in the Netherlands (1999–2000) he transmitted Belyustin's *Arcanology of Light*, together with his commentary, which was published in an elaborated form, together with Belyustin's original text, in Moscow in 2018.

With its Christian mystical character, Tomberg's *Meditations* stands also as an influential factor in this Russian tradition. It was translated into Dutch on the recommendation of Stepanov, who valued the work of Rudolf Steiner and knew also the writings of the Russian anthroposophists Nikolai Belozvetov, Gennady Bondarev, and Sergei Prokofieff.

| Maria V. Dorogova | Vsevolod V. Belyustin | Vladimir G. Stepanov |
| (1889–1981) | (1899–1943?) | (1941–2011) |

From the anthroposophical point of view, the French Hermeticists are an odd mix. Among them we find St.-Yves d'Alveydre, with his influential, conservative doctrine of synarchy (from 1877)[12] and

---

12. Osterrieder, *Welt im Umbruch*, 341–56.

the problematic political occultist Papus, whose Martinist order cannot be legitimately traced back to Saint-Martin. Tomberg may not have been well apprised of Papus' political manipulations. He did, however, emphasize the Christian aspirations of the "mature Papus," which stemmed from his late acquaintance with the French miracle-worker Maître Philippe of Lyon, who practiced "sacred magic" in Tomberg's sense. In French Hermeticism, ceremonial magic was practiced above all, whereas for Tomberg only sacred magic (theurgy)—as expressed in the healings of Christ, in Christian worship, and in the making of a sign of the cross—was legitimate.

Tomberg considered Hermeticists as making up a community whose members he called "Friends," and whose ideas he did not trouble to criticize, but instead corrected. By means of his reinterpretation of the symbolic images of the Major Arcana of the Tarot, he wanted to give this tradition a clearly Christian direction. In Letter III he pointed out most explicitly the dangers of magic when used to enforce the mage's personal will rather than the divine will. In Letter X he placed alongside the principle of the *snake* as the "great magical power" (as taught in the school of Eliphas Lévi) the principle of the *dove*, symbolizing the Holy Spirit. And in Letter XXI he wrote about the "Faustian test" of the arbitrary (or personal and ceremonial) magic with which Saint-Martin, Eliphas Lévi, Paul Sédir, and Papus had had to struggle before finding their way to the divine magic, mysticism, and gnosis of Christian Hermeticism.

Tomberg may have helped the "destiny-group" of Hermeticists, even after their passing. On this assumption, we may perhaps be in a position to better understand the remark in Letter XIV that, while writing *Meditations*, the author many times felt the "fraternal embraces" of these "friends." In fact, through his purification of certain aspects of the Hermetic tradition, Tomberg was able to contribute to the transformation of forces that had their roots far back in dark magical practices of Ancient Egypt. It is relevant to note here as well that this ancient Egyptian "karma" was at work also in those Masonic lodges which, since the seventeenth century, have destructively influenced European politics.

Tomberg wrote that he had "forty years of study and meditation of the Tarot behind him." This does not mean, however, that he had

Valentin Tomberg and the *Ecclesia Universalis*

been continuously engaged with it. He had been familiar since 1917 with Russian arcanology, in which spiritual knowledge was collected in an encyclopedic manner. In 1938, as we know, he met in the Netherlands the great Tarot expert Gérard van Rijnberk, who stood in the French tradition of Martinism harking back to Papus. Tomberg spoke with van Rijnberk frequently about the symbolism of the Tarot. From 1959 onwards he was able to work out his own approach to this symbolism. Although there are no references to the Tarot and the Hermetic tradition in his writings from the 1930s, he nevertheless did read some authors from that tradition, as is apparent from his 1931 review of the *The Hieroglyphic Monad* by John Dee.[13]

In short, Tomberg regarded the Tarot as a later "incarnation" of the *Holy Book of Thoth*, a position in full accord with interpretations given in 1906 by Rudolf Steiner in two lectures on the *Book of Thoth*, of which notes exist:

> The Egyptian *Book of Thoth* consisted of 78 cards, which contained the world secrets. This was well known in the initiation rituals of Egypt. The names of the playing cards descended from those—King, Knight, Keeper of the Tower, Commander-in-Chief, etc., are esoteric denotations. Those who were initiated in the Egyptian Mysteries could read p̄. They could also read the *Book of Thoth*, with its 78 cards depicting all world events from beginning to end—from Alpha to Omega—which one could decipher if they were arranged in their proper order. The book contained pictures of life leading to death and arising again to new life. Whoever could combine the correct numbers with the correct pictures could read the script. This number-knowledge, this picture-knowledge, had been taught from earliest times. It also still had a great influence in the Middle Ages, as for instance on Ramon Llull,[14] but nowadays not much of it remains.[15]

---

13. *Russian Spirituality*, 57–61.

14. Raymon Llull (c. 1232–1315), Catalan mystic and poet whose writings influenced Neoplatonic mysticism throughout medieval and 17th-century Europe, is best known as the inventor of an "art of finding truth" intended to support the Roman Catholic faith in missionary work, but designed also to unify all branches of knowledge. Llull was born on the island of Majorca, and may have died there as well. Interestingly, it was while vacationing on Majorca in 1973 that Tomberg died.

15. *"Freemasonry" & Ritual Work* (Gt Barrington, MA: SteinerBooks, 2007), 375 ff.

England (1948–1973)

The historical origin of the Tarot cards is uncertain. A recent study considers them to be pedagogical aids designed in the fifteenth century in circles around the Platonic Academy of Florence in Italy.[16] For Tomberg (who used the cards of the Tarot of Marseille), however, the meaning of the cards went far beyond pedagogy. For him, each image is an arcanum, a "ferment," which, when contemplated, can stimulate the spiritual and mental life. "The arcana are practical spiritual exercises with the aim of awakening ever deeper layers of consciousness," he writes in Letter IV. Meditative deepening in the images of the arcana can lead to a practical Hermeticism, which, as Tomberg emphasizes at the end of this Letter, is alchemy:

> The ideal of alchemical *transformation* of Hermeticism offers to human beings the way to the realization of true human nature, which is the image and likeness of God. Hermeticism is the rehumanization of all elements of human nature; it is their return to their true essence. Just as all base metal can be transformed into silver and into gold, so all the forces of human nature are susceptible to transformation into "silver" or "gold," i.e., into what they *are* when they share in the image and likeness of God.
>
> But in order to become again what they are in their essence, they must be submitted to the operation of *sublimation*. Now, this operation is the crucifying of that which is base among them and, at the same time, it is the blossoming of that which is their true essence. The *cross* and the *rose*, the ROSE-CROSS, is the symbol of this operation of the realization of the truly human man.[17]

The alchemical realization of our true human nature includes also "the transformation of the system of lotus flowers (*chakras*) into a system that functions through love and for love" (Letter IX). Tomberg relates this realization of our essential nature to the mystery of the second birth "of water and the Spirit" (John 3:5) that is necessary to gain access to the kingdom of God. In Christian Hermeticism this second birth is called the "Great Initiation" (Letter I).

---

16. *Les mystères du Tarot de Marseille*, Arte 2014, https://www.youtube.com/watch?v=UfoyExawsNk.

17. *Meditations*, 96.

Valentin Tomberg and the *Ecclesia Universalis*

In Letter III, Tomberg speaks of the Holy Grail as the mystical Eucharist in which the power of sacred magic has its seat. With such references as these to the traditions of the Rose-Cross and the Holy Grail, Tomberg placed his Tarot book squarely in the great tradition of esoteric Christianity.

According to Robert Powell, contemplative study of the *hermetic philosophy* as presented in the book *Meditations* opens an inner path of *mysticism*, that is, a striving toward union with Christ (or with Christ and Sophia). This path takes place in and through divine love. We may then receive guidance from divine wisdom (*gnosis*), so that in due course we may unite our will with the divine will (*sacred magic*).[18] In a description by Michael Frensch, this path begins with mystical contact with God, after which "Christian Hermeticism leads the meditator through the stages of gnosis, sacred magic, and Hermetic philosophy to the sensuous world."[19] Frensch considers *Meditations* (of which he made the published translation into German) to be the "summary of Christian Rosicrucian wisdom for the twentieth century."[20]

For Tomberg himself, the Major Arcana were "a school of meditation, study, and spiritual effort" (Letter I) in which Christ is the Master. He interpreted the symbols, shared his rich spiritual knowledge, and offered his insights on all manner of subjects. But he did not want to be seen as the originator of the thoughts presented in the book. For this reason he chose to have it published anonymously.[21] Taking this a step further, he addressed his readers as "Unknown Friends" (a term most likely drawn from the "unknown philosopher" Louis-Claude de St. Martin). Readers who are prepared to read the Letters meditatively and to immerse themselves in Christian Hermeticism will thereby become a "Friend" of the author and a participant in his explorations.

18. Communication from Robert Powell.
19. Michael Frensch, "Ein Freund von jenseits des Grabes," *Valentin Tomberg*, Vol. III, 79.
20. Ibid., 85.
21. The author's designation as "Anonymus d'Outre-Tombe" ("The anonymous writer from beyond the grave") was not Tomberg's own idea, but that of his publisher Herder Verlag.

England (1948–1973)

Tomberg worked on *Meditations* for eight years, from 1959 to 1967. He began by writing preliminary studies on the last nine arcana.[22] Maria Tomberg went through the entire manuscript with him. As the daughter of a French countess, her French was better than that of her husband. The book proved to be Tomberg's *magnum opus*. Until his retirement in 1962, he could only work on it in his spare time. And since he was periodically called out of retirement until the end of 1965 to fill in as a substitute at the BBC, it was not until May 1967 that he was finally able to complete the book.

During these years the Tombergs made several trips to places where they could experience for themselves the spiritual history of Christianity. In 1959, 1960, and 1961 they were in Bruges, Belgium. The relic of the Holy Blood of Bruges was authentic for Tomberg.[23] In 1963 they moved from Peppard, where they had lived since 1956, to Caversham near Reading (both west of London) to the house at 3 Newlands Avenue where their son Alex had lived with his family before moving to Holland.[24] After this move Valentin and Maria

---

22. For the preliminary studies still known to exist, see *The Wandering Fool, or Love and Its Symbols: Early Studies on the Tarot* (San Rafael, CA: LogoSophia, 2009); included also as a supplement to the recent (2019) Angelico Press edition of *Meditations*.

23. Tomberg spoke of this in a letter to Ernst von Hippel dated September 4, 1959 (Hippel Archive): "We have visited the Chapel of the Holy Blood several times, but only on three occasions when the reliquary was exposed.... Now, regardless what others may say, we know through *experience* that the relic is genuine. For on the first occasion, hardly had the elderly priest with trembling hands laid the glass tube containing the relic out on a silken pillow and spoken the words 'Come ye, who would venerate the Holy Blood' than an inexpressible light flooded the chapel, and a shaking came over the soul, a shaking surely very like the shaking of the earthquake that occurred as the words 'It is fulfilled' were uttered. It is not the soul-shaking alone, however, that testified to the reality of the Holy Blood, but also the wonderful after-effects of our encounter with the relic. By this I mean that one became centuries younger (that is, rejuvenated in a deeper sense); the soul in all its faculties and interests was enlivened and refreshed: all became more interesting, life more colorful, the imagination richer, thoughts more clear and true...." Heckmann and Frensch, *Valentin Tomberg*, Vol. I.2, 342.

24. The gifted Alex Tomberg studied languages at Cambridge and then worked as a colleague of his father in the BBC service. In the Netherlands he got a job with Shell. He had no connection with the Anthroposophical and Hermetic work of his father.

visited them, as well as Maria Louise van Rijnberk, several times. In the spring of 1964, and again in 1965, they took Louise van Rijnberk along on their trips to Florence and Assisi. Ernst von Hippel, now professor emeritus, had in the meanwhile moved to Perscheid in the Rhineland-Palatinate, where the Tombergs were regular guests from the summer of 1966.

Already in January 1965, Gertrud von Hippel had begun translating the Tarot book into German. In June 1972, the first German edition appeared under the title *Meditationen über die Großen Arcana des Taro*.[25] In 1980, the publisher Aubier published the first French edition, *Méditations sur les 22 arcanes majeurs du Tarot*, which went through several editions. Originally, Paul Derain in Lyon was to have published the book, but Tomberg did not agree with the many adaptations to French colloquialisms made by the publisher. In 1983, the Catholic publishing company Herder published *Die Grossen Arcana des Tarot* in a new translation. The Catholic philosopher Robert Spaemann wrote a preface; and the Catholic theologian Hans Urs von Balthasar, an introduction. Naturally, this made the book more accessible to German Catholic readers. The English translation by Robert Powell, entitled *Meditations on the Tarot: A Journey into Christian Hermeticism*, was published in 1985. In 2020, Novalis Verlag published a new German translation by Michael Frensch which contains no forewords or introductions by other authors.[26]

The French edition was extensively discussed by Antoine Faivre, the influential professor of the history of esoteric and mystical currents in modern Europe at the Sorbonne in Paris. He writes that the book "is probably destined to become one of the most important works of the so-called modern Western esoteric currents."[27]

---

25. Valentin did not get around to checking the whole translation, for lack of time (he was by then already busy with his text on Lazarus). He relied on Gertrud von Hippel, after reading the translation of Letter I.

26. *Meditationen über die Großen Arcana des Taro. 22 Briefe an den Unbekannten Freund*, trans. and ed. by Michael Frensch (Steinbergkirche: Novalis Verlag, 2020).

27. Antoine Faivre, "Analyse der Meditationen über die 22 Großen Arcana des Tarot de Marseille," in *Valentin Tomberg*, Vol. II, 132–75.

England (1948–1973)

The book was very well received in certain Catholic circles. The well-known Benedictine monk Bede Griffiths wrote in a letter: "It is simply amazing. I have never read such a comprehensive exposition of the *philosophia perennis*."[28] Trappist monk Basil Pennington remarked: "It is without doubt the most extraordinary work I have ever read. It has enormous spiritual depth and insight."[29] Thomas Keating, also a Trappist monk, wrote: "This book is, in my opinion, the greatest contribution to date towards the rediscovery and renewal of the Christian contemplative tradition of the Church Fathers and the High Middle Ages."[30]

Pennington and Keating were among the founders of the *Centering Prayer* movement that arose in the United States in the 1970s, and that emphasizes the contemplative prayer of inner silence practiced by the early Desert Fathers of the Church. Tomberg stood in this contemplative tradition, which includes Teresa of Avila, the Orthodox tradition of hesychasm (in which the Jesus Prayer plays a central role), and the pilgrims and hermits of ancient Russia.

Meditations was included in the Harper Collins list of the 100 best spiritual books of the twentieth century. Translations in German, English, Russian, Portuguese, Spanish, Italian, and Dutch have been published. Chinese, Danish, Hungarian, and Swedish editions are in preparation, or have recently appeared.

The Last Years

Even before *Meditations* was completed, Tomberg had finished in early 1967 another work, on "The Three Kingdoms" (of Nature, Man, and God). It was dedicated to his son Alex. He had also begun work on a book centered on the theme (also found in *Meditations*) of "The Miracle of the Resurrection of Lazarus in World History," completed in 1970. A third work, "The Proclamation on Sinai," was completed in May 1972. Toward the end, Tomberg began another

---

28. Shirley Du Doulay, *Beyond the Darkness: A Biography of Bede Griffiths* (New York: Doubleday, 1998), 237.

29. *Catholic Fidelity*, November 23, 2007: https://www.catholicfidelity.com/centering-prayer-by-dave-armstrong/.

30. Thomas Keating, *Catholic Book News*, Commonweal (May 23, 1986), 309.

Valentin Tomberg and the *Ecclesia Universalis*

new work, which he called "The Breath of Life," but did not live to finish.[31]

These texts, written in German, are "esoteric Christian" writings, not specifically Catholic writings. The same holds true of Tomberg's views on the three "feminine" aspects of God (Mother, Daughter, and Holy Soul) as presented in "The Proclamation at Sinai," and which he also touched upon in *Meditations*. This extraordinarily significant theme had in fact already been developed to some extent nearly thirty years earlier in the Our Father Course.[32]

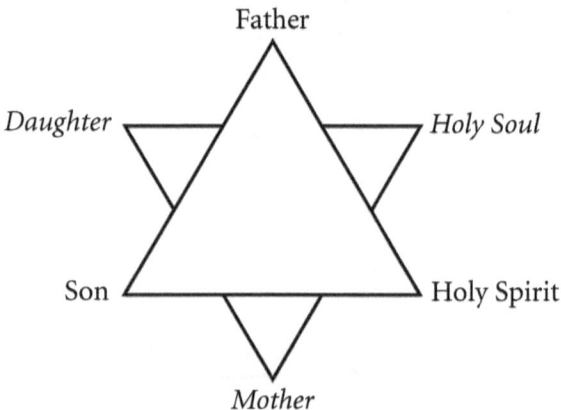

31. These four works were published together by Element Books in one volume in 1985 as *Covenant of the Heart*, and by Lindisfarne Books in 2006 under the title *Lazarus Come Forth!* Angelico Press has prepared new translations for all four texts, arranged now in three separate volumes: the first text as *Lazarus: The Miracle of Resurrection in World History*; the second, as *The Proclamation on Sinai: Covenant and Commandments*; and the combined third and fourth texts as *The New Evolution of the Good: The Three Kingdoms and the Breath of Life*. All three volumes are scheduled for publication in 2022.

32. Catholic theologian Wilhelm Maas, an associate of Cardinals Joseph Ratzinger (later Pope Benedict XVI), Karl Lehmann, and Hans Urs von Balthasar (but also a student of the work of Rudolf Steiner and Valentin Tomberg, and a scholar of Buddhism and Islam as well) wrote two in-depth articles on the theme of Sophia and the "Feminine Trinity" which will be included in a collection of his articles to be published by Angelico Press (along with articles on the representations of papal infallibility and the Jesuits in the work of Steiner and Tomberg). They can be found in the original German under the titles "Tombergs Sophia-Lehre" and "Maria-Sophia und die leuchtende Trinität" in Heckmann and Frensch, *Valentin Tomberg*, Vol. I.2, 609–23.

England (1948–1973)

In his last studies, Tomberg sheds the light of his meditations and his wisdom on the miracle of the raising of Lazarus and its implications for the spiritual and cultural history of humanity, on the Decalogue, and on the Kingdoms of Nature, Man, and God. As in his earlier *Meditations*, his esoteric Christian views on topics that are familiar in exoteric Christianity are enriched by insights from the traditions of Jewish mysticism and Platonism, and from depth psychology as well. They demonstrate that Christianity is the ongoing resurrection of all truth and all love from our spiritual and cultural history. They "will have their home in the Church of Christ, which will then be the all-embracing (catholic) unity of all things and beings who are striving for timeless wisdom," as he wrote at the end of his work on the Lazarus miracle. This is indeed the *Ecclesia universalis*.

It should also be mentioned in connection with the original German publication of these late works that its editor, Martin Kriele made significant cuts in two places in the text on Lazarus. Firstly, some pages on reincarnation were excluded (presumably because this teaching was felt to be contrary to Roman Catholic doctrine), although, ironically, the pages thus deleted demonstrate, quite to the contrary, that belief in reincarnation is *not* dogmatically excluded but is just as much a matter of personal discretion as was for many centuries the since-discarded almost universal belief in the geocentric theory of the solar system. It is perhaps to be regretted that the many Catholics for whom reincarnation is an experiential fact[33] have not stepped forward to protest such censorship. In any event, as Tomberg wrote, many choose to remain silent about it.[34]

Secondly, Tomberg's critical remarks about the Second Vatican Council (1962–1965) were also removed. Tomberg believed both

---

33. A 1990 Gallup poll found that 25% of American Catholics believed in reincarnation. More recent polls have shown higher figures for Germany (27%) and the UK (41%); and for "mainly Catholic" countries, 25–33%. More research is needed in this area, but clearly these percentages point to a significant segment of Catholics. See www.christian-reincarnation.com/ReincBelief.htm for a general overview.

34. Carro von Benwick, *Tombergs hermetisches Wirken in Anthroposophie und Kirche* (Schönach: Achamoth Verlag, 2001), 69–72.

Valentin Tomberg and the *Ecclesia Universalis*

that the Church has a duty to guard the unity of tradition, and that the laity could bring about renewal "from below" in a process that often took a long time. But what happened at the Council instead was that the Church itself opened its windows to the world and adapted to the spirit of the times at the expense of tradition. Tomberg also criticized the abolition of Latin as a liturgical and sacred language, the problematization of the celibacy of priests, and, furthermore, the Church's attitude to mixed marriage and contraception.[35] In the current English edition these excised portions are restored. In these matters Tomberg showed himself to be a devout Catholic—though not without his own views.

Kriele described Tomberg as a man who, by extensive daily and nightly prayer work, made an effort "to offer practical help to numerous deceased in purgatory. For him, 'heaven' was the presence of angels and other personal beings filled with concrete life."[36] In view of this juxtaposition of the themes of reincarnation and purgatory, we cite at length an important passage from *Meditations*:

> You see now, dear Unknown Friend, *why* the Church was hostile to the *doctrine* of reincarnation, although the *fact* of repeated incarnations was known—and could not remain unknown to a large number of people faithful to the Church with authentic spiritual experience. The deeper reason is the danger of reincarnation *by way of the ghost*, whereby one avoids the path of purification (in purgatory), illumination, and celestial union. For during earthly life, humanity could succumb to the temptation of preparing for a *future* terrestrial life, instead of preparing for purgatory and heaven. To prepare for a future terrestrial life instead of preparing for the confrontation with Eternity amounts to ... evading purgatory and the confrontation with Eternity. One ought during earthly life to prepare for this meeting with a fully awakened consciousness, which is *purgatory,* and for the experience of the presence of the Eternal, which is *heaven,* and not to prepare for a future terrestrial life, which would amount to the crystallization of the

---

35. Ibid., 73–76.
36. Martin Kriele, "Meine Lebensbegegnung mit Valentin Tomberg," in *Anthroposophie und Kirche: Erfahrungen eines Grenzgängers* (Freiburg: Herder, 1996), 148–58.

England (1948–1973)

"body" of a ghost. It is worth a hundred times more to know nothing of the fact of reincarnation, and to deny the doctrine of reincarnation, than to turn thoughts and desires towards the future terrestrial life and thus to be tempted to resort to the means offered through the promise of immortality made by the serpent. This is why, I repeat, the Church was, from the beginning, hostile to the idea of reincarnation and did all that it could so that this idea would not take root in consciousness—and above all in the human will.

I confess that it is only after hesitation, due to objections of a very serious moral order, that I have decided to write of the danger that the doctrine of reincarnation entails, and above all of that abuse that can be—and is, in fact—made of it. It is the faith that you, dear Unknown Friend, understand the weight of responsibility that presses on each person who sees himself treating reincarnation not as belonging to the domain of esoteric (i.e., intimate) experience, but as an exoteric teaching to popularize—called to convince everyone—which has determined me to speak of the practical abuse of the fact of reincarnation. I *implore* you therefore, dear Unknown Friend, to have the good will to examine, in the light of moral conscience, the question whether the way of treating reincarnation in exoteric teaching that has been adopted and is practiced in general both by representatives of the French occult movement of the nineteenth and twentieth centuries and by Theosophists, Anthroposophists, Rosicrucians, etc., is justified and desirable.[37]

Valentin Tomberg (c. 1969)

---

37. *Meditations*, 361–62 (italics added).

Valentin Tomberg and the *Ecclesia Universalis*

After the completion of *Meditations* in 1967, years followed in which Valentin and Maria were plagued by illness. In May 1969, for health reasons, they traveled with Maria Louise van Rijnberk to Gnadenwald near Innsbruck (Austria) for six weeks to recover. Ernst and Gertrud von Hippel joined them for a fortnight. In the autumn of 1972, the Tombergs and von Hippels spent another holiday together near Limburg (Germany). The von Hippels then invited Valentin and Maria to spend a holiday together in C'an Picafort on the island of Majorca (Spain).

The Tombergs arrived there by air on January 3, 1973. Their close friend Bernhard Martin and his wife, and Fritz von Hippel and his wife, came to Majorca also. On February 9, Maria suffered a slight stroke that paralyzed her left side. She was to be flown back to England, but on the 13th, Valentin suffered a fainting attack and a cerebral infarction, causing paralysis on the left side. He died in Palma hospital on February, 24, 1973, and was buried four days later in the Catholic section of San Cristobal of Palma's Municipal Cementerio in one of the customary carved graves there. This grave was later exhumed. Maria was flown to England on March 4th, where she died just over two weeks later while hospitalized in Reading on March 23, 1973. As noted before, when asked on an earlier occasion by Eva Cliteur about provision for their old age, Valentin had predicted that they would die together. The trip to Majorca proved to be the farewell trip for them both.

PART II

The Significance of Valentin Tomberg

6

The Controversies

During his early years, Valentin Tomberg was active in the Anthroposophical Society with the healing intention of strengthening the connection of its members with the spiritual world and with the living Christ. In his subsequent focus on the philosophy of law, he sought to contribute toward restoring the moral basis of law in divine law. As he then turned toward the Catholic Church, his spiritual work was directed at stimulating a revival of spirituality by drawing upon the resources of esoteric Christianity. Finally, he strove to cleanse the Hermetic tradition of its prevalent abuse of magic and to make it accessible as a spiritual path of which Christ is the Master.

These healing impulses were aimed at strengthening humanity's connection with God and with the spiritual world. This connection had grown tenuous in the wake of the Middle Ages with the gradual development of the free personality, the consequences of which had in Tomberg's own time broken virulently upon society in the guise of Communism and Nazism.

The Catholic Church that Tomberg joined in 1945 was a very traditional one. At that time, an ecclesial anti-modernism and social conservatism prevailed, in which Tomberg found his place both as a believer and as a jurist. He was convinced that the Church should educate the faithful morally, and that Christian politics should serve justice. Interestingly, such ideas were diametrically opposed to what Rudolf Steiner had intended with his book *Philosophy of Freedom*, with his ethical individualism, and with his vision and practical efforts toward what he called "social threefolding." Through these three initiatives Steiner had hoped to facilitate the *transition* from

Valentin Tomberg and the *Ecclesia Universalis*

the ecclesial, moral, and social order of the Middle Ages, based on what he called the "rational soul," to a new order belonging to the modern age of what he called the "consciousness soul"—a new order, that is, deriving from the spiritual, moral, and social impulses of the free human being.

In a reflection on the legitimate development of the modern soul found in Letter V of *Meditations*, Tomberg contrasted "hope in man" with "hope in God." For his part, he placed his hope in God in order to overcome the spiritual crises that had come to manifestation in the two World Wars, crises that had brought him personally much tragedy and continual upheaval. In his view, the project of Anthroposophy—which, like Renaissance humanism, placed its hope in the free, emancipated human being—had collapsed during the regime of National Socialism. In contradistinction to Tomberg, Steiner had elected to build upon the power of human beings to connect themselves with the spiritual world from below through inner work. Tomberg, in his philosophy of law and in his Hermetic philosophy, followed the opposite path, taking its start from above in the spiritual world—that is, leading from the above to the below.

Considered in isolation, however, both these paths are necessarily one-sided. The path from above to below can lead to an authority-bound conservatism, whereas the path from below to above can lead to a misguided confidence in human freedom. In order to develop inwardly and to commit to a new spiritual way of life, free individuals must not only find within their own "I" the *source* of their spiritual, moral, and social intuitions; they must also be prepared to *receive* inspiration and guidance from the spiritual world. When the blending of these two qualities is achieved, the two paths work in unison. The collaboration of God and man achieved in this way represents, in truth, our solemn task for the future.

It seems that, in trying to respond to the need to set the stage for these two paths to enter into and enhance collaborative synthesis, Tomberg could not avoid becoming the center of several controversies. From 1931 onwards he was attacked by circles around Marie Steiner in Dornach. Around 1940, he faced similar problems within the Dutch Anthroposophical Society. Later, with the renewal of interest in his writings in the 1980s, the subject of "Anthroposophy and the Catholic Church" came to the fore critically, and sometimes acrimoniously, in various anthroposophical journals and other venues. Some of Tomberg's articles from the 1930s were republished in the journal *Erde und Kosmos*. The magazine *Info3* (1988/5) published articles by Wolfgang Garvelmann and Karl Boegner on Tomberg, as well as an interview with Martin Kriele. These exposures led to another wave of criticism. Matters went so far that in 1995 Tomberg was declared to be a Jesuit opponent of Anthroposophy (an accusation Steiner also did not escape, having been attacked by Annie Besant, the president of the Theosophical Society)! The truth of the matter, however, is that these controversies had less to do with Tomberg than they did with crises and unresolved issues still festering in the Anthroposophical Society itself during this period—issues that, unfortunately, continue to plague objective discourse among many of its members.

The Criticism of Marie Steiner

As mentioned in Part I, on January 7, 1934, Roman Boos published a critique of Valentin Tomberg's Studies of the Old Testament in the Society's newsletter.[1] Boos did not trouble to discuss the *actual* research presented in the book, but instead narrowed his sights to criticizing Tomberg's simple statement (which was only a reiteration of Rudolf Steiner's oft-repeated position on the matter) that the Anthroposophical Society could only maintain itself through a steady, conscious relationship with the spiritual world. That is, clinging to what had by now become for many the "tradition" of what "Herr Dr. Steiner had said" could not alone keep the Anthroposophical Movement quick with life; for when ongoing spiritual research falls silent, so too does further revelatory insight. And this in turn can only lead to hardening of hearts, and, in due course, to the death of the movement.

Albert Steffen, Marie Steiner, and Guenther Wachsmuth, members of the Executive Council of the Anthroposophical Society, had apparently come to regard as their primary duty "standing guard"

---

1. Roman Boos, "Eine unwahre Behauptung," in *Nachrichtenblatt* (January 7, 1934).

Valentin Tomberg and the *Ecclesia Universalis*

over Rudolf Steiner's work, with the unfortunate consequence that emphasis was diverted from what (both sadly and ironically) Steiner himself had established the Board to encourage and oversee in the first place: the need for *new* spiritual insights in the School of Spiritual Science! From such a prejudiced starting position it is certainly not to be wondered at that, in face of the appearance of another individual showing clear signs of the ability to carry on just such new spiritual research in the spirit of Steiner's *own* hopes, the tragically misguided individuals concerned would feel "threatened"— fearing the "undermining" of what they regarded as *their* authority. Indeed, Marie Steiner herself said, in connection with Tomberg, "we have no need of a new initiate."

In a letter of January 12, 1934 to Marie Steiner, Tomberg complained of hatred directed toward him on the part of Boos. He wrote that he had never felt well received in Dornach, and that he had experienced mistrust even on his first visit in 1929. He pointed out to Marie Steiner that he had prefaced his Studies of the Old Testament with the absolutely clear statement that "he owed everything to Rudolf Steiner." But he also did not neglect to mention Steiner's own statement that there are always Christian initiates working upon the earth. He wrote that the notion of a "one-time revelation" confined to the years 1902–1925, to which nothing essential could be added "for centuries to come," could only lead to a mood of despondency in the field of knowledge, and thereby have a fatal effect on the life of the Society. Finally, he asked Marie Steiner whether or not his active contribution to the life of the Anthroposophical Society was wanted.[2] This plain question speaks volumes, for it demonstrates his readiness to withdraw from the Society, were she to give a negative answer. As matters turned out, Marie Steiner did write a reply, probably at the end of February 1934, but it was never sent. The key points of her criticism, however, which were also mentioned in two letters of March 1934 to other correspondents, and in a letter and a draft letter of 1936,[3] were given as:

---

2. Rudolf Steiner Nachlassverwaltung, Dornach. Partially quoted in Heckmann and Frensch, *Valentin Tomberg*, Vol. I.1, 164–67.

3. Ibid., 171–76; also 180–81, 233–34, 504–8.

The Controversies

- Youthful aberration, bias, and arrogance: Tomberg was put in charge of the School of Spiritual Science in Estonia too soon. He sees himself as a continuator of Rudolf Steiner's work and acts as though he is the new initiate. He does not understand how unique Steiner's work is.

- Tomberg has called his Studies "anthroposophical" without the consent of the Board.[4] On this account, he represents a different esotericism, and so has excluded himself from the School of Spiritual Science.

- Vanity is caused by self-conceit, which Tomberg feeds excessively.

- Vanity and pride, which make him a target for temptations.

- Dependence on Maria Belozvetov. Her will connects with the part of Tomberg's soul still controlled by passions and desires.

- Imprisoned by a wave of erotic mysticism, which has swept over Tomberg and some of his circle.

- Caught up in a web of certain intentions at work in the soul of Nikolai Belozvetov, which Belozvetov cannot himself see because he is possessed by them.

Marie Steiner believed that Nikolai Belozvetov was more the cause of evil than was Maria Tomberg. She spoke in his case of a "silent, suggestive possession." She called him the "prophet" of Tomberg. Even so, she *did* like Tomberg, and for some time cherished the hope that he would "come to his senses" again. That is why she was at first reluctant to make a peremptory determination in this matter. Given the circumstances as they played out, it would not be unreasonable to consider that Marie Steiner's primary objection to Tomberg at that juncture was that she had a personal antipathy for the woman he had chosen to marry.

Such criticisms of Tomberg were never addressed to him personally. Nor were specific details or charges, to which he could have responded, ever forthcoming. Marie Steiner herself did not know the situation in Tallinn from her own experience. Her criticisms

---

4. As if the word "anthroposophical" was trademarked!

Valentin Tomberg and the *Ecclesia Universalis*

were based solely on the opinions of people who for some reason (regarding which no information has been made available) already harbored a dismissive attitude towards Valentin and Maria Tomberg, as well as towards Nikolai Belozvetov. A possible factor might have been (although this is supposition on our part) that Marie Steiner would surely have been familiar with Rudolf Steiner's statement that one should not take on the role of spiritual teacher before attaining the age of forty. And so (in addition to her other criticisms) perhaps she considered it virtually impossible that a young person like Tomberg, only thirty-four at the time, could be so engaged in spiritual-scientific research and have already achieved the personal, conscious contact with the spiritual world it requires. A salient fact that needs mentioning here, however, is that Tomberg stepped forward as an *actual* "spiritual teacher" in the full sense of the expression only in 1940 (i.e., precisely when he *was* forty years old) when he inaugurated with an intimate circle his masterly and extraordinarily profound Our Father Course.

Marie also knew that Rudolf Steiner had sometimes advised newly-married couples to wait two years before doing deep esoteric work. She may rightly, then, have had some general grounds for concern. But even if this general consideration of a personal reservation be granted, how could she, who knew virtually nothing firsthand regarding Tomberg's personal situation or motives, possibly arrive at a sufficiently informed opinion on so intimate a matter as whether Tomberg had been so "astrally charged" in his friendship and marriage to Maria Belozvetov that this alone "disqualified" him for esoteric work? Moreover, just what is one to understand by "astrally charged" in the first place?

Even with the best will in the world it is difficult not to suggest that in the final analysis Marie Steiner categorically rejected the possibility of *any* individual spiritual research that would take Anthroposophy further after Steiner's death. "From his creation of Anthroposophy we shall be able to draw for centuries to come," she wrote in her unsent letter to Tomberg. Like Roman Boos, Marie Steiner did not respond to Tomberg in terms of the actual *content* of his work. Tragically, it was she (a central figure in the birth of the Anthroposophical Society from its very inception) who ultimately

The Controversies

played the leading role in driving Tomberg and his work from the center of Anthroposophy in Dornach.

Regrettably, such "criticism from Dornach" revealed the complacency of a Board that no longer functioned according to its *actual mandate*, but focused instead on maintaining its spiritual "prerogative." Seen from this gravely flawed perspective, the independent and indisputedly spiritually-gifted Tomberg obviously posed a "threat" to the circle around Marie Steiner, who for whatever personal reasons had fallen into the error of confusing their mandate to steward and cultivate ongoing spiritual research with autocratic authority to "guard" Steiner's work as a sort of "deposit of faith"— one they felt they had to defend at all cost against any "incursion" of possible contributions and continuations by a new generation of spiritual researchers operating at or near an "initiatic" level. The way in which the leading anthroposophists in Dornach elected to deal with Tomberg painfully illustrates the incapacity of a Society so preoccupied with "preserving" Anthroposophy that it proved unable to objectively assess the spiritual quality of Tomberg's work. Instead, he was attacked personally on the basis of qualities they believed they saw in him, whether rightly or wrongly, but in any case almost exclusively on no other basis than hearsay. Naturally, taking care to protect and preserve a legacy as broad and deep and future-directed as that of Rudolf Steiner *is* an important and legitimate concern. But as is so often the case with the legacies of such outstanding teachers, it may be that the Board members we have mentioned identified themselves more with preserving the "uniqueness" of their teacher (and perhaps, by conflation, their own uniqueness in that regard) than entering spontaneously, open-mindedly, and open-endedly—and with no sense of special entitlement—into the needs of those endowed with the requisite capacities for the sort of independent spiritual research Steiner had himself called for, and that constituted the very raison d'être for the establishment of the School of Spiritual Science in the first place. After all, its mandate was, precisely, to encourage and sponsor such further research, and those capable of conducting it!

Valentin Tomberg and the *Ecclesia Universalis*

Willem Zeylmans van Emmichoven

Of Willem Zeylmans van Emmichoven we have already had much to say in Part I. He was the General Secretary of the Anthroposophical Society in the Netherlands. As such, he was responsible for the development of Anthroposophy there. Naturally, potential tensions were associated with the sudden appearance in the Netherlands of an independent researcher like Valentin Tomberg, who, in addition, had himself previously held an equivalent office as General Secretary of the Anthroposophical Society in Estonia. As was by then quite well known, Tomberg's activity was focused more on the moral-Christian core of Anthroposophy, and Zeylmans' more on practical work arising out of Anthroposophy (schools, medicine, agriculture, etc.). Their representative groups had quite distinct qualities. However, there was no indication of personal issues of a challenging sort between Tomberg and Zeylmans at the time.

Problems did arise however, as we have described before, when Tomberg shared results of his esoteric research with members of his group, for example on Nazi occultism, and talked about previous incarnations of members of his group.

For instance, according to Leendert Holleman, Tomberg once visited the Prinsenhof Museum (the residence of William of Orange) in Delft with some friends from his circle. This must have taken place between 1939 and 1942. Holleman had heard of this visit from his relative Maria Louise van Rijnberk, who may have been present.[5] According to this report, when viewing the paintings in the museum, Tomberg explained which of the portrayed people from William of Orange's circle had been reincarnated in his circle. He is said to have told them who among them, in a previous life, had been one or another of the significant figures upon the canvas. Admittedly, this may be an unfamiliar and discomfiting topic for many readers, and, taken out of context, a hazardous one. We include this brief mention of incarnational attributions only to point out that such matters are almost universally inadmissible for a

---

5. Notes of J.E. de Groot from his conversation with L.J.W. Holleman (March 8, 1985). Author's archive.

spiritual teacher, because they can make the work unfree and perhaps evoke ghosts from the past, regardless whether the attributions are true or false. This must not, however, lead us to entirely discount the importance of furthering our own self-knowledge in this domain, and (at least in principle) of moving toward a setting where deepening insight into this field may be "hygienically" attained. In any case, another interpretation of these attributions is also possible, based upon the "principle of analogy." Tomberg had previously employed "historical analogies" to describe configurations of people in Tallinn. It appears to have been in this sense that in a notebook entry dated May 6, 1933, he jotted down a short series of names of friends, which he laid out in connection with the names of one or another of the Apostles, after which he added as a parenthetical qualifier "in principle." The simplest interpretation of this penciled note would be that Tomberg was thinking of something like twelve "Apostolic types" or "collectivities," in accordance with which he was indicating to which such type or collectivity he felt those whom he mentioned belonged. More than this cannot be said with any certitude.

In a certain sense, this subject of reincarnation, and establishing actual examples, stands before us as a great challenge for the future. For the most part, we lack the maturity of consciousness and the requisite moral capacities to make headway in such spiritual research without giving way to inflation and self-delusion. What is clear is that far too many frivolous games are played on this field (most often with a cast of prominent historical figures), and that these most often lead to unfortunate consequences. Such games were rather popular among anthroposophists, and also, for a time, with Valentin and Maria Tomberg, Stefan Lubienski, and Ernst von Hippel. In Tomberg's circle they concerned his own previous "incarnation," those of the people around him, and of Willem Zeylmans. To the author of this book these supposed incarnations do not make sense, except perhaps as historical analogies.

During the war years, the members of the Dutch Anthroposophical Society heard about the conversation between Zeylmans and Tomberg. After the war they heard from Lubienski about an "incarnation" attributed to Zeylmans as a former enemy of Tomberg.

Valentin Tomberg and the *Ecclesia Universalis*

When Tomberg's later move to Catholicism also became known after the war, many Dutch friends (and others who had till then been generally sympathetic) turned away from him.

The Bodhisattva Question

Over the decades, some people who knew Valentin Tomberg, or read his writings, came to associate him with the Maitreya bodhisattva.[6] As understood in the tradition of Buddhism, bodhisattvas are spiritual teachers who pass through many incarnations before attaining the buddha-dignity. As a result, they reach a higher level of consciousness, and thereafter need not incarnate again in a physical body. After Siddhartha Gautama (563–483 BC) ascended in this way to the buddha-dignity, the developmental path of a new bodhisattva began—that is, the Maitreya.

Rudolf Steiner first spoke about the bodhisattvas in 1904 and 1905, and again in 1909–1913. He described them as individualities ensouled by an archangelic being as far as their physical body (or sometimes only as far as their etheric body). It is said that five thousand years are required for a bodhisattva to attain the buddha-dignity, during which time this high being incarnates approximately every hundred years. About a century before Christ, according to Steiner, the Maitreya incarnated as Jeshu ben Pandira, the leader of the sect of the Essenes at that time. His task in that life was to point to the near approach of the *physical* incarnation of Christ. In the twentieth century, according to both Steiner and Tomberg, the mission of the Maitreya was to proclaim the *etheric* incarnation of Christ. As the future Maitreya Buddha, this present bodhisattva will be a "bringer of good through the Word" and have the task of preparing humanity to fully fathom the Christ impulse of love.

According to Steiner, this bodhisattva in his twentieth-century manifestation was to incarnate in a human being as his "vehicle" between that individual's thirtieth and thirty-third year. This personal vehicle, into whom the Maitreya was to incarnate, would experience this incarnation within his being as "a tremendous change" of

---

6. Hereafter, usually given simply as "Maitreya."

The Controversies

life—a process in which his soul would be, as it were, "exchanged" in such a way that, as an individuality, he would thereafter be "a very different person than he had been up till then." Steiner declared on November 4, 1911 that this individual was already embodied and would in due course become the "actual" proclaimer of the Christ in his etheric garment.[7] In the summer of 1921, the well-known Lutheran theologian (and first leader of the Christian Community) Friedrich Rittelmeyer asked Rudolf Steiner whether the bodhisattva had already been embodied on earth at that time and received the answer: "If we live another fifteen years, we can still experience something of it."[8] This statement, then, indicates some time in the year 1936. Unfortunately, however, the Anthroposophical Society collapsed as a unified whole in 1935, and so could not become the Maitreya's field of activity. When reporting his interchange with Steiner, Rittelmeyer added: "This is what he said. Everything else is playing with words." After quoting this same answer in his notebook, Walter Johannes Stein[9] added his personal conclusion that "Jeshu ben Pandira was born at the beginning of the century."

Now, Tomberg stated in 1940 in the Our Father Course, in connection with the fourth part of Steiner's Foundation Stone Meditation (which describes the interaction between the head and the heart), that the Christmas Conference of 1923 had arisen from the spirit of the Maitreya: "This Christmas Conference was to be a preparation for the work of Maitreya ... who began his work in 1932, 1933."[10]

After Steiner's death, voices were raised that Steiner himself had been the Maitreya, although he himself had clearly stated that, as regards his own individuality, "he had nothing to do with Jeshu ben

---

7. Rudolf Steiner, two lectures on Jeshu ben Pandira, in *Esoteric Christianity and the Mission of Christian Rosenkreutz* (Forest Row, UK: Rudolf Steiner Press, 2001), 93–129.

8. Friedrich Rittelmeyer, *Meine Gespräche mit Rudolf Steiner* (Stuttgart: Urachhaus, 2016), 37.

9. W. J. Stein (1891–1957), an intimate student of Rudolf Steiner, was a spiritual researcher in his own right, especially of the legends of King Arthur and Parzival. He later moved to England, where he edited the short-lived but spiritually significant British Journal *The Present Age*.

10. Our Father Course, week 16.

Valentin Tomberg and the *Ecclesia Universalis*

Pandira" (who he had himself identified as being an earlier embodiment of the Maitreya). In two lectures delivered in 1930, Elisabeth Vreede spoke out strongly against these voices.[11] Of course, this does not exclude the possibility that Steiner may have been "inspired" by the bodhisattva when he spoke of the second coming of Christ in the etheric world. In fact, Steiner devoted a series of lectures to the subject of such intimate "collaborations," especially of leading guides of humanity, to facilitate the fulfillment of various missions.[12]

Tomberg was obviously another candidate for the bodhisattva: at the age of thirty, he had *in fact* appeared as "a comet from the East" (words of Ernst Lehrs), composing impressive articles and demonstrating a refreshingly lively style of lecturing. In truth, from the beginning of the 1930s until the end of the Our Father Course in 1943, Tomberg was one of the few anthroposophists who (together with Friedrich Rittelmeyer, Hermann Beckh, and Emil Bock) dedicated themselves—in harmony with what Steiner had said about the Maitreya bodhisattva—to the deepening of Christology and to speaking of the second coming of Christ in the etheric world.

On March 14/15, 1933, Tomberg wrote in his notebook:

During Rudolf Steiner's lifetime, the bodhisattva was not there. [...] Doctor [Steiner] himself—"that is clear"—was not [he]. Who it is, he may not say, for it belongs to the task of the Anthroposophical Movement that the bodhisattva be recognized.[13]

Around 1940, John Daniskas asked Tomberg directly if he was the bodhisattva. Jan van der Most was also present, and in a letter to Michael Frensch in 1989 stated that Tomberg strongly denied this and pointed in a different direction.[14] This statement by Tomberg that he was not the bodhisattva was only published in 2016. This does not exclude the possibility, of course, that Tomberg may have

---

11. Elisabeth Vreede and Thomas Meyer, *The Bodhisattva Question* (Forest Row, UK: Temple Lodge Publishers, 2010).

12. See *The Principle of Spiritual Economy* (Hudson, NY: Anthroposophic Press, 1986) (CW 109).

13. Tomberg Archive, Steinbergkirche.

14. Michael Frensch, "Ein Freund von jenseits des Grabes," *Valentin Tomberg*, Vol. III, 47.

The Controversies

been "inspired" by the bodhisattva. Stefan Lubienski touched upon this in a letter of October 19, 1953, to Eva Cliteur:

> Tomberg, insofar as he is bodhisattva (and one does not uninterruptedly fulfill such a task, but only from time to time), is a focal point—or better, a rainbow—of the moral Christ in the etheric world.[15]

A full statement by Lubienski on this theme has survived from a later period in a reference made by an unknown correspondent:

> Stefan hinted to me that Tomberg had been in immediate connection with the future Maitreya-Buddha at a certain period of his life. Later on, this source of inspiration was eclipsed, leading in the end to his (for Lubienski) enigmatic transition to the Catholic Church.[16]

In a letter from Cornelis Los (a Dutch priest of the Christian Community) to the above-mentioned priest Luba Husemann, dated May 26, 1978, it can be inferred that Husemann assumed that Jeshu ben Pandira, as bearer of the bodhisattva, had been reincarnated in Valentin Tomberg, because in his letter Los stated that, based on his personal experience with Tomberg, he could not imagine such an identification.[17] Martin Kriele wrote in 1996 that he knew for a certainty "that in Valentin Tomberg the Christ messenger announced by Rudolf Steiner, the so-called 'bodhisattva,' had been present."[18] Robert Powell, translator of Tomberg's *Meditations* (and some other works) into English, shares this conviction, and regards Valentin Tomberg as the successor to Rudolf Steiner. In Powell's view, Tomberg was unable to assume his intended activity owing to the problems in the Anthroposophical Society.[19]

---

15. Letter of Stefan Lubienski to Eva Cliteur (October 19, 1953). Tomberg Archive, Steinbergkirche.
16. Helmut Finsterlin, "Verschiedene Informationen über Valentin Tomberg," in *Erde und Kosmos* (1986/2).
17. Letter of Cornelis Los to Luba Husemann, May 26, 1978. Central Archive of the Christian Community, Berlin.
18. Kriele, *Anthroposophie und Kirche*, 186.
19. Robert Powell and Keith Harris, "The Transition" (2014), included in Claudia McLaren Lainson, *The Circle of Twelve and the Legacy of Valentin Tomberg* (Boulder, CO: WindRose Academy Press, 2021), 427–65.

Valentin Tomberg and the *Ecclesia Universalis*

Willi Seiss, a publisher of Tomberg's anthroposophical writings, wrote that Tomberg was not the bodhisattva, but that in his Christology he was inspired by the bodhisattva (as in the Our Father Course). According to him, the bodhisattva teaches the way to Christ, and can "enter the human organism when the [necessary] conditions are created [...] in the forehead, throat, and heart chakras."[20]

Michael Frensch, who translated and was jointly responsible for the publication of the German edition of *Meditations*, and who prepared a revised translation in 2020, addressed the matter by suggesting that the temporary "indwelling" of the bodhisattva with Tomberg around 1932/33 may help explain "why he was able to explain the Bible so competently afterwards."[21] Frensch pointed out in this connection that shortly before, in 1931/32, an important turning-point had taken place in Tomberg's life. This turning-point may have started in July 1931, when he was in Helsinki attending the class lessons read by Marie Steiner.[22]

The Catholic Church

During the war, Tomberg came to realize that the collapsed Anthroposophical Society lacked the spiritual wherewithal to resist the forces of evil. The development of the consciousness soul, which might have fostered this capacity, had failed in this respect. He came to the conclusion that the Catholic Church represented the sole bulwark against National Socialism and Bolshevism. For him, this Church was also the only sufficient undergirding for the new moral-legal order that would have to emerge after the war. In his legal writings, he strongly emphasized this moral force of the Church.

According to Martin Kriele, Tomberg officially joined the Catholic Church in 1945, but had become quite familiar with it already in 1944, when he and his family lived with the von Hippels in Bad

---

20. Sebastian Niklaus and Björn Steiert, "Der Impuls von W. Seiß zur Gründung der FhaB," *Valentin Tomberg*, Vol. III, 162–63.
21. Michael Frensch, "Ein Freund von jenseits des Grabes," 82.
22. See page 26.

The Controversies

Godesberg. While there, he had made a practice of accompanying their daughter Elisabeth to Mass each morning.[23]

A recently acquired source (notes of seven conversations that Bernhard Martin, a member of both the Anthroposophical Society and the Christian Community, had with Tomberg between 1944 and 1948),[24] casts light on Tomberg's turn toward the Catholic Church and away from Anthroposophy, the Christian Community, and Protestantism generally during this period. Regrettably, the fragmentary notes of these conversations do not place everything Tomberg said in an adequate context. They were jotted down during the conversations, and were not intended for others. Only with this caveat do we venture to make any reference at all to these sparse notes. Here, Tomberg's feelings stand out, which is seldom the case in his letters. He was both disappointed in Anthroposophy and shocked by the circumstances of his time. This is the state of mind out of which he was then assessing Anthroposophy. Martin himself wished to maintain his connection with Anthroposophy and would not let himself be diverted from this intention.

Tomberg recommended the Catholic Church and the Rosary to Martin. On July 20, 1947, he told him that it was also possible to remain united with Steiner while at the same time being a member of the Church. According to Tomberg, after Steiner had been spiritually excluded from the Anthroposophical Society, he himself was free. That is, he had not connected his personal karma with the Society. Martin wrote regarding their conversation that Tomberg "wants to serve humanity, which today is only represented by the Church!" Also, that "the Catholic Church is victorious in the struggle (1945). The Eastern Church is shattered. Everything else has failed.... The Church has also failed in part, but not in essence."

---

23. Communication from Gabriele von Hippel-Schäfer to Wolfgang Gädeke (January 27, 2021).

24. In early 2021, these notes were transcribed and commented upon by Wolfgang Gädeke. The relevant document, *Bernhard Martin und Valentin Tomberg— Ihre Gespräche in den Jahren 1944–1948*, has been deposited in the Central Archive of the Christian Community, in Berlin, Germany.

Valentin Tomberg and the *Ecclesia Universalis*

The Rosary Prayer of Valentin Tomberg

Tomberg wrote to Ursula von Hippel in the summer of 1971: "This is the Rosary that we pray every evening. It is based on the conviction that there is eternal Fatherly love and eternal Motherly love, because God is perfect love. So the Trinity of God is a hexagon and not a triangle only." It follows below:

Glory be to the Father, and to the Son, and to the Holy Spirit, as it was in the beginning, is now, and ever shall be, world without end. Amen.

Glory be to the Mother, and to the Daughter and to the Holy Soul, here and there, and in the circle of circles, everywhere and always. Amen.

Our Father,
Who art in heaven,
Hallowed be Thy Name;
Thy kingdom come;
They will be done on earth as it is in heaven.
Give us this day our daily bread;
and forgive us our trespasses, as we forgive those who
    trespass against us;
and lead us not into temptation,
but deliver us from evil.
For Thine is the kingdom and the power and the glory,
Forever and ever,
Amen

———◉———

Our Mother
Who art in the darkness of the underworld.
May the holiness of Thy Name shine anew in our remembering.
May the breath of Thy awakening Kingdom warm the hearts
    of all who wander homeless.
May the resurrection of Thy will renew eternal faith unto the
    depths of corporeality.

The Controversies

Receive this day the living memory of Thee from human hearts,
    who implore Thee to forgive the fault of forgetting Thee,
And are ready to fight against the world's temptation
    which has led Thee to existence in the darkness,
That through the deed of the Son, the immeasurable pain
    of the Father be appeased
by the liberation of all that exists from the misfortune of the withdrawal.
For Thine is the home, the bounty, and the all-mercy
for all and everything in the round of Existence. Amen.

Hail Mary (seven times), each time ending with an I-am saying from the Gospel:

Hail Mary, full of grace
The Lord is with thee.
Blessed art thou among women, and blessed is the fruit of thy womb:

    1 *Jesus, who is the resurrection and the life*
    2 *Jesus, who is the light of the world*
    3 *Jesus, who is the Good Shepherd*
    4 *Jesus, who is the bread of life*
    5 *Jesus, who is the door of the sheep*
    6 *Jesus, who is the way, the truth and the life*
    7 *Jesus, who is the vine*

Holy Mary, Mother of God, pray for us sinners
now and at the our of our death.
Amen:

Glory be to the Father, and to the Son, and to the Holy Spirit, as it was in the beginning, is now, and ever shall be, world without end. Amen.

Glory be to the Mother, and to the Daughter, and to the Holy Soul, here and there, and in the circle of circles, everywhere and always. Amen

Valentin Tomberg and the *Ecclesia Universalis*

Martin noted on August 19, 1944, that the change of bread and wine in the consecration at Mass moved Tomberg to his core every time he participated in it; also that he had "gone" to Catholicism, not been "drawn" to it—that is, it had become clear to him that it was to be his "workplace." What this means exactly is not clear, because there is no question (as just referenced above) but that the cult was very important to him. Until the end of his life he participated intensively in the sacramental life of the Roman Catholic Church. Yet he did not "identify" himself wholly with it, for on August 19, 1944, he also said to Martin that his life's journey had started in the Church of the East, then moved via Anthroposophy to Ecumenism.[25] And on September 12/13, 1946, according to Martin, he described himself as "supra-confessional." As in the case of the already mentioned Vladimir Solovyov, Tomberg adopted a position embracing all the Christian confessions. During a two-day visit (September 13/14, 1947) with the Tomberg family in Mülheim, Martin noted down the following synopsis of a conversation on the overall organism of the Church:

a) Its physical body: all the baptized.

b) Its etheric body: all human beings, both the living and the dead; all saints.

c) Its astral body: Mary-Sophia, the Mother of God, the [Spiritual] Hierarchies. Mary as the way to Christ.

d) Its "I": Christ.

Protestantism left out b and c (the saints, Mary, the feminine principle).

Martin joined the Catholic Church in 1946. Regarding his conversion, he wrote the book *Von der Anthroposophie zur Kirche*, which was published in 1950.[26] But he remained a member of the Anthroposophical Society. A letter received from Tomberg, dated April 16, 1956, makes plain that Martin was of the view "that Cathol-

---

25. "Ecumenism" here includes the union of Catholic and Orthodox Churches.
26. Speyer: Pilger-Verlag, 1950.

icism alone is not enough," and that he harbored the desire "to combine Catholic and anthroposophical elements and to work with people accordingly."[27]

This stance adopted by Martin may have reminded Tomberg that around 1930 the Russian anthroposophists associated with Nikolai Belozvetov had held the view that Anthroposophy should form a connection with Orthodox Christianity; indeed, that the Orthodox Church was the vessel for Anthroposophy. From the letter it seems that as regards this new theme in their friendship on the Catholic Church and its possible relationship with Anthroposophy, Tomberg initially wanted to keep a low profile, so that Martin could gather his own experience with his Catholic-Anthroposophical activity.

In July 1956 Martin received from Tomberg a very detailed answer to his query regarding what a layman can and should do "to move the Church forward in the direction of the living spiritual."[28] Tomberg expressed the opinion that this should not be done "by introducing anthroposophical methods," or "by introducing a 'spiritual science,' which is neither real science ... nor real religion...." This would seem to indicate that Tomberg harbored doubts as to the significance for the Church both of Rudolf Steiner's Christology (together with his announcement of the second coming of Christ) and of his own prior anthroposophical writings. More could be achieved, he said, "by deepening and supplementing the symbolic dimension of Christian culture and of the Bible with what has emerged from the experience of the supersensible in other epochs and other cultural spheres." By this he may have meant, at least in part, the interpretation of religious symbolism developed by C. G. Jung and others, which was not to be understood in terms of science or religious doctrine, but more as "formulas of personal certainty." Tomberg's own *Meditations* can in this respect also be seen as a deepening and complementary contribution by a layman.

Tomberg was well familiar with the Church's double, which he called the "fox" (see below), but nevertheless trusted that the spiri-

---

27. Heckmann and Frensch, *Valentin Tomberg*, Vol. I.2, 268–69.
28. Ibid., 283.

Valentin Tomberg and the *Ecclesia Universalis*

tual core of the Church was still living. He wrote about this in Letter VI of *Meditations*:

> Nevertheless, although God, Christ, the Holy Virgin, the spiritual hierarchies, the saints, the Church (or the Mystical Body of Christ) are real entities, there still exists also a phantom or *egregore* of the Church, which is its "double," just as every man, every nation, every religion, etc., have their "doubles." But just as he who sees in Russia, for example, only the bear, in France only the cock, and in Germany only the wolf, is being unfair towards the country of the Heart, the country of Intelligence, and country of Initiative—so is one being unjust towards the Catholic Church when one sees, instead of the Mystical Body of Christ, only its historical phantom, the fox. In order to see rightly, one has to look rightly.[29]

According to Rudolf Steiner, cultic forms of the Egyptian-Chaldean culture were at work in the Church:

> The ecclesiastical element of cultus and hierarchy, which was a transformation of ancient Rome into the Roman Catholicism that streamed into Europe, is one of the impulses that continue to work as backward impulses throughout the whole fifth post-Atlantean period, but especially in its first third. . . . You know that one post-Atlantean period lasts approximately 2160 years. One third of this is 720 years. So starting with the year 1415 [the beginning of this fifth period], this takes the main period to the year 2135. Therefore, the last waves of hierarchical Romanism will last into the beginning of the third millennium. These are echoes in which the impulses of the fourth [or Greco-Roman] post-Atlantean period assert themselves in the forms of the third [or Egypto-Chaldean] period. But many things work side by side at the same time, so there are other impulses working together with these. Roman Catholicism had its actual climax in the thirteenth and fourteenth centuries.[30]

In his book on Lazarus (1970), Tomberg wrote in considerable detail about the reawakening or "resurrecting" impulses, or intercessions, that had kept Christianity alive, rescuing it again and again

---

29. *Meditations*, 139.
30. *Karma of Untruthfulness II* (Forest Row, UK: Rudolf Steiner Press, 2005), 114.

The Controversies

from degeneration. The first such renewing impulse was connected with Pentecost, followed later, as he describes, by the eremitic impulse and the early Church Fathers, then by the founders of the great monastic orders, then by the thought-cathedrals of medieval Scholasticism, and yet again in the sixteenth century by the movement towards interiorization that commenced with the foundation of the Jesuit Order by Ignatius of Loyola and with the reform of the Carmelite Order by Teresa of Avila and John of the Cross.[31]

In this same context of periodic renewing impulses, or "renaissances" (as he sometimes put it), Tomberg saw, at the time he was writing (late 1960s), imminent signs of another such regeneration. Here he speaks again (in this, his last major work) of the expectation of the appearance of the Maitreya, who will bring a new awakening impulse, "who will teach and exemplify a new path of awakening."[32] On this occasion he did not name Rudolf Steiner in connection with announcing the coming of the Maitreya; but earlier, in Letter XXI of *Meditations*, he had done so, in the words, "of all that has been written and said in public [about the Maitreya], the most correct is what was said by Rudolf Steiner."[33]

Tomberg did not mention there that according to Steiner the Maitreya was to prepare humanity for the return of Christ in the etheric world, but did say that he considered the task of the future Maitreya Buddha to be the fusion of spirituality and intellectuality, of prayer and meditation. In Letter XXI he wrote that the Maitreya bodhisattva expected by the Buddhists, and the Kalki avatar (the predicted tenth avatar of the Hindu god Vishnu, whose birth will mark the end of the "Dark Age") expected by the Hindus, will manifest in a single personality in order to realize this fusion. For his part, Steiner had spoken of the task of inspiring the spiritualization of the intelligence as that of the Archangel Michael.

Tomberg was of the view that ecclesial Christianity (the "exoteric" Church of Peter) and Johannine Christianity (the "esoteric" Church

---

31. *Lazarus: The Miracle of Resurrection in World History* (Brooklyn, NY: Angelico Press, 2022), 167–70.
32. Ibid., 178.
33. *Meditations*, 614.

Valentin Tomberg and the *Ecclesia Universalis*

of John, which includes as well Rosicrucianism, Anthroposophy, and Hermeticism) together form the Universal Church of Christ—what we have called the *Ecclesia universalis*. In letter XIV of *Meditations*, he wrote:

> It is the same with Christianity. It is *one* and indivisible. One should not—one cannot!—separate from the so-called "exoteric" Christianity its gnosis and mysticism, or so-called "esoteric" Christianity. Esoteric Christianity is entirely *within* exoteric Christianity; it does not exist—and cannot exist—separately from it. Christian Hermeticism is only a special vocation within the universal Christian community—the vocation specific to the *dimension of depth*. Just as there are in the universal Church vocations to the priesthood, monastic life, religious knighthood, etc., so there is a vocation—as irresistible and irrevocable as the others—to Hermeticism. This is a vocation to a life lived in consciousness of the *unity* of cult (or Christian sacred magic), revelation (or Christian sacred gnosis), and salvation (or Christian sacred mysticism), just as the unity of the whole of mankind's authentic spiritual life throughout its entire history always was, is, and always will be *Christocentric*. Hermeticism is the vocation to live the universal and eternal truth of the prologue of St. John's Gospel.[34]

For Tomberg, esoteric Christianity represents the "dimension of depth," which often seems lost to view in ecclesial Christianity. Indeed, the Roman Catholic Church of his time had turned against Anthroposophy. And Steiner, for his part, had said of the Catholic Church that it "does not want what is coming in the future."[35] In face of such a "stand off," it comes as no surprise that for the esoterically-minded who remain committed to the Church, Tomberg's vision opens a new perspective on the future of Christianity and offers renewed hope. Tomberg rarely wrote about the Roman Catholic Church as it actually existed in his day. He addressed, rather, its ideal archetype, which has its roots in early Christianity. When he writes about the Catholic Church, he most often means the Universal Church of which the Roman Catholic Church and the Orthodox

---

34. Ibid., 390.
35. Rudolf Steiner, answer to a question after the lecture of December 16, 1904, in *Temple Legend* (CW 93).

The Controversies

Church form a part. In his introduction to the second German edition of *Meditations*, Catholic theologian Robert Spaemann beautifully captures the spirit of what Tomberg meant by the "depth dimension" of the Church:

> What lies closest to the author's heart, however, is opening a path for all seekers after Wisdom, all Hermeticists, Theosophists, and Anthroposophists, to the one Church—that of the apostles, of God-become-Man—as their true spiritual living-space, as the spiritual homeland from which, whether they will or no, they must daily draw life, and without whose prayers and sacraments, the realities to which these latter correspond must surely disappear entirely from our world. His gratitude for this God-given spiritual living-space is most stirring in its warmth and depth. From the Catholic Church he does not expect a corresponding gratitude toward Hermetic wisdom-seekers and initiates, but only that it might clear out a humble corner for any who, in accord with their vocation, can do no other than walk the path of analogy and correspondence on the track of the mysteries (both great and small) of Reality—from time to time making most remarkable discoveries. Whether from this last-mentioned corner (which indeed, according to Christ's own words, is the most privileged) a new impulse may proceed from the Church, feeling itself obliged to respond with gratitude also, is a matter beyond human competence alone to answer. But signs that such a response may indeed prove possible are mounting.[36]

The controversies and consternation that arose in the wake of Tomberg's turn to Catholicism mainly concern two issues: his positive assessment of Ignatius of Loyola, and what we can call his "Hermetic" view of the dogma of papal infallibility. Steiner often spoke of Jesuitism as a spiritual stream that opposes Anthroposophy, that systematically extends the principle of authority in all areas. He maintained that Jesuitism distances human souls from the supersensible (thereby precluding the possibility of a spiritually complete understanding of Christ), that it seeks to establish the secular rule of the

---

36. Ibid., vii–viii.

Valentin Tomberg and the *Ecclesia Universalis*

Church more so than knowledge of the spirit, and that it does not concern itself with building a bridge between faith and knowledge.[37]

On October 5, 1911, in an important lecture in Karlsruhe, Steiner condemned the Jesuit way of thinking, which, he maintained, unilaterally and dangerously emphasizes the "Jesus" principle to the detriment of the "Christ" principle, and aims to strengthen the human will in such a way as to enable the Jesuits to work further by this means upon the will of other people. This spiritual path is said to take its origins in the *Spiritual Exercises* of Ignatius. To illustrate his point, Steiner described the meditation Ignatius gives for the fourth day of the second week of the *Spiritual Exercises*:

> The pupil must now visualize Jerusalem and the plain around Jerusalem; King Jesus with His hosts, how He sends out His hosts, how He conquers and drives off the hosts of Lucifer and makes Himself King of the whole earth—the victory of the banner of Jesus over the banner of Lucifer.[38]

Steiner points out that the Jesuits were obliged to obey the pope. He described them as a fighting force that defended the interests of the popes with all possible means; and furthermore, that they were responsible for the dogma of papal infallibility. In view of these easily misrepresented assessments, we should point out that in this lecture Steiner was, in effect, rebuking the "Jesuitism" that could all too readily emerge from this particular meditation which he had selected from the *Spiritual Exercises*, and not the man Ignatius of Loyola himself and the broader impact of his work. Furthermore, Steiner's discussion of the *Spiritual Exercises* was far from complete. He left entirely out of account the continuation and further development of this very same meditation, which describes a moral struggle in which the meditant is enjoined to move towards "spiritual poverty" of the highest degree, towards the desire to be reviled and despised: toward humility, that is, and all the other virtues considered as a whole. The struggle for the "earthly King Jesus" pic-

---

37. See Wilhelm Maas, "Das Thema 'Jesuitismus' im Werk Rudolf Steiners," in *Novalis* (1996/10).

38. *From Jesus to Christ* (London: Rudolf Steiner Press, 1973), lecture one (October 5, 1911).

The Controversies

tured early on in the meditation turns later into a struggle for the "eternal King Christ" which is waged by spreading the gospel and proclaiming the Christian path of virtue. Such much-needed further contextualizing of Steiner's reading of the *Spiritual Exercises* as given in the cited lecture (and elsewhere) is taken up in detail by Klaus Bracker and Wilhelm Maas.[39]

On a later occasion, Steiner himself presented other points of view on Ignatius and Jesuitism. On September 9, 1924, for example, he declared that Ignatius could no longer be said to be connected with his Order in the same way as at its founding, and that the "impulse of will" he had given it was, though undeniably great, one-sided. He also said:

> People still ascribe the present development of the Jesuits to Ignatius of Loyola. But it no longer has anything to do with him. Ignatius of Loyola reincarnated a long time ago, and of course he has separated himself from the movement completely... and so the Jesuitic movement... is no longer connected with Ignatius and is active in an Ahrimanic way.[40]

We must therefore separate the spirit of the man Ignatius of Loyola from what has become of his order and what is sometimes pejoratively referred to as "Jesuitism" in a more political sense. In Letter XXI of *Meditations*, when speaking of Ignatius, Tomberg did not concern himself with Jesuitism *per se*, but instead solely with the importance of Ignatius:

> St. Ignatius of Loyola, the founder of the Jesuit Order, was a master not only of prayer but also of meditation. One could say that this latter to a large extent prefigured the fusion of spirituality and intellectuality, of prayer and meditation [which is the mission of the Maitreya bodhisattva].... I am well aware that St. Ignatius does not enjoy unreserved admiration either among Protestants or

---

39. Klaus J. Bracker, "Rudolf Steiner, Ignatius von Loyola und das Königtum Christi," in *Novalis* (1996/3), and "Das Problem des unverwandelten Dualismus bei Sergej O. Prokofieff," in *Novalis* (2003/1–2); and the German Catholic theologian Wilhelm Maas, "Kreuz ohne Rosen?" in *Novalis* (1996/10). See also Willi Seiß, "Ignatius von Loyola und seine Exerzitien," in *Novalis* (1996/10).

40. Steiner, *The Apocalypse*, lecture 5 (CW 346).

Valentin Tomberg and the *Ecclesia Universalis*

among Catholics themselves... [that] at best he has gained the cold respect of the more perceptive intellectuals of the two confessions. [...] With regard to St. Ignatius of Loyola, it is not only his heroic effort to unite spirituality and intellectuality which interests us... but also, and above all, the fact that St. Ignatius began as a "fool in Spirit" and that he succeeded in attaining to the wisdom of perfect equilibrium between the world of mystical revelations and the world of human tasks and actions.[41]

The second theme concerns the dogma of the papal infallibility, which for Steiner was a "blasphemy," and something deeply "anti-Christian." This dogma was proclaimed in 1870. In 1931, Tomberg had written: "The dogma of infallibility is a definitive break with free spiritual life, decreed from Rome."[42] Some thirty-five years later, in his *Meditations*, he took this theme up again in an inimitable, Hermetic manner, describing the pope in his office as the representative of "moral logic" and "guardian of the sacred pentagram of the five wounds." This pentagram, he wrote, is "the active sign of personal sacred magic." When the pope pronounces something *ex cathedra*, he is doing so in the state of the Hanged Man (Letter XII). It is thus that the dogma enters "from above." But in the letter on Arcanum XIX we also find the opposite way. Here, the dogma is said to arise from "below," in the depths of the soul of the individual believer, whence it gradually penetrates into prayer and liturgical life until, finally, it is proclaimed by the pope. This is what Tomberg called "the leading of the Church by the Holy Spirit."[43] These two paths by which a dogma comes into being stand side-by-side in his work. Tomberg did not resolve this contradiction. Indeed, perhaps he did not experience it *as* a contradiction, because in Hermeticism the way from the above to the below and the way from the below to to above coexist.

It is not clear to this writer why the issue of papal infallibility was

---

41. *Meditations*, 615.
42. *Russian Spirituality*, "The Possibilities of Development in Eastern Christianity," 116–21.
43. Wilhelm Maas, "Valentin Tomberg, Rudolf Steiner und die römisch-katholische Kirche—Ihr Verständnis der päpstlichen Unfehlbarkeit," *Valentin Tomberg*, Vol. II, 323–48.

The Controversies

addressed at all in *Meditations*. In any event, Tomberg's Hermetic view of infallibility (which was bound to strict conditions) is detached from theological considerations *per se*. For what may be true on the symbolic level by means of analogical thinking, may well lose its argumentative force outside of Hermeticism. It is worth mentioning here, incidentally, that in any case only once since 1870 has a pope's "infallible magisterium" proclaimed a new dogma, namely that of the dogma of the Assumption of Mary from 1950. Tomberg later told Eva Cliteur that this dogma originated from the community of believers.

As a matter of personal discretion, Tomberg was of course entirely free (even if an anthroposophist) to associate himself with the Catholic Church. The anthroposophical authors Sergei Prokofieff and Christian Lazaridès, however, saw fit to accuse him in 1995 of having become a "Jesuit enemy" of Anthroposophy. Their "argument" was made on the basis of the fact that in his thirties Tomberg had functioned as a class reader of the School of Spiritual Science, which, to these inadequately informed authors, was erroneously taken as evidence of spiritually "betraying" the "Michael School." By fabricating such an enemy image in their book *The Case of Tomberg*, they in essence merely set up a "straw man" who (to their satisfaction, at least) they could then easily "take down." The main problem with this accusation is that they do not distinguish between Ignatius' individuality and the Jesuitism that arose in his order. They gave no evidence of any positive appreciation whatsoever of Tomberg's life intentions, and even less of his life's journey. As already mentioned, Stefan Lubienski was able to appreciate, assimilate, and solve the "Tomberg problem" in a loving way on the basis of a lifetime of direct personal experience, and in particular his expressed experience of the Christ impulse in Tomberg until the end of his life.

The Christian Community

Tomberg's relationship to the Christian Community remains one of the mysteries of his biography, along with those of his joining the Catholic Church and his apparent lack of significant interest in the practical work of Anthroposophy. As we have mentioned before, in 1931 he shared Nikolai Belozvetov's view that Russian anthroposo-

Valentin Tomberg and the *Ecclesia Universalis*

phists had no need of the Christian Community because the Orthodox Church sufficed for their cultic sense. The two friends also opposed the presumption, current at the time (as mentioned earlier) on the part of one or more priests that the cult of the Christian Community is destined to replace all other Christian liturgical practices—that, in essence, the Christian Community is the Church of the future for all humanity!

In 1935, Tomberg had read and positively assessed the writings of the Christian Community priests Friedrich Rittelmeyer, Emil Bock, and Hermann Beckh, although he may not yet have been familiar with the liturgy of the Christian Community. If he was not already familiar with it at that time, his friend Ernst von Hippel (who was then an active member of the Christian Community, and in whose house the Act of the Consecration of Man in Königsberg was performed) could have introduced him to it in 1936.

The founding circle of priests of the Christian Community was made up of a Lutheran pastor and mainly young theologians. From the point of view of the Orthodox Church (of which Tomberg was then a member), and also from the Catholic point of view, the Protestant Churches had fallen away from the true faith as sects, for in the Reformation most of the sacraments had been lost, as had the veneration of Mary and the saints, the culture of prayer and fasting, the bond with the dead, the heavenly hierarchies, and the importance of good works. Tomberg shared this view, which seems to have formed the basis of his attitude towards the Christian Community. He regarded it as a Protestant movement.

As mentioned in Part I, Tomberg visited Emil Bock in Stuttgart in the autumn of 1942, most probably at von Hippel's instigation. We do not know what the intention was, or what the two men may have talked about. It is quite possible that Tomberg wanted to talk about the meaning of Maria-Sophia, as has been suggested by some. However that may be, the meeting proved unfruitful. At that time Tomberg may also have met the Christian Community priest Luba Husemann, who was very interested in his writings, even taking the initiative of distributing them to others.

Although in 1935, in his *Studies of the New Testament and the Apocalypse*, Tomberg had praised highly and recommended the theological works of Rittelmeyer, Bock and Beckh, as far as is known he himself never wrote about the Christian Community itself—with the sole exception of some references in Bernhard Martin's notes of conversations with Tomberg between 1944 and 1948. According to these notes, on August 19, 1944, Tomberg criticized the Christian Community on the grounds that it had compromised with the politics of the Anthroposophical Society. Emil Bock had indeed taken sides against Ita Wegman in the Dornach divisiveness that led to the splitting of the Board (which had been set up by Rudolf Steiner himself), and furthermore had voted in favor of the wholesale exclusion of members holding other views in 1935. At a minimum, this would make it understandable that, according to Tomberg, the Christian Community only developed on track up to 1934, when the destructive influences just mentioned reached the point of crisis. It needs saying, however, that other leading priests, such as Friedrich Rittelmeyer and Rudolf Meyer, actively opposed the exclusion. In any event, Martin's notes report that at the time of their conversations Tomberg regarded the Christian Community as a "Protestant sect," and, on August 20, 1944, characterized the Act of the Consecration of Man as a "modernized Mass." For him, the Christian Community was not some Universal Church, not some "Church of John." Having no "tradition," it was, rather, a *Gegenwartspilz*, as Tomberg put it, which is to say, something that, like a mushroom, appears suddenly and soon disappears. At best it was a preparatory stage either for the (Catholic) Church or for Anthroposophy. Martin noted that according to Tomberg, the Christian Community's sacraments, instituted by a "Doctor of Philosophy" (that is, Rudolf Steiner), were rightly questioned by the Church.

It cannot be said that this negative assessment of the Christian Community can be attributed exclusively to a simple reaction on Tomberg's part to Emil Bock, and what some have called (rightly or wrongly) Bock's "striving for power" during the first phase of the Christian Community's growth. We need to recall that Tomberg had been baptized a Lutheran in St. Petersburg, and concurrently become acquainted with the rich liturgical life of the Orthodox Church, of which he became a member in the early 1930s. A decade or so later, he had found a new devotional, liturgical, and sacramental orientation in the Catholic Church—a richness informed with devotion to Mary. This was of fundamental importance to Tomberg, for in both the Orthodox and the Catholic Churches, as Martin noted on September 12, 1946, "the way to Christ was through Mary." This maternal principle, Maria-Sophia, was, however, missing in the Christian Community. In fairness, we might at least entertain the thought that Tomberg's emphatic focus on this "Marian" aspect might have prevented him from perceiving in an entirely unprejudiced way the spiritual significance of the renewal of religious life that Steiner had wanted to help make possible in the Christian Community. Documents and records of its founding were not accessible at that time outside the circle of priests, so Tomberg could not have known what Steiner had intended when he agreed to advise the priests. The same applies to what he could have known of the cult and sacraments laid down at that time. It seems fair to say, then, that as regards factual information and direct experience (other than an interview with Bock, and, perhaps, attendance at one or another celebration of the Christian Community's Act of Consecration of Man), Tomberg did not have at his disposal the wherewithal to pass an adequately informed judgment. Whether he had other reasons, or inner resources, that prompted him to express himself as Martin said he did, we cannot know.

Anthroposophy

The final controversy to examine concerns Tomberg's relationship to Anthroposophy and anthroposophists after 1943. We must at the outset distinguish between his relationship to the person of Rudolf Steiner (about whom Tomberg was always positive) and the "culture" of the anthroposophical membership at that time. In *Meditations*, Tomberg praised Steiner's lectures on the four gospels and the heavenly hierarchies, as well as his book *Knowledge of the Higher Worlds* (Letter XV). He wrote that Steiner had made clear that "the center of gravity of cosmic spiritual development" was Jesus Christ (Letter XVII), and had written "magnificent works" such as *Cosmic Memory* and *An Outline of Occult Science* (Letter XX). We have already mentioned how Tomberg appreciated Steiner for his statements about the Maitreya (Letter XXI), to which he added that

The Controversies

Steiner had hoped that his Society would become the bodhisattva's field of activity, but that in this regard he had overestimated it. Tomberg's conclusion—"A new disappointment!"—can perhaps be interpreted as an all too personal echo of his own earlier disappointments with the Anthroposophical Society, since it has no other evident application in the context where it appears in the book.

In his later work *Lazarus: The Miracle of Resurrection in World History* (1970), Tomberg again referred glowingly to Steiner's description of the path of inner development of the whole human being and to his doctrine of the heavenly hierarchies. And in his final completed work, *The Proclamation on Sinai: Covenant and Commandments* (1972), he yet again called attention to Steiner's teaching on the heavenly hierarchies:

> The teaching on the heavenly hierarchies was renewed in the first quarter of the twentieth century by the great Austrian seer and thinker Rudolf Steiner. The depth and breadth of Steiner's contribution to a new understanding of the spiritual hierarchies is such that this theme cannot be seriously considered today without taking into account his remarkable achievement, which, as far as wealth of stimulation, depth and multiplicity of viewpoints, inner lack of contradiction, and organic cohesion, is not to be compared with any seer or thinker—whether of the present, of the middle ages, or of antiquity—for it towers above them all. [44]

Tomberg's attitude towards Anthroposophy became quite critical in the 1940s. As described earlier, on March 30, 1942, the anniversary of Rudolf Steiner's death, he maintained that some time before Steiner died, he had foreseen that his work would collapse—that it had failed. After moving to Germany, Tomberg likewise told Bernhard Martin, on August 19, 1944, that the Anthroposophical Movement had failed, that its impulse had been ineffective. In the same vein, he told Wolfgang Garvelmann in 1945 or 1946 that this impulse had nowhere wrought any real change in life.[45]

The least we can say is that Tomberg's critique of Anthroposophy had three facets.

---

44. *The Proclamation on Sinai*, 134.
45. See page 176.

Valentin Tomberg and the *Ecclesia Universalis*

The *first* facet is clearly laid out in the first chapter of his Studies of the Old Testament (1933):

> To make anything of the facts contained in the Bible, we must employ the means offered us by esotericism. Neither a literary-historic nor an abstractly philosophic method of study can be of any conspicuous use to us in this task—*concrete* esotericism can alone avail. Access to such esotericism has been thrown open to wider circles in the present epoch by the life-work of Rudolf Steiner, who has brought a great part of it before the public in the form of anthroposophical spiritual science. Anthroposophy as it lies before us in Rudolf Steiner's writings and printed lecture-cycles is in itself not actual, concrete esotericism. It becomes so only in the souls of those who not only acknowledge its truths but themselves discern them. Concrete esotericism is only present in the company of living *esotericists*. Otherwise it becomes merely anthroposophically-directed religious, philosophic, scientific, or aesthetic convictions. Concrete esotericism does not consist in the fostering of such convictions, but in the discernment of the facts, interdependencies, and entities of the supersensory world that engender them, and in the fulfillment of the duties and missions that result from them.[46]

This leads us to the *second* facet. At this stage, Tomberg felt that there was too little "concrete esotericism" in the Anthroposophical Movement. In his view, this esotericism had to be grounded in the schooling path of Steiner's book *Knowledge of the Higher Worlds and Its Attainment*. Looking back, according to a note Bernhard Martin recorded on August 20, 1944, Tomberg saw his own work as the continuation of this path of schooling, and was of the opinion that the unwritten "second part" of Steiner's above-mentioned book (had it been written) would have brought a fuller emphasis on Christianity and included a more detailed description of the lotus flowers, or chakras—the various spiritual organs of perception for which Steiner had originally employed terminology from the Eastern religions, because equivalent terminology was not available in the West (a circumstance that needs to be addressed in future). It was pre-

---

46. *Christ and Sophia*, 3 (translation revised).

The Controversies

cisely such a further extension of the path of Christian esoteric schooling that Tomberg had begun to present, especially in the Our Father Course, to his small circle in Amsterdam. Unfortunately, this effort came to a premature end owing to the Nazi occupation of the Netherlands. In short: Anthroposophy was to be a bridge to the Christ experience.

The *third* facet stands out in a later note by Martin, dated September 13, 1946, where we read that Tomberg had remarked that an Anthroposophy that emphasized only Christ could be likened to Protestantism. Anthroposophy, he said, must also emphasize Mary, because "the way to Christ leads through Mary." This is the aspect of Sophia.

In fairness, however, Anthroposophy need not be confined solely to these three facets: concrete esotericism, Christian-esoteric schooling, and Sophia-related work. These facets are also meant to form the inner, esoteric basis for the outer, exoteric, overall anthroposophical cultural project of practical applications in the world. Tragically, however, Tomberg seems not to have found a constructive connection to the proliferation of anthroposophical cultural initiatives that were in full swing during his lifetime. It may be that a contributing factor here was that, as a constitutionally shy Estonian, he did not enter into conversation with strangers easily. His great reticence may have prevented him from entering readily into collaborative friendships with anthroposophists, who for their part were undeniably developing worthwhile practical initiatives, often at great personal sacrifice. Yes, Tomberg did reach many people in the Netherlands with his lectures, but the greater number of his auditors were apparently more interested at the time in practical work arising out of Anthroposophy, and perhaps especially so in the rebuilding years immediately following the war.

For Steiner, Anthroposophy, as a Michaelic impulse, included both the study of spiritual science and its practical applications, for example in pedagogy, where it continues to carry the torch of renewal in the international movement of Waldorf Schools. Tomberg, however, found little or no access to the practical initiatives that were growing out of the new initiatory culture Steiner had set in motion. He might have learned something of this work in the

Valentin Tomberg and the *Ecclesia Universalis*

Netherlands, where his son Alex attended a Waldorf school, but Alex remained there only a year before asking his parents to enroll him in a nearby Catholic school.

Bernhard Martin made a note on September 13, 1946, that, according to Tomberg, "Rudolf Steiner [is] in reality greater than he appears in his activity," that he actually wanted to establish "new mysteries" appropriate to the new stage in human capacities he saw as dawning in the modern world—what he called "a kind of new mysteries of Eleusis." In the ancient mysteries, aspirants had indeed been brought into contact with spiritual beings, but this did not take place in full consciousness, for the reason that such strength of self-aware focus had not yet attained the level it has, generally speaking, in modern times. By contrast, the intention of the "new mysteries" that Steiner hoped to inaugurate with the Christmas Conference of 1923 was precisely to *enable* such contact with spiritual beings in the form of fully conscious communications.

As far as is known, Tomberg expressed a broad critique of anthroposophists for the first time in his conversations with Martin, who noted on June 11, 1944, that in Tomberg's view Steiner had been betrayed by the partisanship and bourgeois attitude of anthroposophists as a whole. They had received wisdom on "credit," he said, but had not exchanged for it for a corresponding "collateral" of morality. On August 19, 1944, Martin noted that, according to Tomberg, what was lacking and needed developing in the Anthroposophical Movement was "moral logic."

In conversations with Martin on March, 30/31, 1946 (as it happens, exactly twenty-one years after Rudolf Steiner's death) Tomberg offered three critiques of the broad cultural project Steiner had envisioned for Anthroposophy.

First, the spiritual world had "oriented" itself perhaps too onesidedly towards Steiner as regards its cognizance of events on earth. This (perhaps initially surprising) notion becomes more intelligible if we recall that according to Steiner spiritual beings cannot see into what is for them the "darkness" of the earth. To the beings of the spiritual world, the "darkness" of the earth is relieved only by shining "points of light" that arise when anything moral in nature is realized there. In thus limiting itself (according to Tomberg, as reported in Martin's note), the spiritual world had in some way, or to some degree, misoriented or over-committed itself with respect to Anthroposophy. It would be difficult to take this note to mean that Tomberg was referring directly to Steiner's own work (as distinct from how it was taken up by the community of anthroposophists), as otherwise it would seem to imply that Steiner had not done anything "morally essential." It was all about "shining," said Tomberg, and he could perceive no such shining among anthroposophists at that time. Were it otherwise, as Martin notes, Tomberg "would have become an anthroposophist immediately!" This statement suggests that Tomberg must have been in a position himself to spiritually perceive such "shining" from afar—because, by the time Martin recorded his notes, Tomberg had hardly any direct contacts left among anthroposophists. It would not be at all out of court, then, to pose the question whether he was in a position to do them justice with this statement—whether, by forming such a black-and-white judgment, he might have overlooked "shining" moral qualities among many individual anthroposophists, if not as a quality of the membership as a whole.

Second, Steiner had elected to present his teaching, including his esoteric research, in "scientific" mode, and this was not to the liking of other initiates, who felt that the time had not yet come for such knowledge to be disclosed in this way. As a result, Tomberg felt (according to Martin's notes) that Steiner

> created a heavy karma for himself, such that all we can do now is wait to see what he will do next. His life was foreshortened. On account of his extraordinary output, he died a premature and painful death. Esotericism was compromised by Anthroposophy.

In Tomberg's eyes, the explanation for this could only have been Steiner's failed attempt to create, alongside its "spiritual-scientific" emphasis, a "new culture of initiation" within the Anthroposophical Society. For as he saw it, the anthroposophical membership did not rise sufficiently to accept this challenge in the wake of the Christmas Conference of 1923. "Never again such an attempt!" was Tomberg's summary comment after offering this tragic assessment.

Third, as Tomberg exclaimed in that same conversation, "To the devil with folk missions!" Here he was referring to Steiner's 1910 lecture cycle on the mission of individual "folk souls."[47] According to Tomberg (as reported by Martin), Steiner had taken into serious consideration the "Völkisches" ("folk" realities), and this could be a dangerous domain. Frankly, we might entertain some reservations as to the sufficiency of this particular abbreviated report, for only a few years earlier, in his Our Father Course, Tomberg had himself spoken in considerable detail about the tasks of European "folk souls." For Steiner, Anthroposophy was connected with the spiritual mission of Central Europe—not only with Germany, but with the neighboring Slavic peoples also. After the First World War, Steiner had hoped to connect Anthroposophy with the Anglo-Saxon peoples through his lectures in Great Britain and his unrealized intention to visit the United States. But with the rise of Nazism (also heavily influenced by "folkish" themes, but, in its case, in an inverted sense), the connection of the German archangel[48] with the German people was severed. On April 19, 1934, Tomberg noted: "The German archangel no longer looks upon the German people. He has averted his gaze from them."[49] Furthermore, in the Our Father Course, Tomberg said that the German archangel had been supplanted and was working in America.[50] Since the war, the relationship of the archangels to their "folks" may indeed have changed. Martin noted that, according to Tomberg, "they roam the earth and are in their own country only one-twelfth of the year. So, no more nationalism." Maria Tomberg added: "It's not about Germany, it's about Europe."

National Socialism had perverted the mission of the German people. Therefore, after Hitler's time, Tomberg did not want to talk about the missions of "nations." For him, it was precisely such "folk realities" that Hitler had so horrendously abused as a false "nation-

---

47. *The Mission of Folk-Souls: In Relation to Teutonic Mythology* (London: Rudolf Steiner Press, 2005).

48. For Steiner, the "office" of folk soul, or, sometimes folk spirit, is under the charge of an archangel. Tomberg addresses aspects of this theme, with special reference to the Israelite folk, in *Christ and Sophia*, 75–77, 89, 91.

49. Transcription of a notebook of Valentin Tomberg, 384–85. Archive of the Freie Hermetisch-Christliche Studienstätte am Bodensee, Taisersdorf.

50. Our Father Course, week 30.

The Controversies

alism." Yes, in *Steiner's* time it had still been possible to speak of "folk spirits" and "missions of nations," but that theme had since grown too dangerous because, since 1933, the demons of the German people had broken loose.

At the beginning of November 1943, Tomberg recorded in his notebook a communication from "Dr." (Rudolf Steiner):

> (Dr.) On his new path (elemental world, the inner world of the earth, the world of human beings), the German archangel will from now on and for all future times be the traveling staff for all beings who go this way (e.g., the Maitreya)—as [that archangel] is now the traveling staff for Christ. He has forever renounced his task as a folk spirit—he does not take part in the circle dance of the movement of the folk spirits. Rather, on his knees, he has asked the Russian archangel to take charge of his people. This seems to have happened.[51]

Tomberg feared that Soviet troops would occupy all of Germany, a fear no doubt exacerbated by his traumatic experiences with the communist regime of 1917–19. He also feared that the Russians would soon have an atomic bomb at their disposal. Partly for these reasons he saw no future for himself in Germany, and in 1948 fled to England, as we have seen. In doing so, he left behind friends (Belozvetov, von Hippel, Martin) in Germany. It may well be said that it was tragic for him that he could no longer imagine a task in Germany—that, for him, the mission of the old Central Europe was past. He could not at that point in his life identify any seeds of a rebirth of that mission. In later historical events, however, this mission did in fact reawaken; and in the many practical anthroposophical initiatives that began to flourish in the aftermath of the war, spread throughout the world as a universal human mission. The impulse of cultural renewal carried on, despite its challenges and its critics.

In seeking to better understand Tomberg's expressed views during this period, it is imperative to hold in mind how he had felt constrained to leave the Anthroposophical Society in 1941. He had been rejected by Marie Steiner and Willem Zeylmans, and a connection

---

51. Transcription of a notebook of Valentin Tomberg, 565–85. Archive of the Freie Hermetisch-Christliche Studienstätte am Bodensee, Taisersdorf.

to the Christian Community had not been established. According to his experience (and let us recall the devastating events earlier brought upon him and his family by the Russian Revolution), what was left of the crisis-ridden Anthroposophical Society (or Societies) did not have the moral strength needed to set up a united front of resistance to the National Socialism and Bolshevism raging at the time. For Tomberg, Rudolf Steiner's project of a "new mystery culture" had failed. At that historical moment, this was perhaps a warranted judgment. Under the oppressive historical circumstances of the time and the eviscerating bickering among parties in the Anthroposophical Society, who can say that Tomberg's (perhaps, to us, pessimistic) assessment of the situation prevailing at the time was in fact not at all unrealistic?

In the chaos of the war, in which keenly perceptive people like Tomberg had a particularly difficult time, he had also to reorient himself inwardly. It seems to us that he found his bearings on the one hand in the Catholic tradition, with its path of the "rational soul," and on the other, in forces coming from the future, from what in anthroposophical terminology is called the path of *manas* (the "spirit self" or higher self)—the "path of the etheric Christ," as he wrote in his notebook in October 1943. Here he gave a brief description of these new paths, which may have been based on a spiritual communication from "Dr." (i.e., Steiner). These paths brought him, then, into what we have called the second phase of his life:

> (Dr.) In the future [i.e., from now on] there will be no more spiritual science, but only the fourteen stations of the cross (which actually represent the seven steps of Christ's Passion in a form more understandable to the world); and, esoterically—the path of Christ is now at the stage of his etheric second coming:
>
> (1) The path in and through the elemental world.
>
> (2) The path into the subterranean spheres [the interior of the earth].
>
> (3) The path into the human world.
>
> All Teachers will follow this path, and teach it—the Maitreya will also follow it to the end.

The Controversies

Thus, there will no longer be a path of the consciousness soul— only the path of the rational soul (the fourteen stations of the cross, or, the seven stages of the Passion) and the path of the *manas* [the higher self]—i.e., the path of the etheric Christ.[52]

What is striking here is the apparent disappearance of the path of the consciousness soul, which, in Anthroposophy, is understood to be the defining path of modern humanity! For Anthroposophy as it exists today, the path of the consciousness soul is *above all* that of Western culture, in which the "Aristotelian stream" predominates. In this stream, the impulse of the Archangel Michael is set against that of the Academy of Gondishapur (which will be described later). Tomberg, however, turned aside from the role of the Aristotelians and their particular task of countering the forces of materialism in modern science and technology. His way was instead that of the spirit-self, or *manas*—the way of the Russian culture, in which the Platonic stream works together with the Sophia impulse.

In an article from 1935, Tomberg described the differences between the Aristotelian and Platonist paths.[53] He showed how, because of the structure of their souls and minds, Western Europeans focus primarily on the perception of external reality, which they strive to understand with their thinking. Such thinking, he goes on to say, must be infused with the will in order to form spiritual concepts. The inner structure of Eastern Europeans, on the contrary, is oriented primarily toward revelations from the spiritual world (as well as toward influences from the subterranean spheres). This *manas* orientation of Eastern Europeans develops through purification of the soul, especially through overcoming pride by practicing humility and learning to *listen* to the spiritual world. Revelations received in this way, however, can also be consciously experienced through skilled concentration and meditation by people from "other parts of Europe" who have absorbed the Michael impulse. Such people must come to the aid of the Russian East, wrote Tomberg.

---

52. Ibid., 582–83.
53. *Russian Spirituality*, "The Spiritual Basis of the East-European Tragedy," 178–95.

Valentin Tomberg and the *Ecclesia Universalis*

⊕

In view of these considerations, we turn now to the question of how to complement this vision of Tomberg with a "third path," that of *I*-consciousness, which has emerged precisely in those "other parts of Europe" he spoke of.

This third path, founded upon the *I* (in contradistinction to the consciousness soul, and the *manas* or spirit-self), is that of Central Europe. Here the other two paths—those of Michael and Sophia, or Aristotelians and Platonists, or consciousness soul and spirit-self (*manas*)—should be brought together in the overarching Christ impulse. In the Russian culture in which Tomberg spent his first eighteen years, there was a deep distrust of the Western culture of the consciousness soul and where it led: individualism, Protestantism, Enlightenment, atheism, materialism, liberalism, Marxism, secularization, rationalism, modern science, technology, the economic struggle for existence. Tomberg shared this distrust.

Anthroposophy, however, aspired to offer the promise of an "I-consciousness culture" in which the negative aspects of the consciousness soul would be overcome, leading *instead* to increasing social consciousness, conscious connection with the spiritual world, spiritual science, moral technology, a threefold society with a culture of freedom, a constitutional state, an economy of brotherhood, and cooperation with the beings of nature. But as matters turned out in the decades following Steiner's death, and especially owing to the role of Germany and National Socialism in the Second World War, in Tomberg's view this promise proved to be unrealizable in Central European culture, at least at that time.

For Tomberg, the development of the consciousness soul had failed. As he saw things, it had therefore become necessary to "fall back" upon the medieval Christian tradition stemming from the age of the rational soul in order to restore the rule of law.[54] Thus, for Tomberg, the principle of freedom (which in practice had devolved into the "arbitrariness" or "license" of power politics) needed now

---

54. It was during this period of crisis that Tomberg began focusing in his writing on law and jurisprudence.

The Controversies

to be supplanted by the principle of authority. Esoterically, the inspirations for the path of *manas* should come from the future, from the activity of the etheric Christ. Looked at in this way, after 1943 we find the path to the Middle Ages *and* the maturation of *manas* conjoined in the life of Valentin Tomberg. Anthroposophy as a way for the Christian development of the consciousness soul seemed no longer possible to him because of the war. But to us, looking back now half a century, it seems clear that the development of spiritual consciousness since the second half of the twentieth century indicates that the cause of Anthroposophy is not yet lost.

Was Rudolf Steiner's work, and the creation of an earthly Michael School for a new spiritual culture, in vain according to Tomberg? In the spiritual darkness of the war he seems to have drawn this conclusion. Or was it more the case that he himself had moved in another direction? In any event, he seemed to have seen no possibility of connecting with it any more. Typical anthroposophical themes disappeared from his work, such as the mission of the folk spirits, community-building, Ahriman, the apocalyptic character of our time, the return of Christ, and the role of Archangel Michael in the spiritualization of thought. For example, Tomberg wrote to Bernhard Martin in July 1956 that, although Ahriman is one of the powers of evil, the Church has important moral grounds for ignoring the "ahrimanic." He saw no reason for extending the Church's teaching in this way. The devil is only as strong as we are morally weak, he believed.[55] In *Meditations* he had much to say about the devil in Letters III and XV, pointing out that God had allowed the devil to be a tempter and a prosecutor. Thus, we see the devil on the one hand as the serpent Lucifer (the tempter in Paradise) and on the other as the accuser ("Satan" in Hebrew) who was allowed to test Job. According to Tomberg, the tradition of the saints shows how people can overcome such temptations and trials.

On the subject of reincarnation, Tomberg remarked to Bernhard Martin on July 20, 1947, that this is not an eternal, but a temporary law, which for that reason the Church cannot proclaim as truth. In

---

55. Heckmann and Frensch, *Tomberg*, Vol. I.2, 275–79.

leading individuals, he said, reincarnation is more a matter of personal sacrifice. In the 1960s, however, in *Meditations*, he referred to reincarnation as an "experienced fact," as neither a truth necessary for salvation, nor a heresy. Reincarnation began with the Fall, and will end one day, he wrote in Letters IV and V.

⊕

The anthroposophically-oriented Our Father Course ended in February 1943. Tomberg's move to Germany a year later to study law and obtain a doctorate in that field led to a break in his biography, and possibly also to the loss of the inspiring relationship with the higher being that some close students of Tomberg's work hold for the Maitreya. After all, a characteristic of this inspiration was the spreading of the new Christ understanding and the proclamation of his second coming in the etheric world, about which Tomberg no longer wrote. From this crisis, which shows similarities with a deep mid-life crisis, Tomberg was as it were reborn, as he himself would later describe it, in a "second incarnation."

We need to be very careful, however, not to oversimplify these matters, or to presume more insight into his deepest motives than is warranted on our part. After all, Tomberg did not distance himself from esoteric Christianity. He did not become a Roman Catholic author of esoteric writings, just as he had not previously been a Greek Orthodox author of anthroposophical studies. Perhaps the least misleading way to characterize his vocation is to say that he became an independent esoteric researcher. The anthroposophical path of schooling and the work of Rudolf Steiner remained valuable to him until the end of his life. In his conversations with Martin, however, he was critical of Steiner's choice of developing a "scientific" approach. As a Platonist in orientation, he had little sympathy for this approach. But even so, he continued to hold Steiner in high esteem until the end. It is therefore difficult to imagine that he could have wanted to level accusations at Steiner with his broad statement that the spiritual world may have injudiciously over-oriented itself toward Anthroposophy and thereby compromised other important spiritual streams. As was said earlier, Tomberg is not known to have ever made any negative statements specifically about Steiner.

The Controversies

⊕

The Anthroposophical Movement had failed. In Tomberg's view, a new attempt should not be made, and the time of folk missions was over. The coming of the teachers of the School of Chartres, which was necessary for the further spiritualization of intelligence, had become uncertain, as he told the young German anthroposophist Wolfgang Garvelmann at this time, because, with the rise of Hitler, everything had changed. In *Meditations*, Tomberg would declare twenty years later that the unification of spirituality and intellectuality (which for Steiner was the task of the Archangel Michael), of prayer and meditation, was the mission of Christian Hermeticism as well as of the Maitreya. Thus, the common project of Aristotelians and Platonists needed to shift now to a "Platonic-religious" project for individual Hermeticists. The Archangel Michael was, then, for Tomberg, "a very special friend and protector of the Hermeticists ... of people who want to unite saintliness and initiation, or who aspire to a Hermeticism that is holy and blessed from above." (Letter XII)

> **Protocol of a Conversation between Wolfgang Garvelmann (1924–2012) and Valentin Tomberg in 1945 or 1946**
>
> WG: Question about the general decline of culture—how does Rudolf Steiner's impulse affect it?
>
> VT: This impulse passed without effect. The Theosophical impulse was actually even greater. Nowhere has there been a practical change of life.
>
> WG: Surely Rudolf Steiner has made access to Christ possible for certain people!
>
> VT: Yes, but only for a small group. The most important thing about Anthroposophy was its scientific emphasis.
>
> WG: Rudolf Steiner spoke of the furthering [of Anthroposophy], of the teachers of [the School of] Chartres coming again. What these bring will not be called "Anthroposophy." But they are coming?

VT: Who says that these teachers may not have reconsidered this? Or that they are even able to make their way through? Or that they even want to? Hitler changed everything. In the blink of an eye, everything has come into flux. What if God the Father should turn away? If further development must shift to other planets?

WG: But still, the Mystery of Golgotha is here!

VT: Yes, that is so, but greater things must come, greater sacrifices. The etheric return must still take place.

WG: So, for now the Church is the "guiding force" of our time?

VT: Yes, in the sense of tradition. Even now it has its saints, like Therese Neumann. There are no anthroposophical saints. Everything else depends on the etheric return. The most essential thing Rudolf Steiner did was point to the etheric return, but it has not yet taken place. Rudolf Steiner, however, was not a prophet, but a spiritual researcher—and he did not choose to instruct by any methodology other than this. Now, a prophet speaks in the name of the Father, and therefore he speaks the truth. What Rudolf Steiner had was knowledge, and knowledge can become false if the causality upon which the future is based undergoes an alteration.

WG: Is it not Christ who was experienced by Max Reuschle?[56]

VT: It is an imprint of the Christ, as takes place in the sacrament—not the etheric Christ. The etheric return will be very different—not for individuals only. There will be a very different, healing, atmosphere. Science will speak [in this regard] of waves.

WG: What does the time of His coming depend on, if not on Him?

VT: On the resistance He faces in the various spheres. He comes in Lucifer's light, but Christ's is the weakest light. Of all forces, He is the least. His light and force differ wholly from any others.

---

56. German writer and archivist (1890–1947), known for his poem "Christ speaks as Lord of Destiny." Tomberg knew him.

The Controversies

Bernhard Martin did not agree with Tomberg's view that the Anthroposophical Movement had come to an end. He remained a member of the Society, and believed that the impulse of Anthroposophy would have to be re-created later. Immediately after the war, Willem Zeylmans (with whom, as we have seen, Tomberg had had problems in 1940) began to work for the renewal of the Anthroposophical Society on an international level. With the cooperation of Emil Bock, Karl König (founder of the Camphill movement), and others, two international meetings were held in 1948. Then Zeylmans started to bring the theme of "the continuing impulse of the Christmas Conference" of 1923 to the fore.

We may surely consider it a missed opportunity that Zeylmans could not work together with Tomberg, for whom the impulse of the Christmas Conference had been the core of his own early anthroposophical work. Destiny had brought these two men (who had already met in 1929) together in 1938 in the west of the Netherlands. Partly thanks to the efforts of Zeylmans, the disintegrated Society could be rebuilt. After years of ongoing deliberations, the Dutch Society rejoined the Dornach Society in 1960. But Tomberg took no notice of this.

On February 18, 1950, in a letter to Nikolai Belozvetov, Tomberg described Anthroposophy as "dry." Anthroposophy, he said:

> had no "living water," for it did not embrace the Virgin Mary. It had the fire, but brought neither holiness nor healing. It brought only more and more postulates and claims. Once the flame of consciousness has been kindled, it gives more and more knowledge of what should be, but does nothing to change what actually is.[57]

After an absence of seven years, Tomberg was back in the Netherlands in 1951. On September 3, 1951, in Amsterdam, he made the following remarks about anthroposophists and Anthroposophy, probably recorded by Eva Cliteur:

---

57. *Valentin Tomberg*, Vol. I.2, 186.

Valentin Tomberg and the *Ecclesia Universalis*

If the followers of Rudolf Steiner had really taken his method seriously, and then worked on themselves, they would all have become Christians and come to a living experience of Christ. [...] The fact that there are so many "old" anthroposophists only means that they are not making any progress, that they are treading water—going back and forth, but not proceeding further in any direction. If they had been proceeding, they would have achieved something. Anthroposophy is not an end in itself, for Christ is the Teacher and His is the way. For the very purpose of Anthroposophy, Tomberg said, is to be an expedient for going the way to Christ.

Tomberg also said that he had delivered hundreds of lectures in order to make Anthroposophy present as a bridge to the experience of Christ. He himself had crossed this bridge, and others with him. But Goetheanism, eurythmy, speech formation etc., were not the main thing. When he was asked about anthroposophical medicine, agriculture, and education, he replied, "These have to prove themselves, to prove their usefulness."[58]

In a long letter to Bernhard Martin in July 1956, Tomberg described the notion of anthroposophists belonging to a chosen "Michael Community" as a delusion of grandeur. He criticized anthroposophists' proneness to belief in authority, which led them to turn Rudolf Steiner into an infallible "antipope." He also criticized their intellectualization of spirituality, which led to "esoteric imprisonment" in a conceptual system. He spoke critically of "the new mysteries of Anthroposophy"; instead of these, he advocated silent, unpretentious mysteries that neither rule nor preach. For him, the task was to establish personal certainty in one's search for truth, not expatiate on spiritual "science," which already by its very designation represents an "intellectualized supersensible."[59]

In Letter XV of *Meditations*, looking back to his own earlier experience, Tomberg wrote that the German anthroposophists had been too preoccupied with evil, and that such a preoccupation with a spiritual quality or entity can all too easily lead to identification with it. As regards this preoccupation with evil, he wrote:

---

58. "Lebenserfahrung von Dr. Valentin Tomberg," Conversations in Amsterdam (September 3, 1951), in *Valentin Tomberg*, Vol. I.2, 212.
59. Ibid., 272–83.

The Controversies

The result is a lame wisdom without wings, deprived of creative élan, that only repeats and comments to satiety what the master, Dr Rudolf Steiner, said. And yet Rudolf Steiner has certainly said things of a nature to awaken the greatest creative élan! His series of lectures on the four gospels, his lectures at Helsingfors [Helsinki] and Düsseldorf on the celestial hierarchies, without mentioning his book on the inner work leading to initiation (*Knowledge of the Higher Worlds. How is It Achieved?*), would alone suffice to inflame a deep and mature creative enthusiasm in every soul who aspires to authentic experience of the spiritual world. But it is the preoccupation with evil which has clipped the wings of the Anthroposophical Movement and which has rendered it such as it is since the death of its founder: a movement for cultural reform (art, education, medicine, agriculture) deprived of living esotericism, i.e., without mysticism, without gnosis, and without magic, which have been replaced by lectures, study, and intellectual work aimed at establishing a concordance between the writings and stenographed lectures of the master.[60]

In the same Letter, Tomberg warned against any intuition of evil. This could lead, he said, to an association with the essence of evil, because one would then identify with evil. "One can grasp profoundly, i.e., intuitively, only that which one loves," he wrote.[61] Since one cannot love evil, it is unknowable in its essence. One can only perceive it phenomenologically. In another context, Steiner wrote, concerning the development of the feeling of gratitude: "Something I do not love cannot reveal itself to me."[62]

After completing *Meditations*, Tomberg commented further on his work within the Anthroposophical Movement in a letter dated September 28, 1967, written in response to a letter from Willi Seiss, who was on friendly terms with Stefan Lubienski. Seiss had written to Tomberg with regard to his anthroposophical writings from the 1930s. Tomberg answered:

> The Anthroposophical Society or Movement was already then, that is to say in the thirties, an intellectually "overfed" one. Even

---

60. *Meditations*, 402–3.
61. Ibid., 403.
62. *Knowledge of the Higher Worlds.*

then there was a veritable "inflation" of points of view, connections, communications, and advice, the quantity of which was so great that one had neither the time nor the strength to really make use of them: its "study" alone would require almost a lifetime. It was an overloaded Society or Movement. What I did, and what I regret, was to contribute to this overload and to this inflation by publishing the writings and lectures you mentioned. More was added to the excess.

However, I had the intention and the hope of bringing about a focus among the members on the essentials, i.e., inner work in the sense of *Knowledge of the Higher Worlds* and Christology, and to bring the Society back from peripheral activities and interests to the core of true esotericism. However, this has failed. So I regret having tried.

As for the Anthroposophical Society, it no longer exists in the sense intended at the Christmas Conference, namely as a Society rooted in the esoteric and focused on the esoteric. A *corpus mysticum* of the A.S. no longer exists. It is now a question of individual people and their angels, and of what they make personally of the material [the legacy of R. Steiner] on their own path of destiny. The Society is no longer an esoteric unit or entity but merely a "Society" in the same sense, for example, as the Kant Society, which also continues to care for Immanuel Kant's legacy. It is of course good that Rudolf Steiner's legacy not be neglected, for it deserves to be preserved and cared for, and to be lived—that is, as esoteric schooling.

I am not writing this because I assume that you, dear Mr Seiss, have a different opinion, but to say that I regret having made an attempt, similar to that of Julian the Apostate,[63] to bring something to life that was dying.

I wish you every success on your journey.

Yours sincerely, Valentin Tomberg[64]

In the draft of a second letter to Willi Seiss, written on March 9, 1970, but not sent, Tomberg elaborated on the "scientific" claims of

---

63. Flavius Claudius Julianus (AD 331–363) was Roman emperor from 361 to 363, as well as a notable philosopher and author in Greek. His rejection of Christianity, and his promotion of Neoplatonic Hellenism in its place, caused him to be remembered as Julian the Apostate in Christian tradition.

64. *Valentin Tomberg*, Vol. I.2, 474–75.

anthroposophical spiritual science and pointed to a new beginning in his biography, which separated him from his work in the 1930s:

> Most esteemed Mr. Seiss,
>
> Here is a late, but thoughtfully considered, reply to your letter of January 15, 1970, which I have read and pondered very carefully. My main question, and concern, is how I might spare you a costly disappointment. For a disappointment must inevitably follow, were you to journey to Reading to meet me in person. You would not find in me the same person who emerged as the author of the Anthroposophical Studies in the thirties, seeking to reorient spiritual science toward its core—for the simple reason that he is not here any more, he no longer exists.
>
> The author of the Anthroposophical Studies of the Old and New Testaments was a man whose purpose had been to rescue Rudolf Steiner's life-work—spiritual science—from its trivialization and petrification by redirecting it to its core. But the "inner successor" of this same man today is of the opinion that a "spiritual science" is not possible, and never can be—for even if it were brought back to its core, it would only further swell the stream that propels its mill of death, enabling it to grind out yet another batch of "fossilized" intellectual concretions. Furthermore, such a spiritual science was never really possible, because, right from the beginning, it lacked the criteria that define what is meant by "science": universal validity and verifiability.
>
> This being so, if we look more closely at this so-called science of the spirit, we find that with regard to its religious aspect it was in reality a free or personal [*auf eigene Faust*] theology; and with regard to its anthropological and psychological aspects, it was a generalizing of personal depth-psychological experiences. Clearly, then, since these latter are mystical in nature, they can make no claim to being scientific, i.e., universally valid and verifiable.
>
> It follows that, in the final analysis, the convincing power of so-called spiritual science rests, psychologically, upon the trusting compliance of a group of people of particularly like-minded inclination, and, objectively, upon the confidence that group is willing to place in what this spiritual science attests to—that is, in its authority. Now, not even a pope has ever been accorded such authority as has the "spiritual researcher" or "initiate" Rudolf Steiner. For popes advocate on behalf of tradition, with its scores

Valentin Tomberg and the *Ecclesia Universalis*

of witnesses, whereas "spiritual researchers" do not draw upon tradition, but instead bring forth and interpret their own experiences. Regardless of the man Rudolf Steiner's own intentions in this regard as a spiritual researcher, his followers have so elevated his authority as to rival that of the pope. In effect, they have made him into a kind of "antipope." None of this is spiritual science. I do not mean by this, however, that there is not now, and never has been, such a thing as spiritual knowledge. I mean only that spiritual knowledge is not science, but is inner certainty, which is a state that cannot be imposed on others—at least without renouncing the claim to be universally valid and verifiable. For spiritual knowledge is based on personal experience of the most intimate sort. Thus, it can only be shared (if it is shared at all) within an intimate circle of companions brought together by destiny.

This is the spiritual change that has been wrought in the Valentin Tomberg of the thirties. He no longer has any relation to spiritual science. He can no longer see any purpose in it.

You see, most esteemed Mr Seiss, you would not find here the Valentin Tomberg of the thirties. The distance separating me from him today is as great as that between two incarnations.... One might even say that I ought now to be called by another name, although for civil reasons that is not possible. Today, nothing lies further from me, or would exhaust me more, than to be obliged to endure the ashes of the anthroposophical past being stirred up again.

Do please save yourself the shock of disappointment and spare me from discussions about the my earlier "Studies," methods of working, and similar things, which are now so very far from my thoughts. Today my life is prayer and contemplation; that, and only that, is what I live for; not for "study."

Do you understand? asks and prays
Your faithful friend,
Valentin Tomberg[65]

In his book on Lazarus, completed in 1970, Tomberg wrote this incisive remark about Anthroposophy:

---

65. Draft of a letter of Valentin Tomberg to Willi Seiss (March 9, 1970), in *Valentin Tomberg*, Vol. I.2, 522–23.

The Controversies

Unfortunately, as matters turned out (for reasons we need not enter into here) Steiner chose, or was perhaps obliged, to cast his work in the mold of a science—"spiritual science" (*Geisteswissenschaft*)—such that the third aspect of the indivisible ternary of the way, the truth, and the life, namely *life*, could not adequately be provided for. The strictures that the logic of the Logos had to adopt in order to be framed as spiritual science left little room for pure mysticism and spiritual magic: that is, for life.[66]

Tomberg had already explained the reasons for Steiner's spiritual-scientific activity in the Our Father Course:

> During his life, Rudolf Steiner was faced with the choice of either not speaking out on this theme [of spiritual science] but instead being strongly empowered to work magically, or else speaking out but not working magically at all. He felt it important that as many people as possible should be prepared in their thinking, and in other ways, for the coming of Christ in the etheric, and for this reason denied himself the exercise of the white magical power he held under his sway. The measure of this power which he possessed was incalculable—for such a great individual is not often in incarnation. This is the reason why black magic has been able thus far to tip the balance in its favor.[67]

So much, then, for Tomberg's critique of anthroposophists and Anthroposophy. What can we make of it? In some respects he is undoubtedly on the mark; in other respects his critique has only partial validity because it was expressed from a one-sided perspective at a particular historical moment.

In order to better understand the position Tomberg came to regarding Anthroposophy, it will be helpful to lay some further groundwork. To begin with, Steiner had expected his pupils to become "spiritual scientists" through their inner development. He had hoped that such collaborative inner work would begin to manifest after the Christmas conference of 1923. But nine months later, Steiner had to conclude that this had not happened, and that the

---

66. *Lazarus: The Miracle of Resurrection in World History*, 123.
67. Our Father Course, weeks 38–39.

conference had therefore failed.[68] This did not mean, however, that the impulse for cultural renewal that he had brought totally disappeared from the face of the earth! When Tomberg had published his Studies of the Old Testament in 1933, he had still expected to find fellow spiritual researchers within the School of Spiritual Science. This is unmistakably clear from his introductory words to that volume, which we have already cited:

> Anthroposophy as it lies before us in Rudolf Steiner's writings and printed lecture cycles is in itself not actual, concrete esotericism. It becomes so only in the soul of those who not only acknowledge its truths, but are also able to discern them. Concrete esotericism is present only in the company of living esotericists. Otherwise it becomes merely anthroposophically-directed religious, philosophic, scientific, or aesthetic convictions.[69]

For Tomberg, then, spiritual science does not mean picking out quotations from the complete edition of Steiner's work and placing them in this or that context. Actual spiritual science only begins when, after examining and reflecting upon such contents, we resolve to commence our own spiritual research. Those who merely quote Rudolf Steiner's statements without examining them "with their common sense," and without making an effort to expand these contents through their own inner schooling, are in effect treating Steiner as an infallible authority—as an "antipope," as Tomberg several times put it.

In 1970, Tomberg was of the opinion that there is, and can be, no "spiritual science." He gave two arguments for this. First, he stated that such a project is "inevitably intellectually schematized." This seems to imply that, for Tomberg, "scientific" thought by its very nature does not lend itself to being spiritualized. But is this really so? Is spiritualization of the results of "intellectual research" impossible in principle? Is it really fair to say that such a spiritual transformation of the rational aspect of the intellect has proven impossible for *all* anthroposophists? Is this view perhaps not itself overly schema-

---

68. Gerhard von Beckerath, *Der Leidensweg Rudolf Steiners* (Dornach: Verlag für Anthroposophie, 2011), 227–29.
69. *Christ and Sophia*, 3, revised translation.

The Controversies

tized? Perhaps, rather than an "either-or," Tomberg's approach to knowledge represents a *complement* to what Steiner himself (regardless whether or not this was taken up successfully by many of those who associated themselves with his work) presented as *one aspect* of a broader perspective on paths of cognition, a perspective that—owing to his disappointment in the members (and perhaps also his premature death)—prevented him from further describing. Surely it cannot be said of Rudolf Steiner that he worked with dead, intellectual concepts! His thinking was alive and connected to the heart. Does not Steiner's recurring appeal to our need (indeed, our spiritual responsibility) to develop our higher thinking to the point of union with the love and wisdom of our heart run like a scarlet thread throughout his vast work of some 350 volumes? Did he not tirelessly repeat the universal maxim of all spiritual schools that "we only know what we love"? Without doubt, many of Steiner's students, despite their best efforts, did turn aspects of Anthroposophy into "intellectual schemes." But this only means that they cannot *yet* be called "spiritual scientists" in the full and proper sense (the sense Steiner himself trenchantly expressed in the statement that, for such a spiritual science, "the laboratory table must become an altar"). *True* spiritual science arises from the union of the *transformed* intellectual thinking of the head with the loving, moral thinking of the heart, i.e., through the *spiritualization of intelligence*. In his earlier work, Tomberg himself was perhaps even the most eloquent expositor of *precisely* this insight! Perhaps some biographical factors may help us contextualize and better understand the development of these views. A few such factors suggest themselves.

Tomberg apparently did not actually encounter any "Aristotelian" anthroposophists who had as yet advanced as far as he might have hoped on the path of spiritualizing their thinking in the sense described above. We do know that Steiner felt this way. Had Tomberg's life-destiny been different, though, he might have experienced this capacity in such pivotal anthroposophical "spiritual thinkers" as Ita Wegman, Karl König, Willem Zeylmans, and Ehrenfried Pfeiffer. In our time also there are incontestably some among the "Aristotelian" types who *do* develop new inner capacities and who *do* spiritualize their intellect to one degree or another—alone or in communities of researchers. That such matters are not so often spoken about publicly is, after all, not surprising, given their more intimate nature. It is *our* task to recognize such individuals and their work—which requires of *us* the selfsame efforts toward the spiritualization of *our* thinking that we claim to be looking for in *others*. Perhaps we read a book, or hear a lecture, or engage in a conversation, and intuit a spiritual depth, a new insight, which we suddenly recognize to be just such spiritualized thinking. In truth, to be such a researcher *already* presupposes some level of inspiration by spiritual beings—and this fact alone can speak to us, even if initially as no more than a "sixth sense."

As to Tomberg's second argument for his view that there can be no spiritual science, he stated that spiritual science cannot be a science because its results are not "verifiable and universally valid." In so doing, he judged spiritual science according to the criteria of natural science. Tomberg seems here to have lost sight of the fact that, according to Steiner's *intended* meaning, spiritual science has its *own* criterion of "scientificity"—differing from that of the "universal validity" Tomberg repeatedly invoked in his criticisms—and can only be practiced by researchers who develop the requisite *inner* capacities by following a path of spiritual development appropriate to our own time (such as Steiner developed in numerous books). By working together, such researchers can test each other's research results, even though these results may have come *originally* through unique inner intuition (results, that is, at the antipodes of what is universally valid and thus always identical). Admittedly, this is an entirely *new* kind of science, of which not many scientists are capable at present. One can even wonder whether a better expression for such a science might have been chosen.

Significantly, the English rendering "spiritual science" does not in fact adequately convey the sense of the German original *Geisteswissenschaft*, which, outside the specifically anthroposophical context, would more likely be translated as "study of what is of the mind or spirit." *Geist* can mean mind, intellect, or spirit (with further nuances as well), so it almost begs the question to settle on the one rendering "spiritual science" as a point of contention. The fact that modern natural science leads to universally verifiable results is a

The Controversies

worthy and necessary achievement in its own "Aristotelian" domain. If Tomberg came to regard this as the sole sense of what Steiner intended by the term *Geisteswissenschaft*, he may himself have been adopting a one-sided view of science. Yes, such "Aristotelian" science does work within time-bound paradigms that dictate how research is done to continually test, confirm, and verify unproven hypotheses. But that is not what "spiritual science" in Steiner's sense is intended to signify.

Spiritual science is a *new* achievement. It is based on a spiritual, living thinking that encompasses *all* levels of reality—not only the world of "matter" which science (as usually understood) studies, but also the worlds of life, of consciousness, and of self-consciousness or spirit. According to Steiner's panoramic view, when in the future more people will have developed this kind of thinking, what he intended spiritual science to be will quite naturally come to be recognized as a *further development* of science.

According to Steiner, there are two more fundamental criteria for the scientific character of Anthroposophy: the statements of Anthroposophy must lend support to each other, and they must lead to practical results. And here we must correct a prevalent, one-sidedly optimistic view of spiritual science. Steiner cautioned that spiritual researchers can make mistakes too, especially if they investigate only a limited number of the aspects of the object of their investigation.[70] Spiritual-scientific knowledge is, therefore, always provisional and subject to correctives and new perspectives.

It seems to us that Tomberg may contrast natural science and spiritual science in too absolute a way. His assertion that "there can be no spiritual science," and his consequent lack of confidence in the prospects for its development, may have its background in the cognitive crisis he himself experienced in the 1950s, when he realized that he could only have *personal certainty* about *his* spiritual research, and could not claim "universal validity and verifiability" for it. Interestingly, in the 1930s he had been an inspired spiritual researcher who assuredly *did* seem quite certain of the research he

---

70. In the preface of his book *Cosmic Memory*, Steiner expressly disclaimed infallibility for his spiritual research.

was presenting in his first books! But after 1943 this changed. As mentioned in Part I, Stefan Lubienski even suggested, in a conversation with Dieter Brüll quoted earlier, that Tomberg may have in the meanwhile suffered some alteration in the nature of his contemplative consciousness. After 1950, the spiritual world appears to have spoken to Tomberg in the language of symbols—a language, significantly, that *cannot* be made the subject of science in the usual sense, because, by their very nature, symbols elude definitive interpretation. It is a science of the spiritual dimensions of reality. The symbols of depth psychology, for instance, or more generally of mythology and Hermeticism, are susceptible of ever higher levels of understanding. Of course, this applies also to the *Secret Figures of the Rosicrucians* of the sixteenth and seventeenth centuries, and perhaps most of all to the images depicted on the cards of the Tarot.

By contrast, Anthroposophy investigates not only symbols, but also facts (such as karmic connections), spiritual forces, and beings in the spiritual world. Researchers who have developed "spiritual" or "clairvoyant" abilities (this latter understood literally, as "clear seeing," and not in mediumistic sense the term has unfortunately acquired since the late nineteenth century) should, in principle, arrive at the same result in the case of such connections, of which, then, one or another researcher may continue to discover new aspects.

Discussion about the scientificity of spiritual science can help us understand that we must draw distinctions as between scientific knowledge, intellectually-schematized spiritual knowledge (gained from books), personal spiritual knowledge (gained from our own spiritual experience), and spiritual-scientific knowledge such as may arise when head and heart (that is, when knowledge and wisdom, or "Aristotelian" intellectuality and "Platonic" spirituality are combined).

The fact that precious little authentic spiritual research has as yet been forthcoming in the Anthroposophical Movement may have something to do, not only with the fact that most would-be researchers have not yet been able to adequately develop the requisite faculties, but also with the fact that even though there was a renewed opening up of the spiritual world with the commencement of the Age of the Archangel Michael in 1879, nonetheless, for other reasons, access to it since then seems to have grown increasingly difficult.[71] Perhaps the failure of the Christmas Conference of 1923 and the conflicts in the Anthroposophical Society played a role in obscuring the spiritual atmosphere. When such an important spiritual impulse as that of the Christmas Conference of 1923 is not taken up, it may well be that a "vacuum" is created into which negative beings then rush. Further obscurations of the spiritual world were certainly also set in motion with the seizure of power by the National Socialists, the Second World War generally, the spread of radioactivity, the increasing generation of electromagnetic radiation, and, in recent decades, the formation of the electronic "worldwide web" around the earth.[72] According to their own testimony, when people today develop some degree of spiritual sight or clairvoyance, it often leads first to a "chaotic" perception of images.

A final, critical point is Tomberg's view that Anthroposophy lacks life. It is true that, compared to later and current developments, there was only a modest degree of "living" activity in the practical areas of Anthroposophy up until the 1970s—the time of Tomberg's death. But even so, it is evident that this is not what Tomberg meant by saying that Anthroposophy "lacks life." As we have seen, it was because Steiner developed a spiritual "science," Tomberg wrote, that the aspect of "life" in the Anthroposophical Movement had come close to a standstill. There was no longer room for pure mysticism and spiritual magic—that is, precisely, for "life." As he put it, "sacred magic is that life which was before the Fall.... It is connected to the Tree of Life.[73] But from another point of view, Tomberg's Hermetic idea of life cannot really be so readily applied

---

71. Steiner himself was aware of the problem. He remarked that all too often people no longer have the strength to bring the spiritual to manifestation in physical life. For example, food plants are in a state of degeneration, making it necessary to cultivate new ones. See Paul Emberson, *The Death of Nutrition* (Tobermory: The Etheric Dimensions Press, 2019), 43–59.

72. The sheer enormity of these factors is described with disturbing eloquence in Arthur Firstenberg's *The Invisible Rainbow: A History of Electricity and Life* (Santa Fe, NM: Chelsea Green Publishing, 2020).

73. *Meditations*, Letter III (The Empress).

to Anthroposophy, which has its own "mysticism" (e.g., in meditation, working with the weekly verses of Steiner's *Calendar of the Soul*, and other such verses), and its own "magic" (e.g., in the making and use of medicines, and in working with preparations in biodynamic agriculture).

It is striking that Tomberg's critique of anthroposophists and of Anthroposophy, which can be found in *Meditations* and in *Lazarus*, had come to be noticeably "misaligned" or even of questionable relevance in its *actual* contemporary context. It would be more accurate to say that his assessment illustrates his *own* conflicts at the hands of the self-styled leadership of the Anthroposophical Society as it was during the first half of his life—with which it appears he was struggling still at the end of his life. Quite naturally, it was precisely upon these points of conflict and criticism that he was aggressively engaged by later anthroposophists.

If we keep an open mind, the controversies surrounding Valentin Tomberg can offer us much insight into the failures of the Anthroposophical Society during his lifetime, failures which did indeed occur and did indeed impede what he and many others regarded as the depth of the further contribution he could have made, based on his truly astonishing early work. In the 1930s, most Board members of the Society did seem focused almost exclusively on "preserving" Anthroposophy in the state Steiner left it at the time of his untimely death. They were not open to new spiritual research. The Anthroposophical Society never recognized anyone as the bodhisattva Steiner had said would manifest in the 1930s. At least, it certainly could not accept that this expected successor had worked, or been manifested, in Tomberg.

Furthermore, we can certainly not fail to consider that Tomberg himself may not have been so entirely innocent of these controversies as some who are more partisan-minded would insist. Might he actually have been in some ways vain and ambitious in the thirties, as Marie Steiner alleged (she had said the same of Ita Wegman and Elisabeth Vreede)? After all, even his close friend Stefan Lubienski spoke of Tomberg's pride. Moreover, during his anthroposophical period, Tomberg was apparently not very skilled at dealing with others, as an example will show. In 1938, while traveling back together by boat from a conference in Bangor, Ernst Lehrs complained to Tomberg that he had been unable to sleep because of engine noise, to which the latter replied: "He who carries Christ in his heart cannot be troubled by noise."[74] Surely not the best social hygiene!

Regardless whether Marie Steiner was right or wrong in her assessment, Tomberg's life assuredly proved to be a schooling in humility, the very opposite of pride, as his field of activity diminished further and further after 1940. As early as 1935, he had himself described the path of humility and humiliation, and in particular how the experience of the silence of the spiritual world was necessary for Russians to let their pride die and to open space for the structure of their *manas* (higher self) to mature sufficiently to receive revelations.

Some Dutch anthroposophists from Zeylmans' circle who met Tomberg in the 1930s also remarked on what they perceived as challenging personality traits. The educationalist Max Stibbe found Tomberg's work too schematic. According to Tom Jurriaanse, in whose home Tomberg held a course, his judgments became noticeably black-and-white after the outbreak of World War II in September 1939—that is, he presented his views in such a way that the course participants felt some pressure to agree with him. The general feeling in Zeylmans' circle was that, after 1940, Tomberg had in some sense lost his way.[75] Zeylmans later told British anthroposophist Owen Barfield that Tomberg had worked in a rather destructive way in the Dutch Anthroposophical Movement, that he had attracted a special group who considered him their teacher.[76]

In the Netherlands, Tomberg had taken the decision, considered imprudent by most, to speak of his own and of others' previous incarnations (even if they may have been meant primarily as "analogies") and to form a group that separated itself from others. The

---

74. Communication to Robert Powell from J.E. de Groot (September 23, 1985).

75. Communication from J.E. de Groot based on his conversations with them in 1985 and 1994.

76. Report from priest Oliver Mathews, *Priesterrundbrief* nr. 328 (December 1977), Central Archive of the Christian Community, Berlin, file 6.1.

humanly-warm character of his group work did certainly set it apart markedly from what was more characteristic in anthroposophical circles at the time. Several in his circle followed him also in religious matters, as is shown by their conversion to the Orthodox Church, and in some cases later to the Catholic Church. In retrospect, Wolfgang Garvelmann described Tomberg's effect on others as one of considerable suggestive power.[77]

Tomberg's actual awareness of the more practical areas of Anthroposophy (including the Christian Community) was in fact very limited, and his judgments about them could undoubtedly be seen as one-sidedly negative and unfair. He could no longer acknowledge Anthroposophy as a spiritual science in the way he had done in the 1930s; and after what we feel we have identified as a kind of cognitive crisis, he limited himself in his *Meditations* to the interpretation of symbols and the description of the Christian-Hermetic initiatory path. His deep connection with traditional Catholicism remained a mystery to anthroposophists, including his friend Lubienski. Interestingly, no controversy arose, however, around Tomberg's vision of the second coming of Christ.

In his later activity as Hermetic philosopher, Tomberg did not speak of the second coming of Christ in the twentieth century. This had not yet become visible in nature, as he had originally thought. Rudolf Steiner's description of the second coming of Christ, who would appear to humanity as a comforter, counselor, and helper (which he gave on October 1, 1911, in his lecture on "The Etherization of the Blood") has, on the other hand, been confirmed many times since 1933.[78] Tomberg must have known this lecture, because it appeared in 1932. Nonetheless, the number of people who have perceived Christ with their natural etheric clairvoyance seems to have been smaller than Steiner had anticipated.

---

77. Communication to the author (July 23, 2001).

78. Rudolf Steiner, "The Etherization of the Blood," lecture of October 1, 1911, in Rudolf Steiner, *Esoteric Christianity* (CW 130). Gunnar Hillerdal and Berndt Gustafsson, *We Experienced Christ* (Forest Row, UK: Temple Lodge Publishing, 2016); Rolf Tschanz (ed.), *Vom Christus-Wirken der Gegenwart* (Dornach: Verlag am Goetheanum, 1991); Anton Kimpfler, *Ankunft und Wiederkehr des Christus* (Dornach: Verlag am Goetheanum, 2001).

The Controversies

Time Spirits of the Cultural Epochs

What Steiner called the fifth cultural epoch (which began in 1413) is the period during which the consciousness soul is to develop. The task of the Anthroposophical Movement was meant to be that of promoting this development spiritually in preparation for the next cultural epoch, which he called the Slavic. According to Steiner, each such cultural epoch lasts 2160 years,[79] and has its own inspiring time spirit. This temporal rhythm is further subdivided into a sequence of seven shorter "archangelic" periods, or rulerships, of about 354 years each, of which the present Michael rulership (which began in 1879) is one. When one cultural epoch succeeds another, the after-effects of the preceding epoch persist through approximately the first third of the succeeding one. This means that the fourth, or Greco-Roman, epoch, continues to influence our own fifth, or European, epoch until approximately 2133 (1413 + 720). From *another* point of view, however, the third, or Egypto-Chaldean cultural epoch, is *mirrored* in our fifth epoch. This is because there are in total seven such cultural epochs, of which the first three mirror the last three along the mediating axis or reflective plane passing through the central, fourth epoch. Thus, in our present fifth cultural epoch, the third cultural epoch is mirrored—i.e., is gradually reappearing, reawakening, or, in the end, being resurrected in reverse sequence (at a higher level) in a metamorphosed, Christianized form.

On June 12, 1910, Steiner described how, in the epoch of the consciousness soul, a separate Christian time spirit is also at work, *apart* from its own "proper" time spirit. This other, separate time spirit was formerly the time spirit of the Greek epoch, which, after having fulfilled that mission, became in turn the spirit of ecclesial Christianity, and, as such, is linked to the archangel of Roman culture. Furthermore, within this constellation also (as mentioned earlier in connection with the cosmic law of a central mediating axis or reflective plane), the time spirit of the epoch of ancient Egypt is also

---

79. That is, one-twelfth of the well-known Platonic Year of 25,920 years, itself based on the astronomical phenomenon of the precession of the equinoxes.

Valentin Tomberg and the *Ecclesia Universalis*

at work. Thus we have what Steiner called a *trifolium* or "cloverleaf" made up of the simultaneous collaboration of the time spirits of the third, the fourth, and the fifth cultural epochs.[80] To a great extent, then, forces from the past still determine the spiritual life of the present, and in a quite complex array.

Now, it is possible to consider the particular character or stamp of Tomberg's life and work as bearing the signature, quite precisely, of the inspirations of the three time spirits just mentioned. Thus, from 1920, we see Tomberg as working with the inspirations of the time spirit of the present, *fifth*, culture epoch, in which the consciousness soul develops. Immediately after World War II, however, we find him holding the view that the development of the consciousness soul and its attendant free "I" had failed. It seems premature to this author, however, to speak of such a *definitive* failure of the core mission (that of the consciousness soul and the free "I") of our fifth epoch. After all, the two-millennia-long development of this epoch only began in the fifteenth century, and will endure for many more centuries to come.

It was in the spiritual darkness of WWII that Tomberg "built his ark." For him, the rock of the "I" and of the consciousness soul had receded amid the horrific events of the war, and so he sought another rock, one that could resist the unleashed forces of evil. This rock he found in the Catholic Church. In taking the step of entering the Church he was, in effect, allying himself with a force hailing from the *fourth* cultural epoch. In Letter XI of *Meditations* he wrote that the experiences of the Hermetic way prove "that the Roman Catholic Church is in fact a depository of Christian spiritual truth," adding that its teaching on "the three monastic vows of obedience, chastity, and poverty constitute the very essence of every authentic spirituality."[81] Tomberg had in fact already elaborated these vows in the early 1940s as exercises for the development of the consciousness soul in his Our Father Course.

With his turn to the Church of Rome, as also his "Hermetic" interpretation of papal infallibility (which is rejected by the Ortho-

---

80. *The Mission of Folk Souls* (CW 121).
81. *Meditations*, 281.

The Controversies

dox Church), Tomberg distanced himself from the Orthodox Church, although he did not formally choose to leave it when he turned to the Roman Catholic Church, even though as far as we know he did not concern himself, at least personally, with the Orthodox Church after 1942. In *Meditations* he refers for the most part to theologians of early Christianity, with few allusions to the Orthodox tradition *per se*.

Whereas Tomberg the jurist turned to the religious-moral order of the Middle Ages, Tomberg the Hermetic philosopher turned to a tradition hailing from the *third* cultural epoch. Thus, the anthroposophical researcher Tomberg became, in turn, a conservative Christian, a jurist, and an Hermetic philosopher. Such a "return" to the undoubted sources of our own cultural epoch can surely have a healing effect, but only if *at the same time* it transforms otherwise inhibiting forces from the past in such a way as to "make room" again for the free unfolding of the "I," which had been a casualty of the forces of opposition that lay behind National Socialism and Bolshevism. It is important to emphasize in this connection that Tomberg remained an *independent* esoteric researcher in his Hermetic work and in his esoteric meditations, even while he was seeking to revive the Roman Church "in the service of" the Church of John. The Tarot symbols that he interpreted in *Meditations* arose from a culture based on hierarchical structures, the same structures encountered in Hermeticism as an earthly reflection of the angelic hierarchies. The symbols of the Emperor and the Pope lead back to the Egyptian Pharaoh and High Priest. What Tomberg wrote about the importance of the principle of authority in society and about the infallibility of the pope are like "echoes" from ancient Egypt. In Letter V of *Meditations* Tomberg writes trenchantly about the significance of the hierarchical order:

> The impulse of freedom—of hope in emancipated man—has built up and demolished a great deal. It has created a materialistic civilization without parallel, but at the same time it has destroyed the hierarchical order—the order of spiritual obedience. A series of religious, political, and social revolutions has ensued.
>
> But the hierarchical order is eternal, and obedience is indispensable. Now, new hierarchical orders are beginning to be estab-

lished, replacing obedience by tyranny and dictatorship. For he who sows the wind reaps the whirlwind ... this is a truth that we are learning with so much suffering today.[82]

In these words we stand witness to the great drama of the age of the consciousness soul. The impulse towards freedom, which emerged at the end of the Middle Ages from the awakening of the human individual, calls into question the hierarchical order in society. It is, any longer, only in *spiritual life* that a hierarchical order still makes sense today, because people differ markedly in respect of their consciousness, talents, and abilities, even as do master and pupil. The old social order can no longer determine the whole of society, as was the case in the Middle Ages. Power at the top of society has become decadent and corrupted by scandals. Today, power must be vested in the whole of society, empowering the people. Beneficent spiritual powers have tried to guide this democratic development, but decadent forces from the past have wrought chaos and established its inverse: a new coercive rule. With the rise of Communism, National Socialism, Fascism, and Technocracy, the development of the "I" was thus, if not aborted, at least significantly disrupted.

The ancient social order was formed as a pyramid, with an initiated priest or priest-king at its pinnacle. In the Middle Ages there emerged the hierarchical order of the three estates: clergy, nobility, and peasants. Over the ensuing centuries the exercise of power shifted from the religious elite, by way of the political "one percent," to an economic elite, so that today it is the financial elite who sit atop the modern iteration of a pyramid. Behind the great cultural, political, and economic institutions of our time we may discern the recurrence of hierarchical structures of Egypt or Rome—but out of step now, and unsuited to properly govern humanity and guide the development of the consciousness soul and the free "I."

With the vision of a threefold society formulated by Rudolf Steiner in 1917, the conditions can be created for each and every person to become active in all three fields of social life (culture, politics,

---

82. Ibid., 119.

and economy). In the cultural sphere, all should be able to freely develop their talents and their inner life. In the political sphere, all should have equal rights and be able to shape the social order together with others. In the economic sphere, all should be willing to work for all in solidarity. This social triad still awaits its realization as the way to a Christian social order for our epoch of the consciousness soul.

The earlier and still all-too-present pyramids of power must be transformed by the further development of "I"-consciousness. Only thus can the pyramid become "individualized." Looked at in this way, the individual human being can be understood symbolically as a pyramid, i.e., as a conscious connector of earth and sky, of matter and spirit. But to overcome the outdated Egyptian-Roman social order that has gained a foothold "atavistically" in our time, each of us, in our "I"-development, must become our own "pope" (keeper of the keys to the spiritual world), our own "emperor" (executor of political power), and our own *eco-nomos* (economic decision-maker).

On the threshold of the development of the consciousness soul stood the great Italian poet Dante Alighieri (1265–1321). In lines 140–142 of the twentieth-seventh canto of his *Purgatorio*, Dante's guide Virgil bids him farewell, raising to awareness, as Mario Betti has noted,[83] two aspects of the new consciousness soul (the "inner imperium" and the "inner papacy"):

Libero, dritto e sano è tuo arbitrio,
e fallo fora non fare a suo senno:
per ch'io te sopra te corono e mitrio.

Free and upright and sound is thy free-will,
And error were it not to do its bidding;
Thee o'er thyself I therefore crown and mitre![84]

German Dante expert Karl Vossler translated these lines in 1942 as "Be your own Emperor and Pope." *This is the voice of the free human being.*

---

83. Mario Betti, "Dante Alighieri und die Bewusstseinsseele," in *Das Goetheanum* (August 30, 1992).
84. Longfellow translation.

Valentin Tomberg and the *Ecclesia Universalis*

When the symbols of the Emperor (the Pharaoh) and the Pope (the High Priest)—the male archetypes of political and spiritual power—are thus directly related to our *personal* lives, the defence of a hierarchical order for *society* is no longer a necessity for Hermetic philosophy. For the transformation of this order by the free "I" then becomes possible. Tomberg's traditional Catholic comments do not belong to the essence of Tarot symbolism either. For Tomberg, the return to the past was an emergency measure to salvage European culture in what he saw as a stop-gap, hopeless situation. Our *actual* future, however, depends on the *further* development of the "I." With his Tarot book, which was set up as a system of spiritual exercises for the *individual* (the "Unknown Friend") as a path of initiation, Tomberg hoped to contribute to this.

We can find and develop within ourselves the qualities of the symbols of the Emperor and the Pope, as well as the qualities of the symbols of the other Tarot cards. This is the path of "transformation, transubstantiation, and transmutation of human consciousness," the path of the reunion of the "true self" with the "lower self," of the "image of God" with the "likeness of God," as Tomberg explains in Letter XVI. It is the path of Rosicrucian initiation, and, as C.G. Jung called it, the process of individuation.

With his Tarot book, Tomberg gave a new Christian direction to French Hermeticism. For many years the book did not have a noticeable influence in the Catholic Church (there is, however, a photo of Pope John Paul II showing on his desk the Herder edition of *Meditations*, for which Catholic theologian Hans Urs von Balthasar wrote an introduction). But that seems now to be changing. More and more contemporary Catholics have come to give credence to Tomberg's view that the Church needs the esoteric "dimension of depth" to keep stimulating its psychic and spiritual development. After all, ever since the close of the Middle Ages we have lived in the epoch of the consciousness soul, the epoch in which our becoming free persons is the theme. Both Tomberg's articles and writings from his anthroposophical days, and the wisdom of his *Meditations* and later works, can *support* the development of the consciousness soul.

The Controversies

⊕

Meditations amounts to a school of Christian-Hermetic Platonism in which we can develop our imaginative, inspirative, and intuitive consciousness. Intuition comes from the intimate and profound union of "reason and spontaneous wisdom" (Letter XIX). This school aims at the transformation of the soul into "Sophia," so that, through Her, we may be born into a spiritual, Christ-connected higher consciousness. Tomberg developed his own Sophia doctrine, which bore some relation to Russian Sophianic teaching. For these reasons, *Meditations* can be considered a "Sophianic" book. It has a Sophia quality, as Günter Röschert noted in a review.[85]

Yet another perspective opens up if we consider Tomberg's work in relation to the four mystery currents described by Dutch anthroposophist Bernard Lievegoed.[86] Seen in this light, we may say that *Meditations* has its source in the southern mystery stream—that is, the Rosicrucian stream from the Egyptian and Jewish cultural area, which came to Europe by way of Rome. This stream bears the impulse of the transformation of the physical body into the "spirit-man" or *atman* (the spiritualized physical body). These are the mysteries of death and the resurrection body. From this stream arose the Hermetic tradition (alchemy, astrology, gnosis, magic, kabbalah), the Church, and Roman law.

In accord with the reflective law, or inverse mirroring, associated with the seven cultural epochs mentioned earlier, we may say that, in conformity with this law, Egyptian culture (the third epoch) rises up again in our present (fifth) epoch of the consciousness soul, where it must be transformed, which means to say "brought into connection with the Christ impulse of love." In Tomberg's view, little had been achieved of this transformation in Anthroposophy (which remained so strongly associated with Greek culture), and so he undertook to devote himself to working toward furthering this necessary transformation. The *Emerald Tablet* of Egyptian Hermeti-

---

85. Günter Röschert, "Hermetische Philosophie—zum Spätwerk Valentin Tombergs über den Tarot," in *Die Drei* (4/2004).

86. Bernard C.J. Lievegoed, *Mystery Streams in Europe and the New Mysteries* (Hudson: SteinerBooks, 1982).

cism summarized for him the wisdom (*gnosis*) of antiquity regarding the spiritual development of humanity ("the power of growth and evolution"). He saw the Major Arcana of the Tarot as the second, or late medieval, compendium of meditations on the *Emerald Tablet*. In our time, however, according to Tomberg, Hermeticists must work on yet another, a third, compendium of this wisdom, in order that "the essence of modern wisdom might be saved again from the coming Flood"—this time, however, in a "spiritual" Noah's ark (Letter XVII).[87] Tomberg regarded *Meditations* as a contribution toward this end.

The original *Emerald Tablet* summarized the Hermetic wisdom of the age of the *sentient soul* (the aspect of the soul that lives in the senses), which flourished in ancient Egypt. In later time, the Major Arcana of the Tarot came to embody the transformed Hermetic wisdom of the age of the *rational soul*. In our time, France has been the country particularly associated with the development of the rational soul, and so it was no coincidence that a tradition of French Hermeticism arose there. The third stage—the "ark" just mentioned—was to be a new summary on the level of the *consciousness soul*.

In some respects, however, Tomberg's contribution to this cultural project, especially after the major disruptions on all levels brought about by totalitarianism in the course of two world wars, remained at least partially rooted in the age of the rational soul. This insight can help us better "situate" his conservatism; for as a result, Tomberg made place in his thinking, then, for consideration of the traditional hierarchical structures that had their origins in Egypt and Rome. From the perspective of Anthroposophy, however, precisely these hierarchical structures must be *transformed* in our time, so that, in a free spiritual life, those with greater talents become *servants* of those with lesser. In ancient cultures, the initiates, who were responsible for the social order, considered this service *their* task. But now, in the age of the consciousness soul, we are all meant to achieve the capacity to set about freely creating a new social order *together* out of the power of our own inner "imperial" (or Emperor)

---

87. This spiritual "ark" had been presented by Tomberg twenty-five years before in what proved to be the final weekly meeting of the Our Father Course.

The Controversies

dignity, and likewise freely confronting the powers of evil out of the power of our own inner "papal" (or High Priest) dignity.

Tomberg's Hermetic approach to papal infallibility is, we could say, yet another echo of the past. The Holy Spirit, the Spirit of Truth, must become active in the *individual*. And so, to our mind, his critique of anthroposophists and Anthroposophy in *Meditations* does not really fit into a book concerned with the renewal of the Hermetic tradition. But we can turn this critique around in a positive direction if we come to an awareness that Anthroposophy, as a movement from the below to the above, from the earth to the spiritual world (in contradistinction to earlier hierarchical structures), needs a second, *corresponding* movement from the above to the below to come toward it from the spiritual world. At work in this latter movement from above to below is a stream of *revelation* which in earlier times had actually *created* culture and religion. In our day, however, this stream is carried by spiritual beings who can *only* offer their help to *spiritually-awakened* humanity. In this stream, Sophia meets us as Anthropos-Sophia, who expects us, by purifying our own souls, to open ourselves to this stream.

Anthroposophy is a project of many centuries. On its first outing it ran up against insuperable obstacles, which, it seems, Tomberg undertook to diagnose and try to remedy. In the first half of his life, he offered his help as a Platonist. In the second half of his life, he sought to renew the revelatory current of the old Hermeticism and thereby to open up space in the soul of the reader of his *Meditations* for the Divine Wisdom, for Sophia. That such work provoked controversy was surely inevitable!

The next chapter undertakes to shed light on the development of the "Platonic" and "Aristotelian" streams within which Tomberg's life-destiny ran its course. It paints a picture of the great project of joining spirituality and intellectuality together in a new mystery culture that, in the present epoch of the consciousness soul, and under the guidance of the Archangel Michael, works to spiritualize our intellectual capacity. Tomberg participated in this project also. He did so in one way during his anthroposophical period, and in another way during his Hermetic period. This is what he was born for; this is what he remained faithful to.

7

Valentin Tomberg and the New Spiritual Thinking

On one occasion, Eva Cliteur had on her mind to ask Valentin Tomberg whether he considered himself an Aristotelian or a Platonist. Tomberg sensed what she was about to ask and said, "I am a Platonist."[1] According to this report, Tomberg's life may be contextualized as running its course within the twofold framework of a major spiritual-scientific movement. More particularly, the field of his activity was framed by the need for *cooperation* between Aristotelians and Platonists, or, put another way, between representatives of the Michaelic stream of knowledge and the Sophianic stream of revelation—which according to Rudolf Steiner would have to be realized by the end of the twentieth century in order that the foundations for a renewed spiritual culture might be laid. These two streams, Steiner said, had hitherto flowed in relative independence of each other down the centuries, but had, through preparations made in the spiritual world, made provision to actively cooperate also on earth. Tomberg's work in the Anthroposophical Society serves as a good gauge of just how difficult this cooperation proved to be on its first round.

Platonists and Aristotelians

The Greek philosopher Plato (c. 427–c. 347 BC) and his pupil Aristo-

---

1. Communication from Eva Cliteur to Robert Powell. In Robert Powell and Keith Harris, "The Transition," included in Claudia McLaren Lainson, *The Circle of Twelve and the Legacy of Valentin Tomberg* (Boulder, CO: WindRose Academy Press, 2021), 427–65.

tle (384–322 BC) stand at the headwaters of two philosophical streams that differ fundamentally from each other. Plato held the view that "above" or "behind" the things of the sense world stand ideas that represent their archetype—for example the idea "human being" or the idea "horse." Aristotle believed that these ideas do not manifest themselves in another world, but rather exist as principles of form "in" things. Plato regarded the sense world as a means of reascent to "the above," to the "world of ideas." By contrast, for Aristotle, ideas were a means to better penetrate the sensory world as it presented right before him "here below."

The two methods of knowledge that emerged from this contrast are not mutually exclusive, of course, but complementary. In the Platonic tradition, it is said, thinking is more pictorial; in the Aristotelian tradition, more conceptional. What should we understand by that? Platonists aim to increasingly enlighten their thinking spiritually, starting from *doxa* (mere opinion) and progressing by way of *dianoia* (reasoning intellect) to *episteme* (contemplation of the essence). Thus enlightened, the thinking process is able, then, to render the true spiritual essence of things in pure and unadulterated form. Aristotelians, on the other hand, aim with their exact sensory perception (empiricism) and clearly-defined concepts conforming to its own laws (logic), to better grasp individual earthly things and their overarching coherence, i.e., their "lawfulness."[2]

Plato founded a philosophical academy in Athens in 387 BC, where Aristotle came to study. With some interruptions, his academy existed until the seventh century. From 335 BC, Aristotle taught in his own school, the Lyceum, which had more the character of a scientific research institute. The great conqueror Alexander the Great (356–323 BC) spread Aristotle's teachings throughout his vast empire. Over the centuries, other academies came to be founded, in such places as Alexandria in Egypt, Antioch, Nisibis, and Edessa in the Near East. There, Greek philosophy, Christian theology, medicine, and other sciences were studied.

---

2. Mario Betti, *Platonismus-Aristotelismus* (Stuttgart: Mellinger Verlag, 2003), 25–26.

Valentin Tomberg and the New Spiritual Thinking

In speaking of the cooperation of the Platonists and Aristotelians, we are, in truth, directing our attention to the future of *intelligence itself*. According to Steiner, until the end of the Middle Ages the Archangel Michael was custodian of what he called the "cosmic intelligence." How can this be understood? Cosmic intelligence produces cosmic thoughts. More exactly, cosmic thoughts emanate from spiritual beings, or "intelligences," who generate these thoughts and are their purveyors. As the "spirit of the sun" and leader of the "solar intelligence" (consisting, that is, of all intelligent beings in the sphere of the sun), the Archangel Michael, in cooperation with the intelligences of the planets, had for aeons ensured the wisdom-filled connection of these cosmic thoughts with their concrete realizations.

Of human thought, Steiner said: "All human intelligence comes from Michael in the sun."[3] In earlier times, humanity perceived thoughts clairvoyantly. Initiates were well aware that these thoughts were *actually* revelations from high spiritual beings, or "intelligences." However, in order that others might begin to develop their *own* thought life, and thereby come to act morally with insight and freedom, the Archangel Michael gradually conveyed the "cosmic intelligence" to them. This process of the development of the cosmic intelligence into independent human intelligence commenced during the late pre-Christian centuries, and was completed in the late Middle Ages.

Greek philosophy traces the transition from a wisdom still echoing with the ancient mysteries (as in the pre-Socratic philosophers and the philosophy of Plato) to a thought-world mastered by human beings out of their own inner resources (such as speaks incipiently from the philosophy of Aristotle). The new, "human wisdom" took the form of as "philosophy" (*philo-sophia*, i.e., "love of wisdom"), with which the heavenly wisdom (the Divine Sophia) now formed a connection.

As a servant of the Archangel Michael, Aristotle contributed foundationally to bringing the cosmic intelligence to earth. He did so, in that he and his successors—in what, from that time forward,

---

3. *Karmic Relationships*, Vol. III (Forest Row, UK: Rudolf Steiner Press, 2009) (CW 237), lecture of August 8, 1924.

Valentin Tomberg and the *Ecclesia Universalis*

could be called the "Aristotelian stream"—cultivated a brain-bound form of thinking. By dint of such preparation, this new form of intelligence was equipped, by early modern times, to take hold of the "cosmic intelligence," which, according to Steiner, had been descending gradually into processes at work in the human brain. Now, Steiner held that Aristotle's eternal individuality resumed this process also in modern times, furthering the descent of the "cosmic intelligence." In fact, this continuing presence is the reality behind Steiner's designation of this stream as "Aristotelian." This great spiritual individuality made pivotal contributions at several historical turning-points in this process of descent as it ran its course through the centuries. At the outset of "philosophy" in the Greek epoch, he had brought as treasure from the waning mystery traditions the laws of logic and the doctrine of the ten "categories" (which according to Steiner form a "cosmic script"). From the Greek mystery school of Eleusis, he brought the "cosmological" or "nature" wisdom which, although still preserved at that time, would soon fall into decadence. Likewise, when in the late Middle Ages both this cosmological wisdom and the works of Aristotle finally made their way into Central Europe (by way of Muslim culture through Spain), this same great individuality was again present to assist in the further incorporation of the "cosmic intelligence" in the form of Medieval Scholasticism. Others at that time, more connected with the "cosmological" or "nature" wisdom, further incorporated that wisdom into the spiritual arts, such as alchemy (e.g., the alchemist Basil Valentinus) and the "natural" medicine of the Rosicrucians and others (e.g., the physician Paracelsus and the mystic Jakob Böhme).[4]

Steiner pointed out that until the fourth century AD, cosmic thoughts were carried by high angels, the spirits of form (Elohim), but then descended to the spirits of personality (Archai).[5] This descent to the next lower hierarchic level opened the way for thoughts to appear inwardly in the soul instead of being perceived

---

4. *Mystery Knowledge and Mystery Centers* (Forest Row, UK: Rudolf Steiner Press, 2013) (CW 232), lecture of December 15, 1923.

5. *The Driving Force of Spiritual Powers in World History* (Toronto: Steiner Book Centre, 2007) (CW 222), lecture of March 16, 1923.

Valentin Tomberg and the New Spiritual Thinking

outwardly. From the eighth century onwards, then, individuals began to form their *own* thoughts—and herewith came the danger of *forgetting* the Michaelic origin of thoughts in the cosmic intelligence.

Steiner also noted that certain beings of the hierarchy of the Elohim "remained behind," and, instead of conveying this world of thoughts, kept it for themselves. This gave rise to a spiritual battle between the Archai (the rightful custodians of the intelligence) and the Elohim who had remained behind (inspiring groups of people who were not yet able to develop personal thoughts). Among these latter we may count the scholars of the Academy of Gondishapur, which acquired a strong Platonic streak after the Platonic Academy of Athens was closed by Emperor Justinian in 529, driving anti-Christian philosophers from that Academy to relocate for a time to Gondishapur.

In the sixth century, this academy in the southwest of modern Iran became the center of philosophy and science. It was the place where modern materialistic medicine was born.[6] Scholars of that time still inhabited a cosmic world of intelligence, and, according to Steiner, came to be inspired largely by "luciferic-ahrimanic forces" from the sphere of the fallen angels. Owing to this, in the seventh century, an anti-Christian impulse became active in their academy, which Steiner associated with the number of the solar demon (666). Through this anti-Christian impulse around the year 666, human beings were "pushed" by a kind of "revelation" to receive the consciousness soul together with all its contents precociously, that is, well in advance of its appointed time—in fact, long before the development of the rational soul had even been completed. The intended outcome of this untimely advance to the stage of the consciousness soul was that, long before becoming fully aware of their own "personality," including its shadow sides (this being the domain of the as-yet-to-be-developed consciousness soul), the people of the time would be able, "out of season," to develop the judgment to handle certain knowledge in a "seemingly" moral and wise

---

6. Heinz Herbert Schoeffler, *The Academy of Gondishapur* (Spring Valley, NY: Mercury Press, 1993).

Valentin Tomberg and the *Ecclesia Universalis*

manner. They would have made a leap, as it were, all the way to the middle of the epoch of the consciousness soul (whose appointed time of flourishing was meant to be about the year 2500) nearly two millennia before its appointed hour! An "intelligent" humanity would thereafter have arisen, one with deep insight into the spiritual-earthly, into the transcendental-earthly. But, according to Steiner, this humanity would thereafter have been cut off from any *further* spiritual development.[7] Such a humanity, not having first been able to form their "I" (which is essential to the proper development of the consciousness soul) would in due course have become mental automatons.

This scenario was, however, prevented. In 642, a Muslim army conquered Gondishapur, thereby "blunting" this anti-Christian impulse, as Steiner put it. In a weakened form, this gave rise to "scientific intelligence," which reached Western Europe by way of various stations. Of these, the first was the scientific academy founded in Baghdad under Caliph Harun al-Rashid (c. 766–809) by his advisors and viziers Yahya ibn Khalid and his son Ya'far. Here, as in Gondishapur, Greek philosophical texts were translated and scholars from other countries invited to further develop science. Rudolf Steiner called this Arab phase in the development of the blunted impulse of Gondishapur "Arabism." He characterized "Arabism" on the one hand as a premature development in the consciousness soul of logical and abstract thought, and on the other as the development of "sensuous fantasy."[8]

Steiner reports that in 869 Harun al-Rashid and his counselor (probably Yahya) sought an encounter in the spiritual world with the eternal entelechies of Aristotle and Alexander the Great, whom they "desired to meet again."[9] This meeting occurred, but turned

---

7. *Death as a Metamorphosis of Life* (Gt Barrington, MA: SteinerBooks, 2008) (CW 182), lecture of October 16, 1918 ("How Can I find Christ?"); and *Three Streams in the Evolution of Mankind* (London: Rudolf Steiner Press, 1985) (CW 184), lecture of October 11, 1918.

8. Steiner, lecture of January 14, 1918, in *Mysterienwahrheiten und Weihnachtsimpulse* (GA 180).

9. *Karmic Relationships*, Vol. VI (Forest Row, UK: Rudolf Steiner Press, 2009) (CW 240), lecture of August 14, 1924.

Valentin Tomberg and the New Spiritual Thinking

instead into a spiritual battle, because the eternal entelechies of Alexander and Aristotle had in the interim united with Christ—had in fact only recently returned to the spiritual world following incarnations in the spiritual environment of the Grail family. They made it clear that, as Steiner explained it, what had come about *before* as Aristotle's philosophy in the time of Michael's rulership in Greece must, in the strictest sense of the word, *now* be led into Michael's later rulership as a time spirit, which was set to begin centuries later, in 1879.

Harun al-Rashid in particular wanted to keep hold of what was spreading from his Baghdad court over the Muslim world as Arabism. According to Steiner, the spiritual influence of Harun al-Rashid (and that of Yahya) continued to guide the spread of Arabism across North Africa to Europe, and therewith the development of a materialistic and rationalistic science.

In the Islamic world, the writings of Aristotle were translated into Arabic. Then many commentaries were written on them. Later, in twelfth- and thirteenth-century Spain and Southern Italy, both Aristotle's writings and the Arabic commentaries thereon were translated into Latin. Prior to that, only a few of Aristotle's writings on logic had been known in Western Europe. These commentaries, especially those by Averroës (1126–1198), aroused great opposition among Christian theologians. Thomas Aquinas (1225–1274) fought against the Averroist interpretation of Aristotle, in whose spirit he worked, in his 1270 treatise *De unitate intellectus contra averroistas* ("On the Unity of the Intellect Against the Averroists").

Thomas argued for the individuality of the human spirit, and its immortality. By this means he brought the philosophy of Aristotle into harmony with Christian theology. According to Steiner, Thomas and other representatives of Christian Scholasticism strove to apply human intelligence in the sense of the aforementioned "Michael movement." They remained loyal to the archangel Michael and fought to prevent Ahriman from fully appropriating the formerly "cosmic intelligence" that had now become "earthly-human intelligence."

In "Arabist" Aristotelianism, which persisted in its focus on the sensory world, the spiritual world disappeared from view. The

Valentin Tomberg and the *Ecclesia Universalis*

"ideal" quality of concepts was lost. And so there appeared within medieval Scholasticism from the fourteenth century onwards the current of "nominalism," where concepts came to be regarded as arbitrary "names" of things. In this nominalist stream, thinking became impersonal, earthly, cold, and materialistic; in short, true thinking died. In his second "class lesson" of February 22, 1924, Steiner spoke of precisely this death of thinking: "The death of thinking was gradually preparing itself since the year 333 of the post-Christian era." Ahriman was killing thinking.

A further step on this road to the death of thinking may be seen in the Fourth Council of Constantinople (869/70), when the Western Church Fathers condemned the "two-soul" doctrine of the Greek patriarch Photius. This doctrine held that there is both a sinful lower soul and a sinless higher or "spiritual" soul. In the context of his lectures, Steiner (perhaps owing to the complexity of the archaic Council wording) tended to oversimplify this condemnation of Photius's doctrine of a "spiritual aspect" of the soul as "an abolition of the spirit." His point was well taken, nonetheless, because one could argue that awareness of the "spirit," which in the centuries before the Council had still been clearly distinguishable, diminished by stages in the Western world until, at the time of the Council's condemnation of the doctrine of Photius, what had previously been understood as a lingering spiritual "aspect" of the soul was (in accord with this Council) formally snuffed out. Significantly, according to Steiner, this Council took place when, in the spiritual world, the "hosts" of Aristotle and Harun al-Rashid were battling one another. And later, in the materialism of the nineteenth century, thinking even as only an aspect of the soul died; for then, not only was the spirit abolished, but (for the consequent materialist) the soul also.

In contrast to the "Christianized" Aristotelianism of Thomas Aquinas and his students, "Arabized" Aristotelianism of an Averroist and nominalistic bent developed in the sciences. The Italian astronomer Galileo Galilei (1564–1642) took up his own position in this latter context, criticizing traditional Aristotelianism as dogmatic. He catalyzed a separation of philosophy and science, just as the Islamic Aristotelian Averroës had earlier advocated the separa-

Valentin Tomberg and the New Spiritual Thinking

tion of philosophy and faith. In a subsequent stage of this process, science came to be separated from ethics as well. Galileo turned the scientist into an objective observer, intent only on what can be measured. His mathematistic view of the world was as far as could be from the descriptive-empirical attitude of Aristotle, who had advocated attending to phenomena and experimentation.

Francis Bacon was the leading continuator in his time of the struggle begun against Christian Aristotelianism by Harun al-Rashid. In his writings, Bacon advocated an experimental science that regarded all spiritual ideas as "empty idols." In his work *Nova Atlantis* (1626) he described a utopian state where scholars conducted their experiments in a research institute that he called the House of Solomon. The adage "knowledge is power" goes back to Bacon, as do the ideas that the aim of science is "to torture nature in order to reveal her secrets," and that nature should be "docile and enslaved."

Rudolf Steiner describes Bacon's activity and influence after his death as prodigious. His passing released, as he put it, materialistic "idols of thought" into the spiritual world, which then became active as demons, and even penetrated the supersensible Michael School. The demons that remained became the inspirers of materialism in the nineteenth century.[10] Bacon was the first to develop a method of data processing with a binary (a-b) code and thus, according to English researcher Paul Emberson, became "the father of the computer."[11]

Modern science emerged in the seventeenth century from the combination of abstract conceptualization and sensory perception focused on what can be measured. Its worldview is mechanistic: phenomena are studied according to the model of the machine, so that, as one example, the human heart is considered to be a pump.

According to Steiner, until the beginning of the fifteenth century, most of humanity was made up of "heart" people. They "thought

---

10. *Karmic Relationships* VI (CW 240), lecture of August 27, 1924; and *Karmic Relationships* IV (CW 238), lecture of September 16, 1924.

11. Paul Emberson, *From Gondischapur to Silicon Valley*, Vol. 1 (Tobermory: Etheric Dimensions Press, 2009), chapter 2.

Valentin Tomberg and the *Ecclesia Universalis*

with their hearts." Since the end of the Middle Ages, however, most have gradually become "head" people. To this end, in a kind of "cosmic storm" at the time of the supersensible Michael School, the highest spiritual hierarchies (Seraphim, Cherubim, and Thrones) led the cosmic intelligence into the nerve-sensory structure of the human brain. The "cosmic intelligence" became thereby humanity's own intelligence.[12] From the fifteenth century onwards, this transformation led to the emergence of a new organ in the brain. This organ releases hidden forces that transform the brain in such a way that, since the end of the nineteenth century, humanity has gained the capacity to acquire spiritual knowledge.[13] European humanity was to go through the modern school of logical and scientific thinking in order then to apply to "spiritual thinking" the capacity to "think in sharp contours" that characterizes Aristotelianism.

⊕

To more accurately and equitably depict the development of European thought, we must now add to what has been said regarding the Aristotelian tradition (which had taken the detours through Gondishapur and Islamic culture to reach Europe) that it was all the while accompanied at some distance by the Platonic tradition under the ongoing inspiration of Sophia. In Plato's philosophy, echoes of spiritual perception and the cosmic intelligence still lingered. Of Plato's writings, only parts of the *Timaeus* were known in the Middle Ages. Only in the twelfth century were two other dialogues added. The *Timaeus* describes how the cosmos came into being and was animated by the World Soul. Not until the fifteenth century did the manuscripts of all Plato's dialogues (about thirty) finally make their way from Greece to Florence, where between 1462 and 1469 they were translated from Greek into Latin by Marsilio Ficino (1433–1499).

Islamic culture had also preserved a Platonic current (it had also played an important role in the academy of Gondishapur), which

---

12. *Karmic Relationships* III (CW 237), lecture of July 28, 1924.
13. *The Bhagavad Gita and the West* (Gt Barrington, MA: SteinerBooks, 2009) (CW 146), lecture of June 1, 1913.

Valentin Tomberg and the New Spiritual Thinking

entered early-on into European Christianity. This current came gradually to manifestation in seven new academies, each of which gave further important impulses to the spiritualization of thought:

1. In Alexandria, Egypt, there was a Greek scientific academy (the *Museion*), a theological school, and a philosophical academy in which, in the third century, Neoplatonism developed. Greek, Egyptian, Jewish, and Christian traditions intermingled there. Furthermore, Neoplatonism influenced the Egyptian Hermetic tradition, which had its origin in the wisdom of Hermes Trismegistus. Hermetic writings contained teachings on the evolution of the soul, on the cosmos, and on God. The idea of reincarnation was part of the Hermetic worldview also. Alexandrian Platonism exerted a significant influence on theology, and played a determinative role in the development of Christian philosophy in Western Europe up until the twelfth century—even outside the court and cathedral schools mentioned below.

2. In the Carolingian court schools, which arose in the ninth and tenth centuries, Platonism was further enriched by new impulses deriving from Anglo-Saxon and Irish culture. From 782 onwards, the Anglo-Saxon scholar Alcuin led the court school in Aachen (Germany). He introduced the study of the seven liberal arts, which was the quintessence of classical education. The aim of this study was the acquisition of "virtuous wisdom." The Irish philosopher Johannes Scotus Eriugena, who led the court school in France in the ninth century, taught the Christian doctrine of the nine hierarchies of angels, as well as a philosophy of nature in which nature was seen as a mirror of God, a revelation of God.

3. In the cathedral schools of the eleventh and twelfth centuries, Platonism blossomed yet again, reaching its zenith in the School of Chartres. Thereafter, from the twelfth century onwards, Platonic thought was superseded by the philosophy of Aristotle in the Scholasticism of the new universities. At the School of Chartres, Platonism went hand in hand with a cosmological "nature-spirituality" of Celtic origin. Rudolf Steiner said of this School that its mood of

soul was permeated by "spiritual, invisible impulses, like shadows cast by the castle of King Arthur and the Castle of the Grail.... Something of the solar Christianity of the Arthurian knights still hovered over the school."[14]

For philosophers from the School of Chartres, such as Fulbertus, Bernardus Silvestris and Alanus ab Insulis, nature was a living being. At the beginning of the creation of the world and of humankind stood the goddess Natura. According to Alanus, the creation of the "new" human being was also inspired by Her. He spoke also of a "new earth," so that we can understand his philosophy as a "Platonism of the Resurrection." We also find this in the Platonic monks of the Cistercian order, who cultivated the earth in their monastic communities.

At this time, human nature was considered to have been created in the image and likeness of God. Because of the Fall, the *likeness* of God had been lost, and every human being had to make a personal effort to heal his imperfect person by working on himself. This had become possible because the likeness had in principle been *restored* by Christ. The *image* of God in human nature, however, had not been lost; it had not been corrupted, but only lost to view. The teachers of Chartres designed their teaching of the liberal arts in such a way that the image of God could reappear on this path of formation of the soul. In this way, the beginnings of imaginative, inspirative, and intuitive thinking could be cultivated in their pupils, so that, in due course, human intelligence could reach the sphere of Sophia, Divine Wisdom.

4. In the Italian Renaissance of the fifteenth century, Platonism appeared yet again, in the Academy of Florence. Here Plato's dialogues were studied, together with other writings from Greek, Neoplatonic, Hermetic, and Kabbalistic sources. This led in turn to the development in Western Europe of sciences (in the pre-materialist sense) that had their basis in a spiritual, Platonic-Aristotelian worldview. Names that come to mind in this connection are the physician Paracelsus, the astronomer Johannes Kepler, and the phi-

---

14. *Karmic Relationships* VI (CW 240), lecture of August 21, 1924.

losopher Giordano Bruno. During this period, the Rosicrucian Brotherhood was active in the background also. Not until the seventeenth century did modern science supersede the beginnings of this "spiritual" science of nature. Thereafter, living nature and the human body were studied increasingly in mechanistic terms.

5. At the end of the eighteenth century, Platonic thinking blossomed again in German classicism, in both literature (Novalis) and in the philosophy of Idealism (Fichte, Hegel, and Schelling). At this juncture, no specific Platonic Academy arose, but instead a network of people in various German cultural centers (extending as well to other countries in Central Europe, such as Poland and the Czech Republic).

6. Another century further on, a similar circle of philosophers, theologians, and poets emerged in the framework of Russian religious philosophy (1880–1950), including the "Sophiologists" Vladimir Solovyov, Pavel Florensky, and Sergei Bulgakov. Although uniquely Russian in spirit, influences of German Idealism and the Platonic tradition interlaced their work. The Russian Revolution of 1917 effectively brought the work of this circle to an end. Florensky was arrested in 1928 and died in a Soviet camp in 1937. Bulgakov was exiled from Russia in 1922, but continued his sophiological work in Paris until his death in 1944. Valentin Tomberg as well as Daniil Andreyev, the author of *Rosa Mira* ("The Rose of the World"), may also be counted among this circle.

7. For the twentieth century, Steiner predicted another return of the Platonic movement, especially that aspect of it which had been carried forward by the Platonist masters of the School of Chartres. They were to become active in the esoteric school he founded in Dornach in 1924. With Steiner's death, this school lost its spiritual leader, but in many countries initiatives continue to take form which, as metamorphoses of the School of Chartres, seek to further their work from an anthroposophical vision of humanity and the world. Such initiatives include research centers and institutions in the field of astrosophy, movement art and other arts, chakra research, Christology,

education, etheric energy, geomancy, Hermeticism, karma research, (curative) pedagogy, Sophiology, spiritual psychology and therapy, even working with nature beings. In all these areas we can learn to connect with our higher self and with the spiritual world. Ideally, Aristotelians and Platonists work together here.

⊕

Rudolf Steiner described that between the death of the leading Chartres Platonist Alanus ab Insulis (1203) and the birth of the leading Aristotelian Thomas Aquinas (1225), a "council" took place in the spiritual world.[15] During the course of this spiritual council the Platonists foresaw that in the coming centuries the human intellect would develop in such a way as to install a materialistic culture of science and technology. This "dead" intellect would have to be spiritualized again after 1879—that is (according to Steiner's teaching on historical cycles and their correlation with the various levels of the spiritual hierarchies) at the dawn of the age of the Archangel Michael, who was to provide the basis for this.

At this council, an "indissoluble agreement" was made between the Platonists (who had only just returned to the spiritual world) and the Aristotelians (who were preparing at that time for a new manifestation in order to resume their part in this common task). The Aristotelian philosophers would be the first to appear, beginning toward the close of the nineteenth century in order to prepare this work. They would return then at the end of the twentieth century in order to work together with the Platonists of the School of Chartres (who would have incarnated in the twentieth century) on the spiritualization of intelligence. They would then cooperate for the first time in history. In August 1924, Rudolf Steiner reminded the anthroposophists of their own expected return at the end of the century, in what has sometimes been called his "Michael Prophecy."[16]

The rise of the intellect is linked to the birth of the independent individual in the late Middle Ages. It led to a loss of perception of

---

15. Ibid., lecture of July 18, 1924.
16. Steffen Hartmann, *Die Michael-Prophetie Rudolf Steiners und die Jahre 2012 bis 2033* (Hamburg: Edition Widar, 2017).

the spiritual world and of the higher forms of knowledge developed in Platonism. Before this happened, the aforementioned Alanus ab Insulis and some other Platonists designed an edifice of knowledge that the German anthroposophist Michael Frensch calls a "cathedral of knowledge," consisting of two sets of cognitive faculties.[17]

Platonic cognitive faculties:

1. The towers—*intelligentsia*, man's highest intelligent faculty, for the perception of the creative thoughts of God
2. The roof—reason for the perception of ideas

Aristotelian cognitive faculties:

3. The walls—formation of concepts with our rational mind
4. The foundation—sensory perception

From the thirteenth century onwards, the Platonic faculties fell away, so that in science only observation and conceptualization remained, leading to the formation of theories and models. The dismantling of this cathedral of knowledge has its parallel in the collapse of the edifice of law erected by Thomas Aquinas, which Valentin Tomberg described in his doctoral thesis as the "degeneration of law."

The groups of leading Platonists and Aristotelians are not so numerous, but they had their pupils in many academies, monasteries, and universities. However, not all of them were linked to Christ, for there were also Islamic Platonists and Aristotelians. Besides these great philosophers and their disciples, we can also speak of Platonic and Aristotelian types of souls. In their pursuit of knowledge, Platonic persons focus on the spiritual world. They open themselves to the stream of revelation from above, whereas, by contrast, Aristotelian persons are researchers investigating the physical world. Platonic types tend to develop their imaginative, inspirative, and intuitive spiritual faculties, whereas Aristotelian types tend to develop their sensory perception and their rational, logically reasoning mind. In general, the Platonic type is more mystical and

---

17. Michael Frensch, *Weisheit in Person* (Schaffhausen: Novalis Verlag, 2000), 254–62.

Eastern European; the Aristotelian type more scientific and Western European. We find this same contrast as between the humanities and the natural sciences. Of course, all human beings possess both types of cognitive faculties and can integrate them through their "I"-activity, so that, in cooperation with others, all can rebuild the cathedral of knowledge and the edifice of law. It was for this very purpose that at the end of the Middle Ages, the Archangel Michael brought together in spiritual council the future custodians of the cosmic intelligence.

The School of the Archangel Michael

According to Steiner, between the fifteenth century, when the age of the consciousness soul began, and the beginning of the nineteenth century, the Archangel Michael gathered the Aristotelians and the Platonists, together with human souls from many other streams, as well as other spiritual beings, in a "supersensible school" for the purpose of preparing them for their task in the twentieth century.

Taken together, the Aristotelians and Platonists made up the "Greek" stream of knowledge among the participants in the Michael School. But there was another stream in that Michael School, made up of participants associated with Palestine in the time of Jesus Christ, when (in accord with the cyclical nature of things) the Aristotelians were for the most part not incarnated, but in the spiritual world preparing for their next earthly life.

Those who were preparing for an incarnation in the Anthroposophical Movement received in the Michael School an "historical overview of the mysteries of humanity." This teaching concluded at the end of the eighteenth century with a cosmic-imaginative cult that lasted for several decades. In one of his karma lectures, Steiner spoke in this regard of "powerful cosmic imaginations expressing what I might call the new Christianity."[18] In effect, this cult served as a "preview" of the new mysteries that Rudolf Steiner had wished to inaugurate at the Christmas Conference of 1923.[19] By "New Mysteries" is meant conscious forms of communication with spiritual

---

18. Lecture of July 18, 1924, in *Karmic Relationships*, Vol. 6 (CW 240), 145.
19. Ibid., lecture of July 20, 1924.

Valentin Tomberg and the New Spiritual Thinking

beings.[20] On earth, this cult found poetic expression in Goethe's 1795 *Fairy Tale of the Green Serpent and the Beautiful Lily.* Steiner's *Mystery Dramas* were also inspired by the events of this supersensible school.

Rudolf Steiner, the leading individual of the Aristotelian movement, gathered people around him from 1902 onwards in order to establish an earthly Michael School. Until the First World War, these were often "souls without a spiritual home" and older people. They were Platonists, as Hans Peter van Manen called them, who on closer inspection turned out to be "platonic" Aristotelians.[21] According to van Manen, these individuals had the task of preparing the *transformation* of Platonism together with Steiner.

Van Manen regarded Anthroposophy as it developed until 1914 as "a Christian metamorphosis of Plato's philosophy at the level of the consciousness soul."[22] It could just as well be called a Christian-Platonic Theosophy. More precisely, it could be called a new form of the Resurrection Platonism of Alanus ab Insulis and other Platonists of the School of Chartres. This renewed Platonism includes important themes that Steiner dealt with in many lectures in 1914. Among these themes are the path of schooling, the Fifth Gospel, the Grail impulse, the Nathan Jesus, the Virgin Sophia, and others from a Mystery Christianity linked to the Gospel of John.

Around 1920, the demographics of Anthroposophy markedly changed: many younger people were now finding their way to it. Some came from a youth movement whose members liked to hike in nature,[23] others were students enthusiastic about the many initiatives then growing out of Anthroposophy. Among these younger people were many scientifically-minded Aristotelians. As matters turned out (unsurprisingly), the older and younger generations did

---

20. Harrie Salman, *The Social World as Mystery Center* (Mountlake Terrace, WA: Threefold Publishing, 2020).
21. Hans Peter van Manen, *Twin Roads to the New Millennium* (Forest Row: Rudolf Steiner Press, 1988), chapter 14.
22. Ibid.
23. A youth movement known at the time as the *Wandervögel* ("wandering birds" or "wayfarers").

not understand each other very well, which naturally played its part in the major conflicts which led to the demise of the Society in 1935.

As regards the larger historical framework of Rudolf Steiner's own role as leader of the Aristotelian stream, we might say that after Thomas Aquinas had transformed the philosophy of Aristotle into a Christian philosophy, Steiner developed it a step further (in his *Philosophy of Freedom*) into the "I"-consciousness activity of intuitive thinking. He then showed, in a further step, how, if this intuitive cognitive faculty has been sufficiently mastered, people of our time can enter the spiritual world in full awareness. But the "new" Aristotelianism that was to have emerged from this had to wait upon a further spiritualizing of consciousness on the part of the Platonists of Chartres. This "spiritualizing" was to involve the development of an expressive, living, moral, creative thinking arising out of the heart's warmth. With his elaboration of the phenomenological method that trains and enlivens our perception,[24] Steiner *prepared* this spiritualization of science (for which Goethe had laid the first foundations in his natural science). Carrying things even further on the path of inner schooling, Steiner's exercises for acquiring higher forms of consciousness were also offered as an ancillary practice to this same end. Aristotelian and Platonic anthroposophists might then have truly built a new "cathedral of knowledge" in the course of the twentieth century. But the sad reality is that after the Christmas conference of 1923, awareness of this pivotal joint task fell by the wayside.

At the Christmas Conference of 1923, Rudolf Steiner refounded the Anthroposophical Society under his personal leadership. Within the new mystery school at its center, the Free School for Spiritual Science, he gave the "first class" lessons in February 1924. However, the

---

24. Using this method, we perceive the world around us as purely as possible, holding back our judgments and concepts. We then allow what we have perceived to resonate within us. Through this connection with things or people, the inner meaning of what we perceive (the essence, the primal image, the message) can be put into words.

Valentin Tomberg and the New Spiritual Thinking

conditions he had set for the success of the new Society were not met. The anthroposophists, who came from different karmic streams in the past and were made up of different generation groups, had to get to know each other and work together in a brotherly and sisterly way. Steiner called this the "harmonization of the karma." On December 25, 1923, at 10 AM, Steiner gave the Foundation Stone Meditation for laying the foundation of their joint work, which, he said, had to be laid in the proper soil, specifying that "the proper soil consists of our hearts in their harmonious collaboration, in their good, love-filled desire to carry the will of Anthroposophy through the world together."[25] Then the being Anthropos-Sophia would be able to incarnate in the spiritual temple that the anthroposophists were meant to build upon these foundation stones.

Before his death, Steiner could only present part of the content planned for the first class—in the form of nineteen class lessons. At the center of the School of Spiritual Science was the General Anthroposophical Section, around which were grouped the other Sections (such as Pedagogy and Medicine) concerned with pursuing spiritual research in their respective fields. As it happened, however, after Steiner's death, the General Section soon came to be limited, in practice, to simply continuing on with those nineteen lessons in a recurring pattern under the authority of appointed class readers.

In what failed to develop in the wake of Steiner's early death, we can see the root-causes of many problems in the further development of Anthroposophy. Steiner's students became active in their respective fields of work, and in the School Sections, but the General Anthroposophical Section—the spiritual center of the Esoteric School—remained empty. Here Tomberg could have become active, for his work encompassed *precisely* what was needed there: Christology and the path of schooling and esoteric development. Other Platonists could then have come forward and contributed further, for example, in the artistic design of the work in the member groups, which usually took place in a very intellectual way. The

---

25. *Proceedings of the Christmas Conference—The Laying of the Foundation Stone* (CW 260a).

School also lacked the nurturing dimension of the anthroposophical social impulse and the new Christianity.

When the Society broke up in 1935, this collapse called into question in a fundamental way the implementation of the already mentioned "unbreakable agreement" of the beginning of the thirteenth century (regarding the planned cooperation between Aristotelians and Platonists at the end of the twentieth century), as Valentin Tomberg expressed it in the 1940s. Rudolf Steiner had anticipated that this cooperation would be dependent on the effect of the impulse of the Christmas Conference of 1923, and also on "the question whether the Anthroposophical Society would be able to cultivate Anthroposophy in the right way and with dedication," as he stated on July 18, 1924 (CW 240). This Aristotelian-Platonic work was to lead to a certain culmination of Anthroposophy. But since this cooperation did not take place in the way Steiner had hoped, it must be taken up again in a resurrection of the anthroposophical impulse, for which the cooperation of the Aristotelians and Platonists is a precondition.

To this end, *both* streams must practice the Goethean phenomenology which in his early epistemological works Steiner had fully expounded. The Aristotelians (who are inclined to live predominantly in the world of intellectual concepts) would primarily cultivate the capacity for "concept-free" sense perception, dispensing with all preconceived theories and models. The Platonists (who are inclined predominantly to live in the world of ideas) would primarily cultivate the capacity to bring that world of ideas into immediate connection with the sense world. As a next step, the Aristotelians could learn from the example of the Platonists to develop their imaginative, inspirative, and intuitive consciousness, and to think with their heart—thus bringing into their thinking spiritual, expressive, living, creative, moral, empathic, and compassionate qualities. By achieving this, they could develop the "heart intelligence" needed to perceive the working of spiritual forces in the sensory world when studying nature, man, and society. The Platonists, on the other hand, could learn from the example of the Aristotelians how to perceive sensory reality more objectively and describe it more precisely. They could learn to enter into the world with the intellect all the way to the point of taking the first steps in transforming it.

Insofar as the great Platonists and their disciples actually did become active at the end of the twentieth century, they may have done so largely outside the Anthroposophical Movement: as philosophers, artists, writers, pedagogues, psychologists, psychiatrists, therapists, ecologists, human rights activists, and, more generally, visionaries with well-developed creative imaginations and moral awareness. By contrast, in our "modern Gondishapur" world we find everywhere initiates and disciples of Ahriman's counter-school, not only in science but also in economics and politics. They are astute, intellectually-gifted, and live in a materialistic mental world. Standing against them as representatives of Michaelic Aristotelianism are researchers, doctors, and other forceful opponents of Ahrimanic forces. Of course, these latter may be working inside and outside the Anthroposophical Movement.

It is not only a question of uniting Platonic and Aristotelian qualities, but above all of actively fostering their cooperation. This encourages a balancing of qualities which then promote further joint research into and connection with spiritual beings. Such collaborative work is a prerequisite for the spiritualization of intelligence that Rudolf Steiner had hoped for.

Michael, Sophia, and Christ

Rudolf Steiner had time before his death to finish only the first part of the first class of the earthly Michael School. This unfinished School did not prove sufficient to make of Anthroposophy, at least in its initial emergence, a significant cultural force. The Michael impulse of the Aristotelians alone was simply not strong enough. A harmonious cooperation with leading Platonists and other individualities would have been necessary for this. It is my conviction that Steiner's goal was to set up the School of Spiritual Science in such a way that *three* impulses—those of Michael, of Sophia, and of Christ—could be brought together.

We can further imagine that in the spiritual world there are three corresponding schools permeating one another, in which spiritual beings inspire and cooperate with the leaders of humanity.

Valentin Tomberg and the *Ecclesia Universalis*

The relationships between Michael, Sophia, and Christ have received relatively little attention in anthroposophical research. In his lectures "The Search for the New Isis, the Divine Sophia," given December 23–26, 1920, Steiner describes how Lucifer had "slain" Sophia, the Divine Wisdom, with the result that, as concerns the cognitive process, the living universe has become a mechanical universe, so that we need to develop what Steiner called "imaginative cognition" in order to open the way to finding Isis-Sophia again.[26]

Tomberg spoke about this in August 1938 in Rotterdam in a lecture on the new Michael Community and its significance for the future. He described how, in the cosmic-imaginative cult of the decades around 1800, the Archangel Michael had resurrected Sophia, Divine Wisdom, in the spiritual world, so that from that time forward she could begin to reveal herself to humanity once more. It is in the awakening memories of this cult that clairvoyant abilities can emerge, Tomberg says, enabling Aristotelians, on the one hand, to become clairvoyant in the study of nature, and enabling Platonists, on the other hand, to see karma—not only past karma but also the karmic consequences of actions in the present. The Aristotelians will do such clairvoyant research on the basis of the consciousness soul. For their part, the Platonists will receive their karmic revelations from the spirit-self (the higher self, or *manas*). In this way, Tomberg says, they will together establish a "spiritual knighthood," a future Michael-Sophia knighthood "in the name of Christ," which will be fully realized only in the next (sixth) cultural epoch.[27]

Steiner describes the Archangel Michael as the custodian of the cosmic intelligence, which, as described above, became human intelligence in the course of the Middle Ages. Aristotle had prepared this transition. Since the end of the Middle Ages, then, human beings have been able to form their own thoughts. This gave rise over the ensuing centuries to the development of the free personality, but brought with it the danger that human thinking overshoots

---

26. "The Search for the New Isis, Divine Sophia" (CW 202), lecture of December 24, 1920.

27. *Inner Development*, lecture 1.

the mark and becomes earthbound and materialistic, and in this way falls outside the range of what our spirit-self can manage to direct. In their time, Thomas Aquinas and the Christian Aristotelians developed their thinking as an individualizing force and thus reconnected their intelligence to that of Michael. In our time, in order to prepare the further salvation of intelligence for humanity and modern culture as a whole, Michael gathered those souls committed to this mission to participate in his supersensible school.

Now, during this process Sophia, the Divine Wisdom, who *personifies* the cosmic intelligence, has gone through her own development as a spiritual being. She also is under the protection of the Archangel Michael. In the *Wisdom Books* of the Old Testament she appears as the "beloved" of the Creator, who created her "at the beginning of his ways" (Proverbs 8:22–31). In ancient cultures she was revered as the Divine Mother of heaven and earth, and also as the primordial Mother of humanity. In Egypt, she was called Isis; in ancient Israel, Asherah. She first *incarnated* in Mary, the mother of Jesus, who thus became "Mary-Sophia."

On the level of humanity, Sophia connected herself with the development of independent human thinking. This thinking came to its first flowering in Greece. As the transcendental being Philo-Sophia, she accompanied the development of human thought. At the beginning of the twentieth century this being underwent a metamorphosis and was born as Anthropos-Sophia. When asked by Walter Johannes Stein when this being had come into existence, that is, when its "conception" had taken place, Rudolf Steiner replied, "When Aristotle took over Plato's task."[28]

In a lecture given during the First General Meeting of the Anthroposophical Society at Berlin on February 3, 1913 on "The Being of Anthroposophy" Steiner said:

> What we receive through Anthroposophy is our very own being. This once floated toward us in the form of a celestial goddess with whom we were able to enter into relationship. This divine being lived on as Sophia and Philosophia, and now we can once again

---

28. Margarete and Erich Kirchner-Bockholt, *Rudolf Steiner's Mission and Ita Wegman*, 52.

Valentin Tomberg and the *Ecclesia Universalis*

bring her out of ourselves and place her before us as the fruit of true anthroposophical self-knowledge. We can wait patiently until the world is willing to test the depth of the foundations of what we have to say, right down to the smallest details. It is the essence of Anthroposophy that its own being consists of the being of the human; and its effectiveness, its reality, consists in that we receive from Anthroposophy what we ourselves are and what we must place before ourselves, because we must practice self-knowledge.[29]

Elsewhere he describes how, as Anthropos-Sophia, Sophia desires to act as guide on our path of development. She reflects us in our true nature. With her help, our thoughts become spiritual. In the Christian esotericism of earlier times Sophia was known as the "Virgin Sophia." By this was meant as well the purified human soul, which in Christian initiation could receive the cosmic "I" (the Holy Spirit).[30]

The relationship between Sophia and the "I" of Jesus Christ has its foundation in the two parts of the primal man Adam that did not enter into the Fall and were preserved in what Steiner called the "Mother Lodge of Humanity." In his Studies of the Old Testament, Tomberg describes Sophia as having absorbed the immaculate "astral" essence of Eve, just as the Archangel Jesus (the Nathan Jesus) absorbed the immaculate "etheric" essence of Adam.[31] Together, these are the feminine and masculine parts of the "Mother Soul of Humanity," which for the first time united with each other in Mary and Jesus.[32]

In a lecture in Tallinn on November 19, 1934, Tomberg described how the archangels working in Northern and Central Europe encountered and mediated the collaboration of the Michael and Nathan Jesus streams in the Anthroposophical Movement as a means of supplementing the union of thinking and will characteristic of the working of Michael with the spirit of love working

---

29. "The Being of Anthroposophy," https://southerncrossreview.org/39/steiner-sophia.htm.
30. *The Gospel of St. John* (CW 103), lecture of May 31, 1908.
31. *Christ and Sophia*, 148.
32. See Michael Debus, *Mary and Sophia* (Edinburgh: Floris Books, 2013), 144–51, 191.

Valentin Tomberg and the New Spiritual Thinking

through the heart, which the Nathan Jesus brings. Michael has his sword. The "weapon" of the Nathan Jesus, however, which touches human beings in their feelings, heals, and enlightens, is love. The "Anthropos-Sophical" consciousness must join together the qualities of Michaelic, the Nathan Jesus, and Christ, he explained.[33]

Here it is important to point out that, according to Rudolf Steiner, since the beginning of the epoch of the consciousness soul, the individual human being can receive a "copy" or imprint of the "I" of the Nathan Jesus, just as in the Middle Ages copies of the etheric body and the astral body of Jesus Christ were incorporated into many people's souls. These copies of the Jesus-"I" are kept in the spiritual world, for all humankind, under the protection of the Brotherhood of the Holy Grail.[34] We can assume that the connection with the being Anthropos-Sophia in the present is a preparation for being able to receive such a copy of the Jesus-"I" in our purified soul (the Sophia-in-us). In this preparation, we work on our double, transforming our soul forces and progressing on our path to insight into higher worlds. This is the sign of Sophia and the Nathan Jesus collaborating within us individually. We may even speak here of a "Sophianic-Nathanic" Anthroposophy, which, as Valerian Schmaeling's letter to Elisabeth Vreede of 1937 shows, played a central role in Tomberg's work in Estonia and Latvia, and later in Holland.[35]

If we look at the whole, we can get an idea of the structure and the task of the School of Spiritual Science. Three stages lead us to the mystery of Michael-Sophia-Christ.

The *first stage* is the proper development of the consciousness soul, for which, according to Steiner, two faculties are necessary: "a truly pure perception of the sensory world" and a "free imagination."[36] The first faculty can be practiced in Goethean phenomenol-

---

33. *Vortragsnachschriften, Aufzeichnungen*, 211.
34. *The Principle of Spiritual Economy* (CW 109), lecture of April 11, 1909.
35. See pages 45–46.
36. *Inner Impulses of Evolution* (CW 171), lecture of September 17, 1916.

ogy, which Aristotelians in particular can learn to practice in their scientific research. The second faculty lies in the field of the Platonists. Steiner called it "a thinking of the heart."[37] Platonists can show us how to develop such heart-intelligence (the higher faculty of Imagination, in Steiner's sense) in order to find Sophia. In this way, thinking is spiritualized: heart and head connect. It is obvious that the Platonist starts out with a stronger connection to Sophia than to the Archangel Michael, and the Aristotelian starts out with a stronger connection to the Archangel Michael than to Sophia.

At the *second stage*, the free, living Imagination brings us into the realm of Sophia, where a new revelation of Wisdom becomes accessible to us, and a spiritual rebirth can take place. As a result of the development of natural or trained clairvoyance, the "etheric sphere" of Christ opens up to this cognitive faculty of Imagination. In his lecture series "The Search of the New Isis, the Divine Sophia" Steiner stated: "Christ will appear again in his spiritual form during the course of the twentieth century; not through the arrival of external events alone, but because human beings find the power represented by the Holy Sophia."[38] That power is the faculty of Imagination at a specific level of cognition. In his book *The Sophia Mystery of Our Time*, Mario Betti writes: "A new wisdom, a living imagination, gives birth to a new human being in the awakening Christ Consciousness." It is here that we touch upon the sphere of what in Anthroposophy is called "spirit self" (the higher self, or *manas*).[39]

At the *third stage*, the connection with the being Anthropos-Sophia prepares us to receive an imprint of the "I" of Jesus Christ. Thus we are on the way to the new man, the new Adam. At the end of this path is the *deificatio* (making-man-divine) about which the Platonist Alanus ab Insulis wrote. In Orthodox Christianity *theosis* (the Greek equivalent of deification) is also at the center of spirituality. This refers to the words of the fourth-century bishop Athana-

---

37. *Macrocosm and Microcosm* (CW 119), lecture of March 29, 1910.

38. *The Search for the New Isis, Divine Sophia* (CW 202), lecture of December 24, 1920.

39. Mario Betti, *The Sophia Mystery of Our Time* (Forest Row, UK: Temple Lodge Publishing, 2013), 73–74.

sius of Alexandria: "God became man [in Jesus] so that man [in the Holy Spirit] might become divine." Aristotelians, Platonists, and representatives of other currents need each other on this path, which, if followed, leads harmoniously to the coming spirit-self culture.

Tomberg's Path as Platonist and Hermeticist
Within the great Michael-Sophia-Christ mystery of Anthroposophy, Valentin Tomberg represented the Christ-Sophia mystery. This lent a Nathan-Sophia quality to his work. As he explained in a 1934 lecture, alongside the Michael stream in Northern and Central Europe, a Nathan-Jesus stream had arisen, directed at the human heart in a spirit of love. The Nathan-Jesus stream seems to have found a special place in the countries bordering the Baltic Sea, especially in Finland, Estonia, Latvia, and Sweden. Here, the Nathan soul lives in the pure etheric world and in the hearts of the people. This can be felt as a mood especially at Christmastime. Likewise, the Sophia impulse spread outward from Novgorod in the Russian hinterland. In rune 50 of the Finnish *Kalevala*, the union of the impulses of the Nathan Jesus and of his mother Mary, who were both connected with humanity in Paradise, appears in the image of Maryatta and her child, who was born in the Finnish forest.

As a Platonic soul from the East, who descended from the spiritual world into the earthly world in a religious stream of revelation (the stream of wisdom), Tomberg was not by nature drawn to what developed in quite a different direction in the Christ-Michael Mystery of Anthroposophy as an Aristotelian science, that is, the stream of action. Platonists are pre-eminently people of the heart. They think with their heart, and their inner orientation is contemplative. Aristotelians, by contrast, are preeminently cerebral people, their inner orientation is intellectual. As a rule, people of the East do not care to connect as deeply with the earth and earthly intelligence as do those of the West. A similar difference, broadly speaking, is often found between men (more focused on earthly matters) and women (more open to spirituality). For this reason, women can help men mature spiritually, just as Platonists can help intellectual Aristotelians open themselves more to the spiritual.

Valentin Tomberg and the *Ecclesia Universalis*

Rudolf Steiner emphasized the need for this spiritualization of intelligence, and mapped out the path to be followed with the help of the Platonists. In the 1930s, Tomberg tried to offer help on this front also, but came to feel that Anthroposophy (which, after all, had been shaped by people from the Aristotelian stream) had itself succumbed to a hardening intellectualization, particularly after Steiner's death.

Of course, the Platonist Tomberg did not shy away from the labor of thinking, and did not leave it to the Aristotelians! He was a close student and expositor of Steiner's epistemological writings. In his study of the tradition of legal philosophy, he worked to concretize abstract legal thinking again. In composing his *Meditations*, he struggled to make his thoughts permeable to the spiritual, so that they might serve his contemplative "Unknown Friends" as spiritual exercises leading further down the path for which Steiner had set the signposts precisely in his early epistemological works. Tomberg invites his "Unknown Friends" to think *with* him, i.e., to spiritualize their own intellectual thinking!

On the basis of the Hermetic tradition, especially in his work on the Tarot, Tomberg developed a spiritual psychology with a new, Sophianic quality. In effect, the Platonic spiritual researcher here becomes a *psychopompos* (a title of the Greek god Hermes), a soul-guide to the underworld who, as mediator between the unconscious and the conscious, leads aspirants on their inner path to initiation toward the Mysteries. Tomberg himself had come to embody the Hermit of the Major Arcana, joining the company, as it were, of those eremitic spirits who withdrew into the deserts in the early Christian tradition, or those *staretzes* (spiritual elders) in Russian culture who likewise withdrew into the forests to lead a life of prayer and contemplation, and as a result became spiritual advisers and helpers to many.

In the ideal image of the "eternal pilgrim," Tomberg was by nature oriented toward the spiritual world. But the circumstances of his life dictated that he enter into and deeply suffer with earthly events. He was poor. He was a refugee. His delicate constitution led him to suffer chronically. He was active in the Dutch Resistance. After the war he dealt daily with the endless suffering of its victims

Valentin Tomberg and the New Spiritual Thinking

in English repatriation camps. Thereafter, for the first sixteen years of his residency in England, his daily work for the BBC confronted him day by day, month by month, year by year, with the onerous burden of scanning the vast ocean of Soviet propaganda broadcasts for any indications that might prove useful to the intelligence services during the Cold War. There he was, "living again" amid the depredation and lies of the Soviet regime from which he had escaped at such great personal cost in 1918. Amid these life challenges, his loving, harmonious relationship with his wife Maria was crucial in helping him navigate life's challenges. They shared similar spiritual capacities and insights, and together formed a small Sophia "academy," which was both a mystery place and a place of contemplation and prayer. On January 1, 1966, Tomberg wrote to Bernhard Martin that their life had taken on the pattern of hermits, which, he said, corresponded exactly to their natures, and that they were living at the time "in a kind of monastery for two."

From the beginning of the 1930s Tomberg had to face many life challenges—among them his role as the first courageous enough to challenge and critique the established order in Dornach. In his critique, he shone a light on four aspects of the Society's "double":

1. Dogmatism and resistance to new revelations from the spiritual world. Here lies hidden the shadow of medieval Catholicism.

2. The incursion of Intellectualism, Arabism, non-Christian thinking.

3. Lack of interest in the "new Christianity," the Maitreya bodhisattva, the second coming of Christ, and the path of esoteric schooling—thereby neglecting central anthroposophical themes.

4. Lack of the feminine quality (Sophia).

At work in these shadows of a dogmatic, non-spiritualized, non-Christian, masculine Aristotelianism, are the forces of the "double" (or what Tomberg was wont to call the *egregore*) of the Anthroposophical Society. These forces throw up a wall through which a Christian Platonist (and any true anthroposophist) cannot easily penetrate. As the forerunner of the expected individualities of the Platonic movement, Tomberg had, as it were, to chisel out space for them, and for himself, in a Society which, after the death of Rudolf Steiner, had fallen into a state of stagnation and inner conflict. The Platonist Elisabeth Vreede supported him in this. Tomberg represented an Anthroposophy that was non-dogmatic and connected to the spiritual world. It was living and imaginative, Christian and Sophianic. These are qualities a Platonist can bring, along with artistic, therapeutic, and social strengths.

The conflicts in Dornach prevented a healthy development of Anthroposophy and led to the breakdown of the Society in the 1930s. During the Second World War, Tomberg considered the cultural project of Steiner's hoped-for "new mystery culture" to have foundered. And so, at the end of the war, he chose to become active in another field of work and lost contact with the Anthroposophical Society as it had come to be. In his assessment, the Society after the war showed only more signs of having lost its way, neglecting opportunities to transform itself in such a way as to offer Platonists an open field of work. The Anthroposophical Society had not been able to "cultivate Anthroposophy with proper dedication," which on July 18, 1924, Rudolf Steiner had said was a precondition for the fulfillment of the "Michael Prophecy." (CW 240)

Had events taken a different turn, Tomberg might have played an important role in preparing for and facilitating the essential cooperation between the Aristotelians and Platonists; but fruitful meetings with the leading officials in Dornach and with the Aristotelians in the various working areas proved unsuccessful. There are complex reasons for this, as this biography has tried to show. Sadly, even tragically, these failures had a decisive negative effect on the destiny of the Platonic movement in Anthroposophy during the post-war period. Many Platonists were marginalized or left stranded inside (or more often, outside) the Anthroposophical Society. Thankfully, in our time, the significance of the Platonists for the healthy spiritual development of Anthroposophy is becoming better understood and valued.

The "spiritualization of intelligence," which did not take place as Steiner had originally hoped within the Anthroposophical Move-

Valentin Tomberg and the New Spiritual Thinking

ment, as a task of the Christian Aristotelians and the Platonists, has yet to be assiduously embraced as a common task for the future. A century has now passed since the foundational Christmas Conference of 1923. A new impulse is needed to cultivate a constructive collaboration of the Aristotelian cognitive faculties with the Platonic Christian intelligence of the heart. Only then can Anthroposophy fulfill its task as a "spiritual science."

The Aristotelian-Anthroposophical work of Rudolf Steiner and the Platonic-Hermetic work of Valentin Tomberg complement each other and need to be understood and appreciated in their complementarity. Steiner worked from the sensory world upwards to reach spiritual insights. Tomberg worked from the stream of revelation downwards. It is from the unison of these two movements that the Michael-inspired science of the spirit—the science of the Holy Grail—can emerge.

In the anthroposophical and Hermetic work of Valentin Tomberg we find seven contributions that can play a role in renewing the impulse of Anthroposophy:

Christology and Biblical Research. Tomberg's first published article (on John's gospel, in 1930)[40] marked the beginning of extremely fruitful work in the field of Platonic Christology, which was continued in further biblical studies, his lectures in Rotterdam, his Our Father Course in Amsterdam, his *Meditations*, and his last writings.

Moral Logic. Tomberg's second published article (on the metamorphosis of logic, also in 1930)[41] echoed a theme that occupied him till the end of his life. He spoke of a logic of the physical, a logic of the living, a logic of the soul (the logic of the heart), and a logic of the spiritual (divine logic). Later on, he spoke of moral logic (or the

---

40. March 2 and 9, 1930, "The Gospel of St. John as a Way Toward Understanding the Spiritual Hierarchies"; see *Russian Spirituality*, 1–12.
41. March 23, 1930, "The Metamorphosis of Logic: The Logic of the Material, Soul, and Spiritual Worlds"; ibid., 12–17.

logic of love). In *Meditations* he wrote: "moral logic is the logic of the head and heart united. It is therefore that which unites meditation and prayer."[42]

Sophiology. The doctrine of Sophia, the Divine Wisdom, goes back to early Christianity in Ephesus, where consciousness of the incarnation of Sophia in the mother of Jesus was preserved. This consciousness spread across Eastern Europe, especially Russia. In the West we find traces of it in the German mystics Hildegard von Bingen (1098–1179) and Jakob Böhme (1575–1624). In Russian religious philosophy, this insight was first formulated in Solovyov's Sophia teaching, which developed further in the twentieth century in the writings of Pavel Florensky, Sergei Bulgakov, and others. Tomberg stood in this tradition also. The continuity of the theme of Sophia in Tomberg's writings, from his earliest article to his final writings, has been examined by Catholic theologian Wilhelm Maas in his article on Tomberg's Sophia doctrine.[43] In his Our Father Course, *Meditations*, and *The Proclamation on Sinai*, Tomberg develops the intriguing idea of a "female" trinity of Mother, Daughter, and Holy Soul, which has to be seen in connection with the "male" trinity of Father, Son, and Holy Spirit. This idea has also been assessed for its theological value by Wilhelm Maas.[44] In the Sophia doctrine, Christianity regains its little-known feminine side.

Russian Spirituality. Tomberg outlined in many articles Russia's unique spirituality and the dangers threatening its development, particularly from Asia. In so doing, he built a spiritual bridge between Central Europe and Russia, which is of the utmost importance for the future.

The Community of Insight. In another article from 1930[45] Tomberg formulated the idea of a community which, by entering into conver-

---

42. *Meditations*, 618.
43. Wilhelm Maas, "Tombergs Sophia-Lehre," in Heckmann and Frensch, *Valentin Tomberg*, Vol. I.2, 609–15.
44. Wilhelm Maas, "Maria-Sophia und die Leuchtende Trinität," ibid., 616–23.
45. September 28, 1930, "The Philosophy of Taking Counsel with Others"; see *Russian Spirituality*, 43–47.

Valentin Tomberg and the New Spiritual Thinking

sation in harmony with the individual insights of a number of free personalities, reaches new heights of insight. He called such communal insights "council decisions." He developed this idea further in the 1938 article entitled the "The Significance of a Free Anthroposophical Group."[46] Steiner described this same way of working as the "reverse cult." A community of insight can grow further into a "community of inspiration," as Tomberg put it in Letter XIV of *Meditations* in reference to the community of living and dead Hermeticists.

Etheric Vision. In two articles from 1931, the theme of etheric vision (which was further elaborated in the Our Father Course) is discussed. In the first article, etheric vision is presented as the result of the strengthening of conscience; in the second, emphasis is laid on how it is prepared for by suffering.[47]

Chakra Research. In his Our Father Course, Tomberg presented his research results on the schooling path and the Christian development of the chakras as a follow-up to Steiner's book *Knowledge of the Higher Worlds*. He also wrote about the chakras in several Letters of his *Meditations*. These findings were expanded and taken further by Willi Seiss.[48] An introduction to Tomberg's chakra teaching was given by Trygve Olaf Lindvig in a 2016 article.[49]

These research contributions from Valentin Tomberg's work belong to the core of esoteric Christianity. The themes of his research testify to the continuity of his work in Anthroposophy and the Hermetic tradition. They can be a source of inspiration not only for Platonic souls, but also for Aristotelian souls, who can discover in them clues for the further development of their spiritual insight.

---

46. Ibid., 48–51.
47. *Russian Spirituality*, "The Deepening of Conscience Which Results in Etheric Vision," 157–62; "Suffering as a Preparation for Etheric Vision," 163–67.
48. Willi Seiss, *Chakra-Werk* (Taisersdorf: Achamoth Verlag, 1992–2007).
49. Trygve Olaf Lindvig, "Die Chakra-Lehre Valentin Tombergs," in Frensch a.o., *Valentin Tomberg*, Vol. III, 112–23.

Valentin Tomberg and the *Ecclesia Universalis*

⊕

As this biography of Valentin Tomberg draws to a close, we believe we have gained enough perspective to now ask how his life might have unfolded had certain events turned out differently: if he had been able to work together with Rudolf Steiner (who was only sixty-three when he died); if there had been more acknowledgment of the young Tomberg from 1931 onwards in Dornach; if (with Steiner still at the helm) the Anthroposophical Society had not fallen apart in 1935; if he had established a good relationship with Willem Zeylmans in 1940; if he had remained a member of Father Dionisi's Orthodox congregation in 1942; if had had had a fruitful meeting with Emil Bock in the autumn of 1942. Events that were not "bound to happen" nevertheless do change people's lives, and this was trenchantly true of Tomberg. As a result, he did not find a suitable place in the Anthroposophical Movement from the 1930s onwards.

Perhaps we may even speak here of a "disintegration" of Tomberg's mission, which could not be realized in a plenary way, owing to the circumstances of the time; and yes, perhaps owing to his own and others' failures. As an associate of Steiner, he might have found his own place in the work of the School of Spiritual Science, especially in the General Anthroposophical Section. He might have worked constructively in the Netherlands with Zeylmans and other Aristotelians on the level of the Michaelic first class; with Marie Steiner, Elisabeth Vreede, and other Platonists on the level of the Sophianic second class; and with Rudolf Steiner on the level of the Christic third class. If we assume that Tomberg was at least inspired by the Maitreya bodhisattva, it was also a part of his mission to announce the etheric return of Christ. It was only when he could no longer work from his greater mission of directing others to the esoteric core of Anthroposophy (inner development and the Christ consciousness) that he was obliged, from 1943 onwards, to reorient his mission of *recall to the spiritual center* in a far broader sense:

- To redefine the moral foundations of the tradition of the law (with Ernst von Hippel).
- To renew the Hermetic tradition.

- To connect ecclesial tradition and esoteric Christianity as constituent parts of the *all-embracing* Church of Christ, which we have called the *Ecclesia universalis*.

If we consider Tomberg's life as *itself* a path of schooling which he had to follow in order to fulfill his mission, we see that he passed through three confrontations with himself: from 1931 to 1940, as a result of Marie Steiner's criticism; from 1940 to 1943, as a result of Willem Zeylmans' criticism; and in the 1950s, during his crisis of knowledge and consequent search for the foundations of inner, personal certainty. We turn now to a fuller examination of these three confrontations.

In 1931, Marie Steiner, with whom Tomberg had until then had a good relationship, became very critical of the influence she believed Nikolai and Maria Belozvetov had on him. Although her judgments were one-sided, it is possible that she had a good eye for Tomberg's weaknesses. Her letters claim that she observed in him indications of arrogance, self-conceit, vanity, and pride. Later, the Dutch doctor Albert Soesman spoke of self-conceit, and, as we have seen already, Stefan Lubienski mentioned a certain pridefulness in Tomberg's nature. Tomberg himself mentions elsewhere *these very traits* as characteristic of Eastern Europeans; and in 1935, he wrote about the path of humility needed to overcome them and to mature the inner structure of *manas*, so that revelations from the spiritual world could be received. In his further life, as we have seen, Tomberg walked this path.

In 1936, after being rejected in Dornach by the circle around Marie Steiner, and with the support of Elisabeth Vreede, Tomberg joined the outcast German, Dutch, and British anthroposophists. Among them were many from the Aristotelian stream, with whom he was, however, not able to establish a productive relationship. The final opportunity for Tomberg to connect with them was in April-May 1940. At that time he was a much sought-after speaker in the Anthroposophical Society and had good relations with leading anthroposophists. After he had been discredited for broaching the topic of reincarnation with members of his intimate circle, the forty-year-old Tomberg, who was in any case predisposed to back away when problems arose, withdrew from the work of the Society when this was suggested to him in the conversation with the dynamic Willem Zeylmans. It was clear that the two men represented very different emphases, which needed to be resolved in a constructive manner. In a sense, Zeylmans became for Tomberg a "guardian of the threshold," from whom he recoiled. The essential criticism leveled at Tomberg was that he did not always leave the members of his group sufficiently free. Assigning reincarnations in a group, even in a game, makes the work unfree; it binds the members to the leader. It is true that some members of Tomberg's circle did "follow him" into the Orthodox Church, and later into the Catholic Church. Some, such as Tom Jurriaanse, allege that their freedom was not fully respected. Here, too, Tomberg followed his path of inner work. Whatever his imperfections may have been, Tomberg spent a lifetime in ever-deepening spiritual self-examination and prayer. On November 27, 1958, he wrote to Bernhard Martin that he had not been involved in personal karmic affairs for some time and no longer took part in such "gossip." In his later *Meditations*, readers are pointedly left free to form their own judgment.

Tomberg could have accepted Zeylmans's criticism, and, rather than feeling that he was in Zeylmans' way, put the greater good of Anthroposophy first and searched out avenues of possible fruitful cooperation with the practical Anthroposophy of the working areas. This missed opportunity did prevent the two from working together on a new anthroposophical impulse after the war. But then again, had matters taken such a turn, his remarkable *Meditations*, and his final works, might not have been written! One must be cautious indeed when second-guessing destiny. In 1941, Tomberg remarked in his Our Father Course that Holland's task was, precisely, to connect polarities.[50] Perhaps there is some irony in this, as Zeylmans and Tomberg, both residing in Holland at the time, did not prove able to overcome their own polarity in this way!

Tomberg could not connect himself with the intellectual Aristotelian Anthroposophy of his time, and the Christian Community

---

50. Our Father Course, week 30.

Valentin Tomberg and the New Spiritual Thinking

seemed to him a Protestant sect. He did not seem able to see that individual anthroposophists, including the Dutch anthroposophists around Zeylmans, could and did nurture their inner life and the Christ impulse in their own way, and that their anthroposophical impulses were not invariably unfruitful. In the spiritual darkness of his time, Tomberg distanced himself from the anthroposophical project of a new culture of initiation, which he considered to have failed. He withdrew from the Society to pursue his own path as a spiritual teacher in his Our Father Course. But then again, what a treasure this Course is! All we may do is try, as best we may, to track these threads of destiny, and find the good in them.

On August 31, 1943, Elisabeth Vreede, who had opened the way for Tomberg to the Netherlands, died in Switzerland. Thereafter, it was as if he was no longer bound to the Netherlands. Soon after, in October 1943, when Ernst von Hippel invited him to come to Germany, Tomberg remarked in his notebook that he wondered where the Archangel to which he had connected himself would send him after the war. The response that came to him may also be a spiritual communication from Rudolf Steiner:

> (Dr. [Steiner]): T.[omberg] is a man who does not predetermine his own affairs. He has chosen this himself, and so it is not possible to say to which country he should go after the war—it all depends on where the angel in whose obedience he has laid down his life sends him. It is the Russian Archangel.[51]

As his conversations with Bernhard Martin show, when Tomberg was in Germany he had to face his feelings about the anthroposophists, the Anthroposophical Society, the Christian Community, Emil Bock, and to some extent Rudolf Steiner himself as well as the German people generally. In addition, there was his fear of Stalin's Red Army—still a looming threat at that time—from which he and his family had had to flee for their lives, and which had then taken his mother's life violently. He had to confront his inner darkness. In his inner crisis, he found support in the Catholic tradition (wor-

---

51. Transcription of a notebook of Valentin Tomberg, page 584, Archive of the Freie Hermetisch-Christliche Studienstätte am Bodensee, Taisersdorf.

ship, the Rosary, and Mary). As Tomberg said repeatedly, in the Orthodox and Catholic traditions, the way to Christ goes through Mary—who, for him, was Mary-Sophia. In 1945, he allied himself as a private person with the Catholic Church. Whether this was part of a "spiritual mission" we cannot say. In 1948, he no longer wished to remain in Germany. During his last years there, he had worked for the English army and taken part in the English program for the re-education of the German people in the war's aftermath. It was this work and these personal associations that led him to England, his next homeland.

Tomberg's studies in the tradition of natural law led him, from the early 1950s onwards, to the question of how his vision of a "regenerated" law could be substantiated. Did this vision have an objective validity or only a subjective one? That was the question, and it led to a third period of self-examination, in which he came to the conclusion that, on spiritual matters, rational proofs do not suffice, for at issue are not scientific conclusions but personal convictions, which hinge on inner certainty and that alone.

As a result of this epistemological crisis, Tomberg distanced himself (as is made clear in a 1956 letter to Bernhard Martin) from the project of Anthroposophy by questioning the "scientificity" of spiritual science itself. Later, he wrote more specifically to Willi Seiss in a letter of 1970 that spiritual "science" is not a real science because its results are not universally valid and verifiable.[52] In his presentation of this epistemological conundrum, however, Tomberg was basing his judgment on a limited definition of science, namely that of *natural* science—and thus, it seems to us, did not do full justice to the *actual* criteria of spiritual science as formulated with admirable clarity by Rudolf Steiner, especially in his early epistemological works and studies in Goethe's scientific phenomenology. Tomberg also seemed convinced that, if subjected to careful conceptual analysis, spiritual science must inevitably succumb to a rigid over-systemization. But in so doing, it seems to us that he may not have adequately appraised the ability of Rudolf Steiner, and of at least

---

52. See page 185.

some other anthroposophists, to also "think with their hearts" and to develop living and spiritual concepts for this purpose.

For Steiner, "knowledge of full reality" arises from the connection of perceiving and thinking. In the particular case of spiritual knowledge, the perceptual component is "supersensible"—that is, it is mediated by "senses" higher than the physical senses. In principle, however, such supersensible perception remains just as provisional as is ordinary sense perception: it still requires assessment by the conceptual component ("sound human reason," as Steiner noted) to disclose correlations with what we already know, so that we may press forward in the relevant spiritual research. This cognitive process is guided by the human "I" and can, in cooperation with others who also possess these faculties, lead to reliable knowledge.

At this stage of his life, Tomberg wished to speak only of personal, inner certainty, and in so doing may not have been able to do full justice to the cognitive process that is possible in the age of the consciousness soul through the development of new "supersensible" faculties of perception. He could not limit himself to exclusively following Steiner on the path to spiritual science he outlined in his book *Philosophy of Freedom* (which is a guide to intuitive thinking and moral intuitions). In Bulgaria, Steiner's contemporary and colleague Peter Deunov had developed a spiritual science in his own way and provided insight into the spiritual laws we need to know for our inner development. In 1943, by contrast, Tomberg sought support in traditions from the past (the age of the rational soul) and in revelations approaching from the future (the age of the spirit self, or *manas*). In so doing, he may have lost sight for a time of the possibilities of the present.

Surrounded by the swirling spiritual darkness of the Second World War, Tomberg came to the conclusion that the development of the consciousness soul had faltered. His natural conservatism led him to fall back on the legal tradition, the Church tradition, and later, also, the Hermetic tradition. But we are now almost eighty years on and must be open to what our own time demands of *us*! Ultimately, it is the balance of tradition and renewal (the stream from above to below and that from below to above) that must be determined anew for each age. We are still, really, only at the beginning of the epoch of the consciousness soul (which will end in 3573), in which, from the activity of our "I" and from our openness to inspirations from the spiritual world, new insights and new impulses can be born.

⊕

Tomberg was not in favor of his anthroposophical works being distributed. However, this did not work out as he had wished, owing to the enthusiastic efforts of Lubienski and others. At the end of his life, he could not hold out much hope that the role of the Church in society would change dramatically, or that there would be a growing need for the sort of spiritual literature he had earlier written. His friend Bernhard Martin, however, who as an anthroposophist, wanted to remain active in these circles in 1956, and did hold out such hope. What we have seen is that the development of the consciousness soul continued. More and more people, detach themselves from the Church and other social institutions dating back to the time of the rational soul, and seek instead their own spiritual insight and spiritual experiences in order to free themselves from the scientific dogmas of materialism.

From this standpoint, the writings of Valentin Tomberg have become important again. His anthroposophical work contains fundamental spiritual insights, just as his Hermetic work offers spiritual and psychological insights that can be particularly valuable for individuals. Many people have been inspired by Valentin Tomberg to connect anthroposophical and Hermetic impulses in their work. In the English-speaking world we can mention, among others, Keith Harris, Claudia McLaren Lainson, Michael Martin, James Morgante, John O'Meara, Joel Park, Robert Powell, Karen Rivers, Robert Sardello, Randall Scott, and James Wetmore.

Elsewhere, the German philosopher Michael Frensch has published articles and books on numerous art-historical, Christological, and philosophical subjects—as well as, more recently, two novels. He revised his 1983 translation of *Meditations* into German from the French, and published it in 2020 through his publishing house, Novalis Verlag. As editor-in-chief, he made the journal *Novalis* the forecourt of a Sophia academy, where work could be done on a renewed Platonism. According to Frensch, this would include the following themes: the resurrection of the mysteries of the feminine, the confrontation with evil by means of "moral logic," a new Platonic theology and spiritual anthropology, research undertaken in communities of insight, reincarnation and karma, the renewal of the Arthurian and Grail mysteries, the revival of Celtic Christianity, and the Christianization of the economy.[53]

The Englishman Robert Powell works as a researcher, seminar leader, and eurythmy teacher in the fields of Hermetic astrology, astrosophy, Sophiology, and meditative and cosmic eurythmy. He translated the book *Meditations* from the original French into English. Starting from the question of the Star of the Magi, he established after a decade of research the chronology of the life of Christ based largely on the extraordinary detail of the temporal indicators given in the visions of Anne Catherine Emmerich.[54] He wrote his doctoral dissertation on the history of the zodiac. Powell is co-founder of the North American Sophia Foundation and the Sophia Grail Circle, and founder of the Choreocosmos School of Cosmic and Sacred Dance. He has written many books on these subjects and been active worldwide since completing his eurythmy training in Dornach in 1982.

The American educator Karen Rivers, the other co-founder of the Sophia Foundation as well as founder of the Rosamira Circle (or, "The Rose of Peace"), seeks to awaken an understanding and respect for all faith traditions. She integrates the work of Rudolf Steiner and Valentin Tomberg in her courses. With Robert Powell she has led pilgrimages to many sacred sites around the world, and for ten years was director of the New Chartres Academy.

The German Willi Seiss (1922–2013) founded the Camphill Heimsonderschule Community in Brachenreuthe, Germany, and played an important role in the development of the mistletoe preparation

---

53. Michael Frensch, "Rudolf Steiner und die Gestalt des Alanus ab Insulis," in *Novalis* (7/8, 2001).

54. See the comprehensive series of volumes on Anne Catherine Emmerich's visions recently published by Angelico Press.

Valentin Tomberg and the *Ecclesia Universalis*

Helixor for cancer therapy. In his compounding of medicines he worked in a Rosicrucian way. Seiss defended Valentin Tomberg against attacks, and in 1982 founded Achamoth Press to publish Tomberg's work. In 1997 he founded Die Freie Hochschule am Bodensee, which has been called the Freie Hermetisch-Christliche Studienstätte am Bodensee since 2011. His serial text *Chakra-Work* and his studies on Hieronymus Bosch came out of his spiritual research. Since Seiss's death in 2013, Catherina Barker has headed the publishing house and the study center, where she also carries on the Hieronymus Bosch research.

Afterword: The Future of Human Intelligence

Valentin Tomberg lived the life of a pilgrim. His life came to a close, as he wrote in 1970, in a life of "prayer and contemplation." Like a hermit from the Egyptian desert, he gathered in the harvest of his life's wisdom in his book on the Tarot. Throughout history, the Platonic movement has repeatedly collected wisdom and made it available to the world. So it was that, ever and again, it provided a spiritual framework within which the Aristotelian movement could acquire meaningful knowledge, and culture could receive new inspiration.

Plato's Academy was an educational institution in which the life of the soul was nurtured, especially in the education of young people—as was also the case in later Platonic academies, in the Carolingian court schools, and in cathedral schools. The Platonically-oriented Cistercian monks were connected in their own way with the Virgin Sophia and with the life of the earth, for example by improving methods of agricultural cultivation. The Platonic Academy of Florence was the very soul of Florentine culture. So, too, coming again in the twentieth century, those in the Platonic stream were meant to have been actively at work developing the intelligence of the heart and devotion to Anthropos-Sophia together with the Aristotelian anthroposophists in the common project of spiritualization of intelligence in a New Mystery culture.

The failure of the greater number of anthroposophists in the months following the Christmas conference of 1923 brought an early end to Rudolf Steiner's activity. This was a world-historical catastro-

Valentin Tomberg and the New Spiritual Thinking

phe. For decades, the collapse of the Anthroposophical Society in 1935 prevented a dedicated fostering of the further development of Anthroposophy as Steiner himself had conceived it. Beginning in the 1970s, unexpected requests for Anthroposophical counsel came from the outside world in the areas of education, medicine, nutrition, farming, etc. This made it possible for the Anthroposophical Society to revive, allowing the greater Anthroposophical Movement to reach a certain culmination, commencing with the end of the 1980s. Those sensitive to reading the signs suggest that anthroposophists from the beginning of the twentieth century have returned in numbers. But all this was not enough to prepare for collaboration with the expected great Platonists of the Chartres School and other cathedral schools. The "unbreakable agreement" between the Aristotelians and Platonists mentioned earlier must, then, be realized now in the twenty-first century.

Many important Platonists may have worked outside the Anthroposophical Movement without being recognized as such. Some, like Russian film director Andrei Tarkovsky and German artist Joseph Beuys, did find their way to Anthroposophy. Other Platonists or Platonic types are working largely unnoticed in Anthroposophy, and in spiritual and Christian-social activities dedicated to the necessary spiritualization of intelligence. It is important that they be recognized, and that their contributions be appreciated.

Among anthroposophists in every country there are "unrecognized Platonists" whose work plays an important role for the future of Anthroposophy, although they rarely find themselves in leading positions. They keep the connection with the spiritual world open and build small Platonic academies, where they work pedagogically, artistically, therapeutically, researching and writing. Aristotelians play an equally important role in the Anthroposophical Movement when they follow the developments in modern materialistic science with the clarity of their thinking and show how, behind the sensory world, spiritual forces and beings are at work.

Without the Platonists, Anthroposophy is in danger of remaining just another "movement of cultural reform," as Tomberg writes in *Meditations*. It could lead to an institutionalized Anthroposophy—perhaps developing important methods, but lacking the fullness of the wisdom and intelligence of the heart. Without the Aristotelians, on the other hand, the Platonists run the risk of isolating themselves from the practical world. But apart from the Aristotelian and Platonic streams, the Anthroposophical Movement also needs people who work from the living Christ impulse of love and who build "Sophianic" communities.

The preparatory work of the Aristotelians did not go well in the twentieth century. Moreover, opposing forces threw up enormous obstacles to thwart the project of the new culture of initiation that this preparatory work was meant to usher in. In 1917, European culture was attacked by the spiritual impulses of the Russian revolutionary Lenin and of American President Wilson. At work in these impulses were the "spirits of darkness" whom the Archangel Michael had engaged in battle between 1841 and 1879, and cast upon the earth. The chaos caused by the First World War and the rise of National Socialism hindered Steiner's work, and in the end his movement lacked sufficient strength to effectively support, further, and realize the impulse of renewal in the aftermath of the Christmas Conference of 1924.

Then, in 1933, the apocalyptic Beast rose from the abyss, as Steiner had predicted. And so, it was in the ensuing spiritual darkness that the return of Christ in the etheric world, which Steiner had also predicted, took place. In short, European culture collapsed during the Second World War, following which the countries of Europe came under the influence of Russian Bolshevism on the one hand, and of Americanism on the other. Materialistic science soon spawned an ever-increasing brood of new technologies, which from the beginning of the twenty-first century has centered on the development of artificial intelligence and universal surveillance.

This brings us to the third manifestation of the Gondishapur impulse ($3 \times 666 = 1998$), wherein the anti-Christian impulse of the solar demon is at work. This commenced already in 1933. The sinister parody of human intelligence now spreading over the world at dizzying speed is the very opposite of spiritual intelligence. It is a global electronic spider web spun by the spirit of lies—by Ahriman, whose actual incarnation in a human being, according to Steiner, can be expected even now. In our time, therefore, the impulse of

Valentin Tomberg and the New Spiritual Thinking

Anthroposophy *must* be renewed. This time, however, with an apocalyptic dimension.

Anthroposophy, as Steiner wanted to develop it, encompasses the whole threefold mystery of Michael-Sophia-Christ. But in practice it is mainly concerned with the Michael impulse. As a Christian Platonist, Valentin Tomberg worked intensively on the religious aspects of this mystery, and thus showed how the Anthroposophical Movement can further enrich its understanding of Sophia and Christ. He was aware of the rise of the opposing forces, those of the dragon from the book of the Apocalypse, who attacks the cosmic Virgin. He experienced the rise of Bolshevism in Russia in 1917 and was one of the few anthroposophists to speak of the demonic forces in National Socialism before the Second World War. In his later work he was especially concerned with the moral actions of the individual human being. He did not pay much attention any longer to the world of Ahriman in which we live today and to the apocalyptic dimension of our time, which had been so important a theme—and rightly so—for Steiner.

To engage in truly meaningful, and thus productive, discussion on the subject of Valentin Tomberg, we must keep in mind the overarching goal Rudolf Steiner had hoped to achieve with the Aristotelian-Platonic project of the spiritualization of intelligence. This goal was the inauguration of a culture of initiation in which human beings connect with spiritual beings in order to nurture universal human qualities and show the way to finding and connecting with our higher self. Achieving this means gaining experiential access to the Michael-Sophia-Christ mystery. The spiritual scientist Rudolf Steiner opened up this great mystery from the perspective of the Michael School. As destiny would have it, however, this was not taken up with sufficient spiritual depth in the Anthroposophical Society.

Tomberg, who worked from a religious impulse and wanted to provide the lacking dimension of depth, found little response. In all fairness, though, the evidence does suggest that Tomberg sometimes had difficulty relating effectively with people from the Aristotelian stream in Anthroposophy and perceiving their merits. Thus, during his anthroposophical period an easy understanding with Aristotelians was for the most part just not to be. In 1946, Tomberg, who himself had a religious point of view, leveled something of a critique against Steiner for having aligned himself too exclusively with science. Still later, he questioned the "scientificity" of spiritual science altogether. His spiritual-religious view (the Eastern European, Sophia aspect) thus became markedly one-sided. But the spiritual-scientific vision (the Western European, Michael aspect) is of course also one-sided. It was in Central European culture that these two should have been brought into harmony with each other through the impulse of Christ. But destiny dealt a different hand.

Anthroposophy has a special concern with connecting the spiritual world and the earthly world. This "scientific" movement from below to above of the Aristotelians and the "religious" movement from above to below of the Platonists complement each other, and *need* each other. Where they truly join together is in the Michael-Sophia-Christ mystery. Tomberg spoke of the cooperation of these two groups in 1938 in Rotterdam in his lecture on the new Michael community as a spiritual knighthood that will bear the motto *Michael-Sophia in nomine Christi*.[55] But he was unable on his own to connect both aspects of Anthroposophy for the common project of the spiritualization of intelligence.

This transformative spiritualization of the intelligence can take place in different contexts. Rudolf Steiner sought to effect this transformation by means of the spiritual science prepared in the supersensible School of Michael. But the Free School of Spiritual Science, which was to carry this out on earth from 1923 onwards through the cooperation of Aristotelians and Platonists, could only be partially achieved. For Tomberg, the project of spiritualizing the intelligence was translated in his later years into a Christian-Hermetic project aimed at helping the "Unknown Friends" reading his Tarot book train themselves in bringing together the intellectual thinking of their heads with the intuition of their hearts. For Tomberg, this personal training was the condition *sine qua non* for bringing science, religion, and art into spiritual unison. In our time, it is necessary that people with many different qualities work together in the devel-

---

55. "Michael-Sophia in the name of Christ."

opment of new spiritual visions and sciences. The Anthroposophical Movement is, however, only one of the arenas where this may occur.

The connection of human intelligence with the "cosmic intelligence" of the Archangel Michael is more urgent now than ever, as artificial intelligence hems us in at breakneck speed, and the philosophy of transhumanism promotes an ever closer connection of the human brain with computer technology. These are phenomena of an automated, Ahrimanic intelligence that offers no opening for the creative and moral activity of the human self. This form of intelligence continues to unfold in the "Academy of Gondishapur" writ large. The spiritual aspects of human intelligence are sorely in danger of being obliterated if, in this distracting digital age, it is not channeled into the areas of upbringing, education, and human interaction. And let us recall that when Tomberg wrote his *Meditations*, these developments were not so apparent as they are today.

In the present reign of initiates from the Ahrimanic counter-school opposing that of the Archangel Michael, it is not an easy matter to stand up for a spiritual culture in the Michaelic-Sophianic-Christian sense. The Ahrimanic battle-forces must be recognized and revealed in their workings. The lies and subterfuge of materialism must be unmasked. The development of intuitive thinking as laid out in Steiner's *Philosophy of Freedom*, and as driven home in Tomberg's fundamental idea of "moral logic," can help us reach spiritual insights and act from moral intuitions in these apocalyptic times. Now, a century after the Christmas Conference of 1923, all that Steiner had hoped to set in motion through the "laying" of the Foundation Stone Meditation can be revisited and renewed. Aristotelians can renew these impulses in the field of science. Platonists, through their characteristic capacities, can receive inspirations for the development of the culture of the future. And those who work out of the Christ impulse of love can found small mystery places where "conversation" with the spiritual world can take place, and where oases of a new spiritual culture can spring forth. But, apart from this way of looking at major streams of humanity, in the end it is *everyone's* task to create new forms of cooperation based on a new social impulse and on uniting in friendship with people from other

Valentin Tomberg and the *Ecclesia Universalis*

backgrounds in spiritual and cultural work. This is the work of building a new future for all humanity. But this can only happen in the context of cooperation with spiritual beings, and in particular in a renewed anthroposophical impulse—under the guidance of Archangel Michael—to rescue human intelligence from the grip of Ahriman and to restore its connection with the "cosmic intelligence" from which it has come to us. Then, the being Anthropos-Sophia can individualize herself in the consciousness soul of humanity, and the intended way to the future Slavic culture of the spirit self can be found and restored. As a pilgrim from the Russian cultural arena, Valentin Tomberg placed before the world his profound anthroposophical, Hermetic, and other esoteric work—done in the service of the *Ecclesia universalis*—precisely to help birth this culture of Christ and Sophia, of Love and Wisdom.

The Writings of Valentin Tomberg

In English translation

Christ and Sophia. Great Barrington: SteinerBooks, 2011. Includes *Anthroposophic Meditations on the Old Testament, the New Testament and the Apocalypse,* and *The Four Sacrifices of Christ.* Earlier published by Candeur Manuscripts, 1983 and 1985.

Group Work. Candeur Manuscripts, 1985 (two articles from 1930 and 1938).

Inner Development. Hudson, NY: Anthroposophic Press, 1992. Earlier published by Candeur Manuscripts, 1983.

Lazarus Come Forth! Great Barrington: SteinerBooks, 2006. Earlier published as *The Covenant of the Heart.* Element Books, 1992. (Includes four separate works, published in new translations in three volumes in 2022: *Lazarus: The Miracle of Resurrection in World History; Thy Kingdom Come: The New Evolution of the Good;* and *The Proclamation on Sinai: Covenant and Commandments.* Brooklyn, NY: Angelico Press.)

Meditations on the Tarot: A Journey into Christian Hermeticism. Brooklyn, NY: Angelico Press, 2020. Includes *The Wandering Fool.* Earlier published by Element Books, 1993.

Russian Spirituality and Other Essays. San Rafael, CA: LogoSophia, 2010. Earlier published as *Early Articles* by Candeur Manuscripts, 1984.

Studies of the Foundation Stone Meditation. San Rafael, CA: LogoSophia, 2010. Earlier published by Candeur Manuscripts, 1982.

The Art of the Good: On the Regeneration of Fallen Justice. Brooklyn, NY: Angelico Press, 2021.

The Course of the Lord's Prayer, Vols. 1–4. Taisersdorf: Achamoth Press, 2015–2016. New edition in press 2022 by Angelico Press.

The Foundation Stone Meditation of Rudolf Steiner. Taisersdorf: Achamoth Press, 2019.

The Four Sacrifices of Christ and the Appearance of Christ in the

Valentin Tomberg and the *Ecclesia Universalis*

Etheric. Taisersdorf: Achamoth Press, 2016.
The Wandering Fool. San Rafael, CA: LogoSophia, 2009. (Early exploratory studies into Arcana XIV–XXII.)

In German
Anthroposophische Betrachtungen über das Alte Testament. Schönach: Achamoth Verlag, 1989.
Anthroposophische Betrachtungen über das Neue Testament und die Apokalypse. Schönach: Achamoth Verlag, 1991.
Degeneration und Regeneration der Rechtswissenschaften. Bonn: Götz Schwippert, 1946; and Bonn: Bouvier/Grundmann, 1974.
Die Grundsteinmeditation Rudolf Steiners. Schönach: Achamoth Verlag, 1993.
Die vier Christusopfer und das Erscheinen des Christus im Ätherischen. Schönach: Achamoth Verlag, 1994.
Grundlagen des Völkerrechts als Menschheitsrecht. Bonn: Götz Schwippert, 1947.
Lazarus komm heraus! Basel: Herder Verlag, 1985. Includes: *Lazarus, Die Verkündung auf dem Sinai, Dein Reich komme, Der Odem des Lebens*.
Meditationen über die Großen Arcana des Taro. Steinbergkirche: Novalis Verlag, 2020.
Sieben Vorträge über die innere Entwicklung des Menschen. Schönach: Achamoth Verlag, 1993.
Vom Völkerrecht zur Weltfriedensordnung. Steinbergkirche: Novalis Verlag, 2022.

Other Publications in German
Aufzeichnungen, Vortragsnachschriften. Taisersdorf: Achamoth Verlag, 2002.
Der Vaterunser-Kurs, Volumes I–IV. Taisersdorf: Achamoth Verlag, 2008–2010.
Der Wandernde Narr. Luxembourg: Kairos Edition, 2007.
Gesammelte Aufsätze. Taisersdorf: Achamoth Verlag, 2013.
Innere Gewissheit. Luxembourg: Kairos Edition, 2012.
Inspirationen zu den Großen Arcana des Taro XIV-XXII. Taisersdorf: Achamoth Verlag, 2007.
Karmische Zusammenhänge bei Gestalten des Alten Testaments. Tais-

The Writings of Valentin Tomberg

ersdorf: Achamoth Verlag, 2003.

Wer war Valentin Tomberg? Seine Rechtswissenschaft, seine wiederholten Erdenleben. Taisersdorf: Achamoth Verlag, 2018.

www.ingramcontent.com/pod-product-compliance
Lightning Source LLC
Chambersburg PA
CBHW022148180426
43200CB00028BA/298